C0-APB-960

THIS ITEM HAS BEEN
DISCARDED BY THE
UNIVERSITY
OF PUGET SOUND
COLLINS MEMORIAL LIBRARY

Authorized xerographic reprint.
UNIVERSITY MICROFILMS, A Xerox Company
Ann Arbor, Michigan, U.S.A.
1969

CHARACTERS
AND
COMMENTARIES

BY
Giles LYTTON STRACHEY

Strachey, Giles Lytton
III

HARCOURT, BRACE AND COMPANY
NEW YORK

COPYRIGHT, 1933, BY
JAMES STRACHEY

*All rights reserved, including
the right to reproduce this book
or portions thereof in any form.*

first edition

Copyright, 1933, 1961 by James Strachey

PRINTED IN THE UNITED STATES OF AMERICA
BY QUINN & BODEN COMPANY, INC., RAHWAY, N. J.
Typography by Robert Josephy

GILES LYTTON STRACHEY

1929

by Lytton Strachey

CHARACTERS
AND
COMMENTARIES

Acknowledgments

Acknowledgments are due to the Syndics of the Cambridge University Press for their permission to reprint the Leslie Stephen Lecture on Pope; to the Oxford University Press (London and New York) for similar permission in the case of the Introduction to Mrs. Inchbald's *Simple Story;* to the Hogarth Press in the case of the Preface to Mr. George Rylands' *Words and Poetry;* and to the editors of the *New Quarterly,* the *Independent* and *Albany Reviews, War and Peace,* the *Woman's Leader,* the *Spectator,* the *New Statesman and Nation, The New Republic, The Century Magazine,* and *The Living Age* in the case of the various essays reprinted from those periodicals.

Contents

ix

IV. LATER ESSAYS

FRONTISPIECE·

Portrait of Lytton Strachey at the age of 49
(Photograph by Kyrle Leng)

I

ENGLISH LETTER WRITERS

FOR this essay, besides the letters and other works of the authors cited, I have consulted no special authorities outside the range of my ordinary reading.

1. The Elizabethans

THE most lasting utterances of a man are his studied writings; the least are his conversations. His letters hover midway between these two extremes; and the fate which is reserved for them is capable of infinite gradations, from instant annihilation up to immortality. But "oblivion blindly scattereth her poppy." The washing-bills of the Pharaohs are preserved to us, but not their love-letters; and the vain chit-chat of Pliny's correspondence has outlived all the gravity of the letters of Tacitus. The end of Time is more favourable to epistolary immortality than its beginnings and its maturity: the barbarism of an early age and the unrest of a vigorous one are alike unpropitious to the preservation of letters. Yet who knows what the present day may not be losing? or what priceless treasures it has not consigned to abolition? Masterpieces lie at the mercy of postmen; preserved correspondences degenerate into culinary employments; and the same flames which devoured a circular may devour a letter from Charles Lamb.

But .imagined losses deserve our lamentation less than known ones; and, when we consider the vanished riches of the past, we may indeed lament with good cause. What has become of the letters of Chaucer, and of Marlowe, and of Shakespeare? These, and a hundred other traces of the renowned minds of former ages, have been obliterated for ever from the world. The crowd of geniuses who adorned the most splendid epoch in our literature live for us merely in

3

a few scattered remnants preserved by chance from out the precious mass which has been taken from us.

"Injurious time now with a robber's haste
Crams his rich thievery up, he knows not how:"

and scants us with some meagre relics, when he might have rejoiced us with the entire bodies of the saints.

What remains to us of the correspondence of the Elizabethan era hardly reconciles us to the loss of the rest; but there is enough to give us a clear view of the main characteristics of the letter-writing of those days. These characteristics are particularly interesting because they offer so many points of contrast with the whole current of what was to be the epistolary style of the future. The most distinctively Elizabethan letters which we possess have no descendants in English literature; they do not form a step in the development of the art of letter-writing; they stand by themselves. It will be well to point out their principal peculiarities, with the aid of illustrations.

The Elizabethan age was pre-eminently an age of action, and some of the finest of its letters were written with the object of forwarding some practical end. What would now be a business letter or a political manifesto became endowed in those days with all the attributes of faultless style. Essex begins a letter to Elizabeth with the following sentence: "From a mind delighting in sorrow, from spirits wasted in passion, from a heart torn in pieces with care, grief, and travail, from a man that hateth himself and all things that keep him alive, what service can your Majesty expect?" And such magnificence of diction was the everyday raiment of an Elizabethan letter. Magnificence, however, could be replaced on occasion by unadorned vigour; with those great spirits the pen was sometimes almost as violent as the sword. Sir Philip Sidney's letter to his father's secretary is a fine example of Elizabethan force.

"MR. MOLINEUX,—Few words are.best. My letters to my father have come to the eyes of some. Neither can I condemn any but you for it. If it be so, you have played the very knave with me; and so I will make you know, if I have good proof of it. But that for so much as is past. For that is to come, I assure you before God, that if ever I know you do so much as read any letter I write to my father without his commandment, or my consent, I will thrust my dagger into you. And trust to it, for I speak it in earnest. In the meantime, farewell."

Apparently, even for that age, this letter was more than usually forcible; for we find Mr. Molineux declaring in his reply that "the same is the sharpest I have ever received from any."

But this combination of practical affairs with literary skill is not the only distinguishing feature of Elizabethan letters. They are even more remarkable for the abundance of their reflexions upon the conduct of life. The crisis of the Reformation had shaken the whole fabric of established thought. Everywhere questions were rising up which had long lain entranced beneath the spell of mother Church; and of these questions none were more important and pressing than the moral ones. The letters of the time show how eagerly men were feeling their way towards the reconstitution of an ethical code. Some of them—such as the letters of Sir Henry Sidney and Lord Strafford to their sons—resemble lay sermons rather than familiar communications. They are filled with maxims, and Latin saws, and careful trains of reasoning; and often, even when their object is not mainly hortatory, their tone is quite distinctly the tone of a moral philosopher. Thus the Lord Chancellor Egerton, writing to Essex to dissuade him from rebellion, says: "I have begun plainly, be not offended if I proceed so. Bene cedit qui cedit tempori, and Seneca saith, Cedendum est fortunae. The medicine and remedy is not to contend and strive, but humbly to yield and submit. Have you given cause, and ye take a scandal unto you? Then all you can do is too little to make satisfaction. Is cause of scandal given unto you? Yet policy, duty, and religion enforce you to sue, yield, and submit to our sovereign. . . . There can be no dishonour to yield; but, in denying, dishonour and impiety. The difficulty, my good lord, is to conquer yourself, which is the height of true valour and fortitude, whereunto all your honourable actions have tended."

It was not only in matters of private morals that this power of gnomic exhortation found vent; the morals of politics came equally within its sphere. "Your father," wrote Sir Walter Raleigh to the young Prince Henry, "is called the vicegerent of Heaven; while he is good he is the vicegerent of Heaven. Shall man have authority from the fountain of good to do evil? No, my prince; let mean and degenerate spirits, which want benevolence, suppose your power impaired by a disability of doing injuries. If want of power to do ill be an incapacity in a prince, with reverence be it spoken, it is an incapacity he has in common with the Deity. . . . Exert yourself, O generous prince, against such sycophants, in the glorious cause of liberty; and assume such an ambition worthy of you, to secure your fellow creatures from slavery; from a condition as much below that of brutes as to act without reason is less miserable than to act against it. Preserve to your future subjects the divine right of free agents; and to your own royal house the divine right of being their benefactors. Believe me, my prince, there is no other right can flow from God."

6

Well would it have been for that "royal house" had it been swayed by such noble counsels! But the right which it preferred to maintain certainly flowed not from God: "The right divine of kings to govern wrong." The elaborate formality of the Elizabethan letter must also be noticed. This effect was doubtless partly produced by the somewhat cumbrous nature of the ordinary prose style, which lent itself much more easily to wealth of ornament than to directness of expression; but it also depended on the fact that the letter was always regarded as a literary exercise. The correspondence of those days was not thrown off in a hurry; letters were given time to mature and grow, and were not despatched till every sentence had blossomed into flower. Those of Dr. Donne provide perhaps the best example of these typically renascent products. They are rich with elaborate discussions upon abstruse questions; they are packed with complicated imagery; they are interweaved with even more complicated compliments. "Sir," Donne begins a letter to Sir Henry Goodyer, "it should be no interruption to your pleasures to hear me often say that I love you, and that you are as much my meditations as myself. I often compare not you and me, but the sphere in which your revolutions are and my wheel, both I hope concentric to God; for methinks the new astronomy is thus appliable well, that we which are a little earth should rather move towards God, than that He which is fulfilling, and can come no whither, should move towards us." Donne's letters exercise the attention of the reader more than most; but the trouble is well rewarded. The more one broods over them the more one realises the originality of his thought, the beauty of his language, and the subtle splendour of his emotion. Such sentences as these repay much labour: "I would not that death should take me asleep. I would not have him merely seize me, and only declare me to be dead, but win me and overcome me."

7

One further passage even more beautiful and characteristic, perhaps, may be quoted from a letter to Sir T. Lucy:
"I make account that the writing of letters, when it is with
any seriousness, is a kind of ecstasy, and a departure and
secession and suspension of the soul, which doth then com-
municate itself to two bodies: and as I would every day provide for my soul's last convoy, though I know not when I
shall die, and perchance I shall never die; so for these ecsta-
sies in letters, I oftentimes deliver myself over in writing
when I know not when those letters shall be sent to you, and
many times they never are, for I have a little satisfaction in
seeing a letter written to you upon my table, though I meet
no opportunity of sending it." After which introduction,
Donne embarks upon a discussion of the question of Grace,
the Primitive Church, St. Augustine, and the doctrine of the
Infusion from God.

The preceding quotations will have sufficiently shown the
gulf which separates the letters of the Elizabethan era from
those of later generations—those of Horace Walpole, for instance, or Gray, or Byron. Since the seventeenth century, the
art of letter-writing has turned aside altogether from the
affairs of practical life, from the business of ethical exhortation, and from the elaboration of literary beauties. Since that
time action has become merely a theme for comment and
description; Latin tags have turned out to be useful as pointing, not morals, but epigrams; and the chief end of stylistic
art has come to be the appearance of a colloquial easiness.
The change has not been without its drawbacks; there has
been a loss of profundity, of seriousness, of grandeur. But
there have been corresponding gains—in lightness of touch,
in clarity, and in play of personal feeling. The old style of
letter is the more instructive; the new is the more entertaining.

The letters of James Howell form the point of transition

between the two schools. In them there appears for the first
time a conscious endeavour to be perpetually amusing.
Howell cared for nothing else; and he attained his object.
He had not a spark of the spiritual fire of Donne; he would
have quailed before Sir Philip Sidney; he would not have
been able to follow Raleigh's arguments; but he possessed
one accomplishment which those great men conspicuously
lacked—he could prattle. It is true that his endless stream
of talk is ornamented after the Elizabethan manner; it
meanders through a grove of the usual conceits and the usual
classical allusions. But it is a stream, and not a piece of artificial water. He touches upon every subject—love, and
Venice, and Socrates, and letter-writing—always with the
same light, affable, engaging touch. He tells a story admirably; he can vividly describe places and things; he can
talk for pages about nothing at all. One extract will suffice
to show his quality:

"I was, according to your desire, to visit the late new-
married couple more than once; and to tell you true I never
saw such a disparity between two that were made one flesh
in all my life: he handsome outwardly, but of odd conditions; she excellently qualified, but hard-favoured; so that
the one may be compared to a cloth of tissue doubled, cut
upon coarse canvas; the other to a buckram petticoat, lined
with satin. I think Clotho had her fingers smutted in snuff-
ing the candle, when she began to spin the thread of her
life, and Lachesis frowned in twisting it up; but Aglaia, with
the rest of the Graces, were in a good humour when they
formed her inner parts. A blind man is fittest to hear her
sing; one would take delight to see her dance if masked; and
it would please you to discourse with her in the dark, for
there she is best company, if your imagination can forbear
to run upon her face. When you marry, I wish you such an

inside of a wife; but from such an outward phisnomy the Lord deliver you, and your faithful friend to serve you."

In spite of its lack of refinement, this is in the true epistolary style. Howell is the direct progenitor of the great eighteenth-century letter-writers.

2. Pope, Addison, Steele, and Swift

IN the troubled sea of History two epochs seem to stand out like enchanted islands of delight and of repose—the Age of the Antonines and the eighteenth century. Gibbon's splendid eulogy of "that period in the history of the world which elapsed from the death of Domitian to the accession of Commodus" suggests at once to our minds the rival glories of his own epoch. Who does not feel that the polished pomp of Gibbon's sentences is the true offspring of the age of Handel and of Reynolds, and yet that it might have been composed as fittingly amid the elaborate colonnades and the Corinthian grandeur of the villa of Adrianus? It is true, indeed, that the comparison might be pushed too far. It would be easy to point out that the eighteenth century was essentially a stage in a great upward movement of mankind, while the golden evening of Marcus Aurelius was succeeded by a night of storm and utter darkness. The eighteenth century was·an era of promise, of expansion, of vigorous and increasing life; the Age of the Antonines was one of intellectual decadence, of moral shrinkage, of gradual but inevitable decline. Nevertheless, when all these underlying differences have been taken into account, there yet remains a residuum of resemblance between the two epochs which is obvious enough. The nature of the resemblance is—if we may use a cant phrase—"atmospheric." The "atmosphere," the "setting" —that complex medium of intimate relations through which every object is presented to our minds—seems to be one and

11

the same when we are considering the younger Pliny and when we are considering the elder Pitt. Both seem most fittingly to live and move and have their being in some well-ordered garden, where the afternoons are long, and the peaches are plump and soft, and the library and the wine and the servants are within comfortable distance. The fact that the brains of the great Commoner turned the scale in the balance of Empires, while those of his Roman predecessor turned nothing of much greater moment than an epigram—that is an irrelevant consideration. Did they not both feel their nectarines ripening in the sun in precisely the same leisurely aristocratic manner? For, if the eighteenth century was profoundly an age of activity, it was also, no less profoundly, an age of leisure. The conflict and torment of the religious struggles, into which the whole energies of the Renaissance had been plunged, were over; the infinite agitations ushered in by the French Revolution had not yet begun. The interval was one of toleration and of repose: of toleration which would have seemed incredible to the age which preceded it; of repose which seems no less incredible to ours. We, from the midst of our obsession of business, of our express trains, our quick lunches, all our hasty, concentrated, conscientious acts, can only look back in wonder upon the days of coaches and of chairs, of pluralities and of sinecures, of jewelled snuff-boxes and powdered hair. What would we say, in our utilitarian fervour, to a statesman who frittered away his mornings in the composition of ribald French verse—in fact, to Frederick the Great? What would we think, in our scientific solemnity, of a man of letters who set about destroying Christianity with no more elaborate an outfit than the Bible and a jest—in fact, of Voltaire? We should surely gasp and stare at such portents almost as much as Horace Walpole would have gasped and stared if he had received, one morning at breakfast, a five-lined whip. The precept "Il faut cultiver notre jardin" has come down to the degenerate descendants of Candide in the form of "Have an eye to the main chance"—a very different exhortation. The twentieth century has learned to cultivate its garden so well that it makes a profit of ten per cent. The eighteenth century cared less for the profit and more for the garden. It spent its leisure in the true process of cultivation. It ripened, and it matured; it did not advance. In art, in thought, in the whole conduct of life, what it aimed at was the just, the truly proportioned, the approved and absolute best. Its ideals were stationary because they were so high; and the strict conformity which they enjoined was merely the expression of a hatred and scorn of everything short of perfection. Whether such ideals were ever realised, whether their realisation was even possible, may indeed be doubted: what cannot be doubted is that they formed the framework of the eighteenth-century mind. Thus, when that period is dubbed the age of "artificiality," there is one sense in which the imputation is true enough. The age was certainly "artificial" in so far as it was the very contrary of being spontaneous; it was a highly elaborate, conventional, concocted age. But that it was "artificial" in another sense, that it was frigid and mechanical and devoid of passion—to suppose this would be to fall into grave error. Doubtless the supposition is often entertained; and it is the more easily held owing to the fact that the great mass of eighteenth-century literature is unemotional. It so happened that the emotions of those days did not seize naturally upon their commonest and most widespread vehicle—the art of writing; they turned instead towards the more recondite arts of painting and music. The wealth of emotion which the eighteenth century brought forth is not to be measured in its poetry; it is to be searched for in the visions of Watteau, of Fragonard, of Gainsborough, in the profound

ENGLISH LETTER WRITERS

inspirations of Bach, in the triumphant melodies of Gluck, and in the divine symphonies of Mozart.

The least emotional body of literature, however, might be expected to offer an exception to its general character in one of its branches, if in no other—that of familiar letter writing. A letter is only less private than a diary; here, therefore, if anywhere, the public conventions of writing are easily overturned, here, where all the particular accidents of circumstance and character, all the moving actualities of life, press forward, in spite of forms and observances, to make themselves articulate. The eighteenth century is no exception to this rule; and he would be blind indeed who failed to perceive emotion in the *Journal to Stella* or the letters of Mademoiselle de Lespinasse. Yet upon the whole the letters of that age partake of the qualities of the rest of its literature to an unusual extent. It was not as a vehicle for personal feeling that the letter attracted the majority of the great eighteenth-century letter writers; it was rather as a means for expressing the delicacies and refinements of personal intercourse. The vast vogue which the letter enjoyed was due to the fact that it formed a natural channel through which the elaborate and leisured civilisation of the time might flow. An eighteenth-century letter is the true epitome of the eighteenth century; and the pair of lovers described by Walpole, who sat all day in one room with a screen between them, over which they threw to one another their correspondence, provide the clearest image of that amazing period.

The group of writers who ushered in the new century possessed the characteristics of the dawning age in a striking degree. The letters which passed about between Pope and Bolingbroke and Arbuthnot and Gay might almost be taken for translations of some of Pliny's epistles. Never was a set of letters less spontaneous and more elegant. They are, indeed, essays rather than letters; the subjects with which they

14

are concerned are the commonplaces, and not the occurrences, of life; one does not think of them as having gone
through the post; their dates and their signatures are mere
rudimentary excrescences; they are the kind of letters which
do not require an answer. "Those indeed who can be useful
to all states," writes Pope to Steele, "should be like gentle
streams, that not only glide through lonely valleys and for-
ests amid the flocks and the shepherds, but visit populous
towns in their course, and are at once of ornament and
service to them. But there are another sort of people who
seem designed for solitude; such, I mean, as have more to
hide than to show. As for my own part, I am one of those
of whom Seneca says: 'Jam umbratiles sunt, ut putent in
turbido esse quicquid in luce est.' Some men, like some pictures, are fitter for a corner than a full light; and, I believe,
such as have a natural bent to solitude (to carry on the
former similitude) are like waters, which may be forced into
fountains, and, exalted into a great height, may make a noble
figure and a louder noise, but after all they would run more
smoothly, quietly, and plentifully, in their own natural
course upon the ground. The consideration of this would
make me very well contented with the possession only of that
quiet which Cowley calls the companion of obscurity. But
whoever has the Muses too for his companions, can never be
idle enough to be uneasy. Thus, Sir, you see, I flatter myself
into a good opinion of my own way of living. Plutarch just
now told me, that it is in human life . . ." etc. Here we have
Seneca, Cowley, Plutarch, and the Muses, and such is the
company one becomes best acquainted with in the letters of
Pope and his circle. The easy flow of the similes, the pas-
toral melancholy of the reflexions, the quiet cultivation of
the style—these things make pleasant reading for anyone
who is content to do without originality and excitement.
Sometimes, especially in the hands of the less skilful per-

formers—of Bolingbroke, for instance—this delicate instrument becomes too obviously an echo; the classical note becomes unduly forced. Some of Bolingbroke's letters are stuffed so full with Latin tags that there is no cake for the plums; and as one reads them, one is inevitably reminded of those frigid images which still repose upon the tombs of eighteenth-century magnates, in all their panoply of toga and perruque.

Pope himself avoided these extremes; yet there can be little doubt that it is his poetry rather than his correspondence which reveals the true nature of the man. His extreme sensitiveness, which expressed itself to the full in his verse Epistles, hardly made itself felt in his prose ones. The poignancy of his note to the Miss Blounts on the death of his father—"My poor Father died last night.—Believe, since I did not forget you this moment, I never shall"—finds few parallels in the rest of his correspondence. There was a trait in Pope's character which goes some way to account for this: his feelings were far more easily roused into expression by dislike than by affection. Scorn, hatred, malice, rage—these were the emotions which, with Pope, boiled over almost naturally into fervent language; it is through its mastery of all the shades of these emotions that his verse has gained its immortality. Unfortunately it is part of the nature of things that one does not write familiar letters to one's enemies. Though Addison figures among Pope's correspondents, Atticus does not. Our loss is great. In the undiscovered limbo of dreams and chimaeras, Pope's letters to Attossa and to Sporus are among the finest examples of the epistolary art.

The greatest of Pope's enemies has not suffered in the same way. We may be sure that we have got the best of Addison. His letters perfectly reflect that charming, polished, empty personality which the *Spectator* has made familiar to the whole world. "My dearest Lord," he writes to the young Earl of Warwick, "I cannot forbear being troublesome to your lordship whilst I am in your neighbourhood. The business of this is to invite you to a concert of music, which I have found out in a neighbouring wood. It begins precisely at six in the evening, and consists of a blackbird, a thrush, a robin-redbreast, and a bull-finch. There is a lark that, by way of overture, sings and mounts till she is almost out of hearing, and afterwards, falling down leisurely, drops to the ground as soon as she has ended her song. The whole is concluded by a nightingale, that has a much better voice than Mrs. Tofts, and something of the Italian manner in her divisions." That is an exquisite piece of writing about nothing at all; and it shows Addison in his happiest capacity—as the master of the flute in prose. But his character had other, and less agreeable, qualities—qualities which Pope seized upon and emphasised with such bitter virulence in his famous lines on Atticus. Pope's picture is of course painted with a malignant hand; but it is a caricature, not a fancy portrait; it represents at least a portion of the truth. In the *Letter to a Lady* Addison's calm consciousness of superiority, his almost priggish self-sufficiency, his complete mastery of the frigidly polite, become only too glaringly obvious. "You have passions, you say, Madam; but give me leave to answer, that you have understanding also; you have a heart susceptible of the tenderest impressions, but a soul, if you would choose to wake it, above an unwarranted indulgence of them; and let me entreat you, for your own sake, that no giddy impulse of an ill-placed inclination may induce you to entertain a thought prejudicial to your honour and repugnant to your virtue." Never was cold water thrown in more refined a manner upon the advances of a lady; the action can hardly be distinguished from a magnificent bow. It is not necessary to remark that Addison was educated at Oxford.

The letters of Steele are as simple as his friend's are elaborate; and indeed their happy *naïveté* is often reminiscent of the preceding age. His notes to Mary Scurlock form a series of exquisite love-letters which might almost have been written by a virtuous and transmogrified Pepys. "Madam," he wrote a few days before his marriage, "it is the hardest thing in the world to be in love and yet attend to business. . . . A gentleman ask'd me this morning what news from Lisbon, and I answer'd she's exquisitely handsome. Another desired to know when I had been last at Hampton Court. I reply'd 'twill be on Tuesday come sennight. Prithee allow me at least to kiss your hand before that day, that my mind may be in some composure. O love! . . ."

The same tone is kept up throughout the correspondence. Many of the letters are nothing but notices of little presents sent to Mrs. Steele by her husband. "I enclose you a guinea for your pockett." "I send you some tea which I doubt not but you will find very good." "I send you seven-pen'orth of wall nutts at five a penny, which is the greatest proof I can give you at present of my being with my whole heart yours, Richd. Steele. P.S. There are but 29 wallnutts." Such are the staple topics of these domestic letters. "For thee I dye, for thee I languish," Steele ends a note to his wife after six years of marriage; and four years later is still addressing Mary Steele as "Ten thousand times my dear, dear, Pretty Prue."

Steele's nature was one of those fortunate ones which are able to transmute the basest accidents of life into occasions for innocent rejoicing. He could not be otherwise than cheerful. The exact reverse is true of Swift. It is not our purpose, however, to discuss the colossal mind of the great Dean of St. Patrick's. Such an undertaking would be no unworthy task for a Shakespeare; less powerful spirits can only prostrate themselves in dumb worship, like Egyptian priests before the enormous effigies of their gods. It would, besides, be beyond the scope of this essay to attempt an estimation of one whose place in literature depends hardly at all upon his achievements in the domain of letter-writing. Swift's letters are all marked with the indelible stamp of his genius; his *Journal to Stella* reveals to us a whole region of his character which would otherwise have remained unknown; and yet, if all this mass of writing were swept away and utterly abolished, Swift's literary stature would be unchanged. It will be sufficient, perhaps, to notice one particular in which that great man's letters (no less than the rest of his writings) differ in a remarkable degree from those of his contemporaries. In every sense of the term, he is the least artificial of writers. His prose style has been aptly compared to a sheet of plate-glass through which every object appears in the form and colour of absolute reality. It is devoid of any ornament which might impede or deflect the underlying thought; it has no sounding cadences, no splendid figures, no elegant antitheses, no verbal wit. Compared with the sober daylight of Swift's style, that of a writer like Voltaire seems to resemble the brilliancy of drawing-room candles, and that of a writer like Sir Thomas Browne the flare of a midnight torch. Unlike all other prose writers in the world, except Pascal, Swift obtains the whole of his effect by his matter, and by his matter alone.

Sometimes Swift's directness of expression is such that it can hardly be distinguished from brutality. His letter to Miss Waring, for instance, forms a curious contrast to the letter already quoted, which Addison wrote in similar circumstances "to a Lady." "Are you in a condition to manage domestic affairs, with an income of less (perhaps) than £300 a year? Have you such an inclination to my person and humour as to comply with my desires and way of living, and endeavour to make us both as happy as you can? Will you

19

be ready to engage in those methods which I direct for the improvement of your mind, so as to make us entertaining company for each other, without being miserable when we are neither visiting nor visited? Can you bend your love and esteem and indifference to others the same way as I do mine? Shall I have so much power in your heart, or you so much government of your passions, as to grow in good humour upon my approach, though provoked by a ——? Have you so much good-nature as to endeavour by soft words to smooth any rugged humour occasioned by the cross accidents of life? Shall the place wherever your husband is thrown be more welcome than courts or cities without him? . . . These are the questions I have always resolved to propose to her with whom I meant to pass my life; and whenever you can heartily answer them in the affirmative, I shall be blessed to have you in my arms, without regarding whether your person be beautiful or your fortune large. Cleanliness in the first, and competency in the other, is all I look for."

Addison's method of refusing a lady was to bow her out of the room; Swift's method was to knock her down. Yet no one could doubt for a moment which of the two men was capable of the deeper affections. No letters are more charged with poignant emotion than those which Swift wrote from London to his friends in Ireland, when Stella was dying. "I have just received yours of August 24," he wrote to Dr. Sheridan in the last of these; "I kept it an hour in my pocket with all the suspense of a man who expected to hear the worst news that fortune could give him; and at the same time was not able to hold up my head. These are the perquisites of living long; the last act of life is always a tragedy at best; but it is a bitter aggravation to have one's best friend go before one. . . . I know not whether it be an addition to my grief or not that I am now extremely ill; for it would have been a reproach to me to be in perfect health when such a friend was desperate. I do profess, upon my salvation, that the distressed and desperate condition of my friend makes life so indifferent to me, who by course of nature have so little left, that I do not think it worth the time to struggle; yet I should think, according to what hath been formerly, that I may happen to overcome this present disorder; and to what advantage? Why, to see the loss of that person for whose sake only life was worth preserving. . . . What have I to do in the world? I never was in such agonies as when I received your letter, and had it in my pocket. I am able to hold up my sorry head no longer."

3. Lady Mary Wortley Montagu and Lord Chesterfield

IT is curious that the two ladies who have won the greatest reputation as letter writers should present so complete a contrast. Lady Mary Wortley Montagu certainly bears out Professor Raleigh's dictum that in the eighteenth century man lived up to his definition and was a rational animal; and "a rational animal" is precisely the last designation which anyone would dream of applying to Madame de Sévigné. "How many readers and admirers," exclaims Lady Mary, "has Madame de Sévigné, who only gives us, in a lively manner and fashionable phrases, mean sentiments, vulgar prejudices, and endless repetitions! Sometimes the tittle-tattle of a fine lady, sometimes that of an old nurse, always tittle-tattle." Nothing could be more unjust; and the injustice obviously springs from an utter lack of sympathy. Lady Mary was the least feminine of women, and Madame de Sévigné was the most. The delicacy, the charm, the tenderness, of the French lady's letters were lost upon the virile mind of the English one. Lady Mary's flashing wit tossed aside the elegance of Madame de Sévigné's with the disdain of a steel rapier tossing aside a piece of silver filigree-work. What could be the value of such a bauble? It was only meant for show!

"Few women would have spoken so plainly as I have done," Lady Mary wrote in the first of her letters to Edward

Wortley; "but to dissemble is among the things I never do." And a certain outspoken clarity is perhaps the most conspicuous characteristic of all her letters. She is always absolutely frank and absolutely sensible; yet she manages never to be heavy. Her wit has that quality which is the best of all preservatives against dullness—it goes straight to the point. If she had been a little less sensible, she would have been an eccentric; if she had been a little less witty she would have been a prig. "To say truth," she wrote, at the age of sixty-six, "I think myself an uncommon kind of creature, being an old woman without superstition, peevishness, or censoriousness." The account was true of all the periods of her life.

Her freedom from prejudice, which was so strikingly demonstrated by her introduction into England of the practice of inoculation, adds a peculiar interest to her letters. Her views on the education of women were especially in advance of her age. "To say truth, there is no part of the world where our sex is treated with so much contempt as in England. I do not complain of men for having engrossed the government: in excluding us from all degrees of power, they preserve us from many fatigues, many dangers, and perhaps many crimes. . . . But I think it the highest injustice to be debarred the entertainment of my closet, and that the same studies which raise the character of a man should hurt that of a woman. We are educated in the grossest ignorance, and no art omitted to stifle our natural reason; if some few get above their nurses' instructions, our knowledge must rest concealed, and be as useless to the world as gold in a mine." She returns to the subject again and again in her letters to her daughter, Lady Bute. "Learning, if she (Lady Bute's daughter) have a real taste for it, will not only make her contented, but happy. No entertainment is so cheap as reading, nor any pleasure so lasting. She will not want new fashions, nor regret the loss of expensive diversions, or variety of company, if she be amused with an author in her closet." And again: "The use of learning in our sex, beside the amusement of solitude, is to moderate the passions, and learn to be contented with a small expense, which are the certain effects of a studious life; and it may be preferable even to that fame which men have engrossed themselves, and will not suffer us to share." "Most people confound the ideas of sense and cunning," she again writes, "though there are really no two things in nature more opposite. It is, in part, from this false reasoning, the unjust custom prevails of debarring our sex from the advantages of learning, the men fancying improvement of our understandings would only furnish us with more art to deceive them; which is directly contrary to the truth. Fools are always enterprising, not seeing the difficulties of deceit or the ill consequences of detection."

These are admirable reflexions, but Lady Mary is not always so serious. Her letters abound in pointed remarks and spicy anecdotes; and her comments on the persons of her acquaintance are usually most amusing when they are most vitriolic. She is at her best when she is telling her correspondent of the history of some "beauteous virgin of forty," and how "after having refused all the peers in England, because the nicety of her conscience would not permit her to give her hand when her heart was untouched, she remained without a husband till the charms of that fine gentleman, Mr. Smith, who is only eighty-two, determined her to change her condition." Or in such a character-sketch as this: "That good creature (as the country saying is) has not a bit of pride in him. I dare swear he purchased his title for the same reason he used to buy pictures in Italy; not because he wanted to buy, but because somebody or other wanted to sell. He hardly ever opened his mouth but to say,

'What you please, sir'; 'At your service'; 'Your humble servant,' or some gentle expression to the same effect. It is scarce
credible that with this unlimited complaisance he should
draw a blow upon himself; yet it so happened that one of
his countrymen was brute enough to strike him. As it was
done before many witnesses, Lord Mansel heard of it; and
thinking that if poor Sir John took no notice of it, he would
suffer more insults of the same kind, out of pure good nature resolved to spirit him up, at least to some show of re-
sentment, intending to make up their matter afterwards in
as honourable a manner as he could for the poor patient.
He represented to him very warmly that no gentleman could
take a box on the ear. Sir John answered with great calmness, 'I know that, but this was not a box on the ear; it was
only a slap on the face.' "

Every reader of Lady Mary must observe, without sub-
scribing to Pope's scurrilities about "Sappho," that a sense
of propriety seems rarely to stand in the way of her sense of
humour. She was the last person to beat about the bush,
when there was a point to be made by plain speaking; and
such were precisely the points which presented themselves
most frequently to her mind. Thus, when she is coarse, she
is always coarse directly; she does not wrap up her meaning
in a veil of innuendoes; so that her indecencies have at
least this merit: they are nothing if not healthy. Nor can
they be denied the saving grace of wit. The following is a
typical passage: "To speak plainly, I am very sorry for the
forlorn state of matrimony, which is as much ridiculed by
our young ladies as it used to be by young fellows: in short,
both sexes have found the inconveniences of it, and the ap-
pellation of rake is as genteel in a woman as in a man of
quality; it is no scandal to say Miss ——, the maid of honour,
looks very well now she is up again, and poor Biddy Noel
has never been quite well since her last confinement. You

may imagine we married women look very silly; we have nothing to excuse ourselves, but that it was done a great while ago, and we were very young when we did it." Who would not be amused by that conclusion? And would it not be a somewhat hypocritical severity to laugh and to condemn at the same time?

Lady Mary's straightforwardness was not without its drawbacks. It is only by striking very hard that one can hit the nail on the head; and Lady Mary, solely occupied with that operation, wasted none of her energies in delicate touches. Her letters are all in one key—the C major of this life. They express no subtleties, no discriminations, no changes of mood. They flash; but with a metallic light. Their writer, one feels, was far too sensible either to sink or to soar; and it is an open question whether she was ever much excited. Describing her discussions with the Jesuits, she wrote: "I have always the advantage of being quite calm on a subject which they cannot talk of without heat." And that was her attitude in every relation of life. Her very love-letters were made up of arguments upon the ethics of marriage. Her philosophy of life, though it was too witty to be dull, was too dispassionate to be true. The real nature of things was hidden from her, because she could never throw herself into its midst. "Why are our views so extensive and our power so miserably limited?" she writes. "This is among the mysteries which (as you justly say) will remain ever unfolded to our shallow capacities. I am much inclined to think we are no more free agents than the queen of clubs when she victoriously takes prisoner the knave of hearts; and all our efforts (when we rebel against destiny) as weak as a card that sticks to a glove when the gamester is determined to throw it on the table. Let us then (which is the only true philosophy) be contented with our chance, and make the best of that very bad bargain of being born in this vile planet; where we may find, however (God be thanked), much to laugh at, though little to approve." It is hardly an exaggeration to say that, to Lady Mary, life was simply—as she describes it—a game of whist. And the rigour of it was what she most enjoyed.

Lord Chesterfield's letters to his son form a fitting counterpart to Lady Mary Wortley's letters to her daughter. They deal with the same subject—education; though the Earl treats it at infinitely greater length and with infinitely greater wealth of detail. His famous letters are, in fact, hardly familiar letters at all. They are a series of elaborate essays upon manners. The theme is always the same; and the endless repetition of it becomes all the more wearisome from the fact that the variations are conspicuously wanting in variety. It is difficult to conceive a fate more terrible than that which condemned the young Stanhope to the weekly bombardment of his father's packet. Even to us, who can read the four hundred letters with the detachment of creatures of another world, they make gloomy and irritating reading. To Philip, who knew that every sentence in them applied in the most personal manner possible to him, who could look back on an endless vista of identical admonitions, and knew that he must look forward to another vista equally infinite, the horror of their perusal must have been unimaginable. "Good God!" he used to read at breakfast, "how I should be shocked, if you came into my room, for the first time, with two left legs, presenting yourself with all the graces and dignity of a tailor, and your clothes hanging upon you, like those in Monmouth Street, upon tenter-hooks!" Could anything be more depressing? But then he had already been informed that "when we meet, if you are absent in mind, I will soon be absent in body; for it will be impossible for me to stay in the room; and if at table you throw down

27

your knife, plate, bread, etc., and hack the wing of a chicken for half an hour, without being able to cut it off, and your sleeve all the time in another dish, I must rise from table to escape the fever you must certainly give me." And in a few weeks he was to learn that "I fear but one thing for you, and that is what one has generally the least reason to fear from one of your age; I mean your laziness: which, if you indulge, will make you stagnate in a contemptible obscurity all your life." The grave was the one refuge from such a persecution; but who could tell that the grave itself would be safe? Might not a letter from Lord Chesterfield follow one even there, with instructions as to how one should deport oneself in that situation?

The main doctrine which lies at the back of Chesterfield's letters has been expressed by La Bruyère in three sentences: "Avec de la vertu, de la capacité, et une bonne conduite, on peut être insupportable. Les manières, que l'on néglige comme de petites choses, sont souvent ce qui fait que les hommes décident de vous en bien ou en mal: une légère attention à les avoir douces et polies prévient leurs mauvais jugements. Il ne faut presque rien pour être cru fier, incivil, méprisant, désobligeant: il faut encore moins pour être estimé tout le contraire." Admitting the truth of the doctrine, were Chesterfield's methods of putting it into practice likely to meet with success? His system of minute instruction falls between two stools—it is either absurdly platitudinous, or uselessly vague. Nobody wants to be told to cut his fingernails so as to make them form segments of circles; and to tell someone to "take the tone of his conversation from his company" is the merest mockery. All the important things in manners are either so easy that it is not worth while teaching them, or so difficult that they can never be taught. Chesterfield never seems to have recognised this. On the one hand, he drummed away on carving and blowing one's nose;

and on the other, he perpetually attempted to inculcate wit
and grace and refinement by the simple process of affirming
them to be important and admirable qualities. In any case,
such a system of instruction would have been absurd; in the
case of Stanhope, an additional fact rendered it peculiarly
preposterous. Chesterfield completely failed to see that character was a question of the slightest importance in education.
He firmly believed, and constantly reiterated, that a man
could learn to be anything—except a poet. If this theory
needed refutation, it received it once and for all at the hands
of Philip Stanhope. No young man, before or since, was ever
more carefully trained in the way that he should go; that he
should shine in politics and diplomacy was the one object
of his father's life, and of his own endeavours. Alas! he shone
in nothing. That was not his nature; and all the pitchforks
of Lord Chesterfield were impotent to change it.

Nor can we be sorry that this was the case. Chesterfield's
scheme of conduct was odious, not because it was immoral,
but because it was blindly conventional. It faithfully crept
after all the unthinking prejudices of the age; it definitely
aimed at the stupid vulgar ideals of stupid vulgar people; it
brushed on one side what was most valuable as trifling and
absurd. Place and power were the ends which Stanhope was
to pursue with all his might; for their sake he was
to flirt with fine ladies, and flatter great ministers; for their
sake he was to learn to dance and to wear clean linen every
day. He was never to be idle a moment; he was never to reflect, nor brood, nor dream. "No piping nor fiddling, I be-
seech you," exclaims his father; "no days lost in poring upon
almost imperceptible *Intaglios*, and *Cameos:* and do not become a Virtuoso of small wares. Form a taste of Painting,
Sculpture, and Architecture, if you please, by a careful examination of the works of the best ancient and modern
artists; those are liberal arts, and real taste and knowledge

of them become a man of fashion very well. But beyond certain bounds, the man of taste ends, and the frivolous Virtuoso begins."

It is pleasant to know that this twaddle produced no effect whatever. Philip Stanhope collected, during his travels, a large library of rare old books. It was among these that the happiest hours of his life were spent; and it must have been with no ordinary sense of relief that he turned, after the perusal of one of his father's epistles, to some quiet quarto or some charming Aldus, to some black-letter Luther, some duodecimo Erasmus, or some vast and venerable Bede.

4. Horace Walpole

THE letter-writing of the eighteenth century reaches its climax in the correspondence of Horace Walpole. The vast period of time which they cover, the immense variety of topics with which they deal, the sustained brilliancy of their execution, give these famous letters a position of pre-eminence unrivalled in English literature, and only paralleled by the letters of Voltaire in the literature of the world. Voltaire, however, threw off his letters in the intervals of a multifarious literary activity—they were little more than incidents in the great work of his life. It would almost be true to say the exact contrary of Walpole. His correspondence was his serious occupation; he did not snatch moments from life to write letters in: he snatched moments from letter-writing in which to live. That he lived so fully, that he was able to indulge in such a variety of occupations and to amass such a wealth of experience, is perhaps almost as wonderful as that Voltaire found the time and the energy wherewith to compile his fourteen volumes of correspondence. In his old age, indeed, Walpole began to degenerate: he wrote letters more and more; he lived less and less. There were occasions towards the end of his life when he deliberately refrained from visiting Lady Ossory, because he knew that then he would have to tell her by word of mouth the anecdotes which he wished to tell her only in a letter. But such conduct was not characteristic of Walpole at his best. He did not spin out his letters, like a silkworm, from

his inner consciousness; he nourished them upon the substantial facts of life. His pages are packed with matter. As
one turns them over, an enormous panorama unrolls itself
before one's eyes. Eminent and brilliant persons, momentous
events, epoch-making books, political intrigues, follow one
another in endless succession. Now one looks in at a mas-
querade at Sir William Hanbury's, now one is at Stowe with
the Princess Amelia, now one is superintending the printing
of Gray's *Elegy* at Strawberry Hill, now one is sitting down
to whist with the "Archbishopess of Canterbury and Mr.
Gibbon," now one is chatting with Madame du Deffand in
Paris, now one is listening to Charles Townshend in the
House of Commons. The vigorous and dazzling world of
Walpole's London lives again before our eyes. We begin to
be intimate with the latter half of the eighteenth century.
We have been led in through the back door to the very central chamber of that great period in English History; and
we see things, not as outside observers, but as familiar friends.

Walpole's activities were so numerous and so various that
readers of the letters are a little apt to emphasise one side
of his personality at the expense of the rest, in accordance
with their own predilections. This was doubtless also the
case with his correspondents. He was probably regarded by
Mann as a politician, by Mason as a man of letters, by Cole
as an antiquary, and by Lady Ossory as a gossip. It will be
well, therefore, to consider his letters from these different
points of view.

I. Walpole's connection with politics was the natural consequence of his parentage. He entered the House of Commons while his father was still in power, and remained a
member for twenty-five years; but it was not so much his
place in the House, as his place among the great political
families, which gave him that inner knowledge of parlia-

mentary workings which is so conspicuous in his letters to Sir Horace Mann. He was thoroughly at home within the narrow circle of the aristocratic society which then controlled the destinies of England. The Lytteltons, the Pitts, the Foxes, the Pelhams, the Bedfords—these were the persons among whom he habitually moved. Besides this, his intimacy with his cousin, General Conway, gave him at one time an almost first-hand acquaintance with affairs. Whether he himself might not have made his mark in politics is perhaps a futile speculation, but it is one which naturally suggests itself to a reader of the letters. It is certain at least that Macaulay's estimate of Walpole's ability was grossly unfair. Walpole cannot be dismissed as an affected and malignant jackanapes. The series of letters to the Earl of Hertford, written while the latter was Ambassador at Paris (1763–5), are sufficient in themselves to show that Walpole was at any rate an acute and sagacious observer, if he was nothing more. But there is some reason to believe that his practice would not have fallen short of his theory. His influence on Conway's party at the time of the Regency Bill (1765) was certainly great, though it was not great enough; and his foresight was proved by the disaster which followed when his advice was neglected. His conflict with George Grenville in the preceding year shows even more clearly how capable he was of taking a practical part in life. Nothing could have been more shrewd and firm than his conduct on that occasion. The qualities which a man must have to be able to baffle and humiliate a Chancellor of the Exchequer were precisely the qualities which would have been most useful to a politician in the time of Walpole.

It is doubtless true that personal motives played a large part in Walpole's politics. But it must be remembered that he never was in any position where the intrusion of personal feelings could lead to any harm; and there is not the slightest reason to suppose that, if he had been in office, he would have allowed his private affections and animosities to interfere with the conduct of affairs. Nor were feelings such as these the only ones which coloured his political views. His hatred of tyranny was certainly geniune; and so was his hatred of corruption. He was not a profound or an original political philosopher, but what principles he had were truly liberal ones; in most disputed questions he was in advance of the majority of his contemporaries. He held the slave trade in detestation. He was bitterly opposed to the American policy of Grenville and North. There was indeed one important topic with regard to which his usual acumen deserted him: he entirely failed to recognise the true significance of the exploits of the East India Company. Clive and Hastings were to him merely types of the successful plunderer who only differs from the common highwayman in that he practises his calling with impunity. But if, in this particular, Walpole erred, he erred in excellent company. It would be too much to expect of a politician that he should be wiser than Burke.

A further instance of Walpole's sagacity is to be seen in the references in his letters from Paris to the condition of France. His jeremiads were never as precise as Lord Chesterfield's, but they display an astonishingly clear appreciation of the trend of events. As early as 1771 Walpole wrote as follows: "For the misery of his people, and for the dangers of his successors (if he escapes himself) the King, I think, will triumph over his country: a victory most kings prefer, not only to peace, but to foreign laurels. The Princes of the blood are firm, without spirit or sense: the nobility have as little of either; the vigour of Parliamentary remonstrances are hushed by the English remedy—bribery: and the people curse the King, the Chancellor, the mistress; and starve." It is interesting to find Diderot writing to Wilkes just a month

later in the following strain: "Imaginez un palais immense
dont l'aspect majestueux et solide vous en imposoit, promet-
toit à votre imagination une durée éternelle; imaginez
ensuite que les fondements s'ébranlent et que vous voyez
tout à coup ses murs énormes se séparer et se disjoindre.
Voilà précisément le spectacle que nous offririons à votre
spéculation." [1]

It is not difficult to explain why, in spite of his position
and his attainments, Walpole never took an active part in
public life. In the first place, the whole cast of his mind was
eminently unsuited to the rough-and-tumble of the parliamentary arena. He could not speak with ease; and in the
heat of battle he would certainly have cut a sorry figure. His
extreme sensitiveness to ridicule, doubtless the main cause
of his abstention from debate, shut off from him for ever
all hope of a political career. Secondly, Walpole's interests
were far from being exclusively political; and it is open to
question whether, even if the highest places had been offered
to him, he would have accepted them. Doubtless he had
ambitions; but he also had Strawberry Hill. His books, his
china, his ladies, his leisure—why should he sacrifice all these
things for the sake of a little uncomfortable power? Was the
game worth the candle, after all?

II. The literary side of Walpole is to be studied chiefly
in the series of letters to Mason, which are little more than
a running criticism of the books and plays of the time. Walpole's taste was certainly not in advance of his age; perhaps
it was on the whole behind it. His admiration of Gibbon
was unstinted; but so was his admiration of Dr. Robertson.
The poetry of Gray he declared to be immortal; but then
he paid the same compliment to the poetry of Mason. These

[1] From an unpublished letter in the British Museum. The date is October 19, 1771.

were all conventional eighteenth-century judgments, which were certainly made by Walpole's bookseller no less than by Walpole himself. But his lack of literary discrimination went further than this. "At present nothing is talked of, nothing admired," he wrote in 1760, "but what I cannot help calling a very insipid and tedious performance; it is a kind of novel, called 'The Life and Opinions of Tristram Shandy,' the great humour of which consists in the whole narration always going backwards. . . . The characters are tolerably kept up, but the humour is for ever attempted and missed." Nothing could be more superficial. It does not seem to have entered Walpole's head that Sterne was a master of English prose, or that one might as well praise the characters of Iago and Macbeth for being "tolerably kept up" as those of Uncle Toby and Mr. Shandy.

The truth is that Walpole's interest in literature as an art was very small. It is only necessary to compare him with Gray, for instance, to see at once how merely skin-deep his literary feelings were. Literature amused him, it interested him; but it never moved him. Reading was for him an elegant recreation, and nothing more. It has been constantly pointed out that his dealings with Chatterton throw no discredit upon him whatever; it is not the business of every rich gentleman to assist unfortunate poets. This defence is complete, but it is irrelevant, unless one fact is clearly recognised—that Walpole belonged to a class which cannot be expected to have a real appreciation of art. Walpole found that he had been deceived by a beggarly young poet; he would have no more to say to him. Nothing could be more natural or require less excuse; for Walpole did not know what a poet was.

Even more marked than his lack of true artistic feeling was Walpole's antipathy to abstract speculation. It was this characteristic which put him altogether out of touch with the

most important literary movement of his time—that great
revolt against the superstition and prejudice of the Past,
which was set on foot by Voltaire, and carried to its height
by the Encyclopaedists. Diderot, d'Alembert, Condorcet,
Hume—these great names only served to raise the contempt
of Walpole. "The *savants*—I beg their pardons, the *philosophes*—are insupportable, superficial, overbearing, and fa-
natic." "The French," he wrote from Paris, "affect philosophy, literature, and freethinking; the first never did, and
never will, possess me; of the two others I have long been
tired. Freethinking is for one's self, surely not for society;
besides, one has settled one's way of thinking, or knows it
cannot be settled, and for others I do not see why there is
not as much bigotry in attempting conversions from any
religion as to it. . . . For literature, it is very amusing when
one has nothing else to do. I think it rather pedantic in society; tiresome when displayed professedly; and besides, in
this country one is sure it is only the fashion of the day.
Their taste in it is worst of all: could one believe that when
they read our authors, Richardson and Mr. Hume should be
their favourites? The latter is treated here with perfect ven-
eration."

It is fortunately possible to be a good letter writer without being even a tolerable critic or philosopher. Though
Walpole's thought was never deep, it was always vivacious;
and excellence of style was meted out to him, though not
the faculty of perceiving it in others. The distinguishing
mark of his writing is a curious mixture of the careless and
the elaborate. He is able to spin the most fanciful similes, to
heap image upon image and embroidery upon embroidery,
and yet to preserve an almost colloquial tone. "Poor human
nature," he wrote to Lady Ossory at the age of sixty-four,
"what a contradiction it is! Today it is all rheumatism and
morality, and sits with a death's head before it: tomorrow it

37

is dancing! Oh! my Lady, my Lady, what will you say, when the next thing you hear of me after my last letter is that I have danced three country dances with a whole set, forty years younger than myself! Shall not you think I have been chopped to shreds and boiled in Medea's kettle? Shall not you expect to see a print of Vestris teaching me?—and Lord Brudenell dying with envy? You may stare with all your expressive eyes, yet the fact is true. Danced—I do not absolutely say *danced*—but I swam down three dances very gracefully, with the air that was so much in fashion after the battle of Oudenard, and that was still taught when I was fifteen, and that I remember General Churchill practising before a glass in a gouty shoe."

Such is a specimen of Walpole's style at its best; and to say that he nowhere, in the whole of his fifty years of correspondence, falls very far short of this level of excellence is no mean compliment. On every page there is the same ease, the same ingenuity, the same constant succession of surprises, the same exquisite balance of rhythm. It is reported of Walpole that he often wrote his letters in a room full of company; and the story is not only interesting as an illustration of the facility with which he wrote. For the precise impression produced upon us by the best of his letters is that they were written by someone who had the sound of a refined conversation still in his ears.

III. No description of Walpole would be complete without an allusion to him as antiquary and connoisseur. The letters are full of references to the various curiosities and objects of vertu which he took so much pride in collecting around him—the Roman Eagle, the medals, the spurs of King Charles, the Domenichinos, the manuscripts, the rare prints —all the multitude of treasures contained in the "Tribune" at Strawberry Hill. There can be no doubt that it was a characteristic of Walpole's mind to be pleased by oddities more easily than by things of more solid worth. He liked Gothic architecture, not because he thought it beautiful, but because he found it queer; and accordingly the Gothic castles (whether of Otranto or of Strawberry) which he himself constructed, were more remarkable for their queerness than for their beauty. His love of peculiarity, however, never outweighed his hatred of the ridiculous; he always remained within the boundaries of common sense. Macaulay's strictures on this head are as exaggerated as the rest of his brilliant diatribe; and indeed, even if Walpole had been carried by his mania for collecting into excesses of folly undreamt of by Macaulay himself, how could we help forgiving them in the face of a passage such as this?—"You are to know, Madam, that I have in my custody the individual ebony cabinet in which Madame de Sévigné kept her pens and paper for writing her matchless letters. It was preserved near Grignan by an old man who mended her pens, and whose descendant gave it last year to Mr. Selwyn, as truly worthy of such a sacred relic. It wears, indeed, all the outward and visible signs of such venerable preciousness, for it is clumsy, cumbersome, and shattered, and inspires no more idea of her spirit and *légèreté* than the mouldy thigh-bone of a saint does of the unction of his sermons.

IV. It is as a commentary on the everyday doings and sayings of the brilliant society of his age that Walpole's letters exercise their firmest hold over the hearts of his readers. At least one-half of the correspondence is taken up with this fleeting unessential side of life, which finds a perfect reflection in the delicate polish of Walpole's periods. His letters to Lady Ailesbury and Lady Ossory, and later to the Miss Berrys, are made up of a stream of anecdotes, of small-talk, of descriptions of fine houses, of accounts of balls and theatricals, of *vers de société,* of gossiping reminiscences of ancient days. After every social event Walpole hurried to send off a comment on it to whichever of his favourite Countesses might happen to be out of town; and when great occasions were lacking, the ordinary occurrences of the day furnish abundance of matter for his pen. "My resolutions of growing old and staid," he wrote to Lady Hervey, "are admirable; I wake with a sober plan, and intend to pass the day with my friends—then comes the Duke of Richmond, and hurries me down to Whitehall to dinner—then the Duchess of Grafton sends for me to loo in Upper Grosvenor Street—before I can get thither, I am begged to step to Kensington, to give Mrs. Anne Pitt my opinion about a bow-window—after the loo, I am to march back to Whitehall to supper—and after that, am to walk with Miss Pelham on the terrace till two in the morning, because it is moonlight and her chair is not come. All this does not help my morning laziness; and, by the time I have breakfasted, fed my birds and my squirrels, and dressed, there is an auction ready. In short, Madam, this was my life last week, and is I think every week, with the addition of forty episodes."

Such was the round of trivial gaieties and dissipations in which most of Walpole's time was spent. But it would be an error to suppose that his intercourse with the men and women about him was always of this ephemeral nature; he was capable both of sincere attachments and of strong dislikes. Everything that we know of him leads us to the conclusion that he was sensitive to an extraordinary degree; and the defects—for defects they certainly were—which he showed in social intercourse, were caused by an excess of this quality of sensitiveness rather than by a lack of genuine feeling. His angry, cutting sentences, his constant mockery of his enemies, his constant quarrels with his friends, all these things were certainly not the result of a coldness of heart. And there was another element in his character which must never be forgotten in any estimate of Walpole's relations with other people—his pride. At heart he was a complete aristocrat; it was almost impossible for him to be unreserved. The masks he wore were imposed upon him by his caste, by his breeding, by his own intimate sense of the decencies and proprieties of life; so that his hatreds and his loves, so easily aroused and so intensely cherished, were forced to express themselves in spiteful little taunts and in artificial compliments. Sometimes for a moment or two the veil is withdrawn. In his account of his quarrel with Gray, for instance, in his letter to Mason, after the former's death, when he says, "I treated him insolently. He loved me, and I did not think he did," one must be very blind indeed to see in such words as those nothing more than a frigid indifference. But perhaps the most interesting of his confidences is in his letter to Conway, written on his sixtieth birthday. It is one of the rare passages in the letters which was obviously not intended for publication. "Though I am threescore today, I should not think that an age for giving everything up; but it is, for whatever one has not strength to perform . . . my spirits are never low; but they seldom will last out the whole day; and though I dare to say I appear to many capricious, and different from the rest of the world, there is more reason in my behaviour than there seems. . . . It would be ridiculous to talk so much of myself, and to enter into such trifling details, but *you* are the person in the world that I wish to convince that I do not act merely from humour or ill-humour; though I confess at the same time that I want your *bonhomie,* and have a disposition not to care at all for people that I do not absolutely like. I could say a great deal more on this head, but it is not proper; though, when one has pretty much done with the world, I think with Lady Blandford, that one may indulge oneself in one's own whims and partialities in one's own house. . . . I will never say any more on these subjects, because there may be as much affectation in being over old, as folly in being over young. My idea of age is, that one has nothing really to do but what one ought, and what is reasonable. All affectations are pretensions; and pretending to be anything one is not, cannot deceive when one is known, as everybody must be that has lived long. . . . Family love and pride make me interest myself about the young people of my own family—for the whole rest of the young world, they are as indifferent to me as puppets or black children. This is my creed, and a key to my whole conduct, and the more likely to remain my creed, as I think it *raisonné*. If I could paint my opinions instead of writing them—and I don't know whether it would not make a new sort of alphabet—I should use different colours for different affections at different ages. When I speak of love, affection, friendship, taste, liking, I should draw them rose colour, carmine, blue, green, yellow, for my contemporaries; for new comers, the first would be no colour; the others, purple, brown, crimson, and changeable. Remember, one tells one's creed only to one's confessor, that is *sub sigillo*. I write to you as I think; to others as I must. Adieu!"

There is something almost austere in the resignation and the disillusionment of these lines. One feels that there are depths beneath. One may not pity; one may perhaps admire.

5. Gray and Cowper

THE main interest of the correspondence of Walpole is that it reflects for us to the full the bustle and glamour of the age in which he lived. The fascination of Gray's letters is of a very different nature; it is almost entirely personal. The subjects with which they deal are not the living momentary actions of every day which we find recorded with such zest in the pages of Walpole; they are the quiet reflected topics which might naturally present themselves to a recluse of any epoch—poetry, and botany, and the beauties of nature, and the almost stationary incidents of University life. But whatever it is that Gray is writing of, we are certain to find the mark of his personality indelibly stamped upon it; everything he lays hands on becomes part of himself; his essence lingers about all his pages, like a subtle and mysterious and pervading scent. As we read on, the attraction which this mind exercises over us becomes stronger and stronger; we cannot tear ourselves away; we begin to be as much absorbed in a catalogue of Latin books and the dates of birds singing as we were in Lady Mary's raciest anecdote or Horace Walpole's most elaborate compliment; we find ourselves becoming endeared to the Cambridge gossip of five generations back; we do not know why this should be, and that very fact intensifies the enchantment. Is Gray's refinement the thing about him which captivates us most? It would, indeed, be difficult to imagine a person more perfectly refined; as Bonstetten said, many years after his friend was dead, "Gray was the ideal of a gentleman." The busy ornament of Walpole's style seems almost vulgar after Gray's easy grace. Gray's prose, though far less studied than his verse, is just as faultless. It is the prose of one who is a complete master of the art of writing; it is natural, yet never weak; expressive, yet never out of taste. It could not have been written by anyone who was not a scholar, nor by anyone who was not a man of the world.

Or is it the breadth of Gray's sympathies which lies at the root of our admiration? This quality of his mind was the natural consequence of his good taste. His literary judgments are always excellent; his enjoyment of Shakespeare did not blind his eyes to the merits of Gresset; he admired Froissart no less than Voltaire. He was passionately fond of flowers and of birds. In his love of nature he was one of the earliest precursors of the school of Wordsworth; and some of the finest passages in his letters are his descriptions of scenery among the Lakes. "As I advanced," he writes to Wharton, describing a mountain walk, "the crags seemed to close in, but discovered a narrow entrance turning to the left between them. I followed my guide a few paces, and lo, the hills opened again into no large space, and then all further way is barred by a stream, that at the height of above fifty feet gushes from a hole in the rock, and spreading in large sheets over its broken front, dashes from steep to steep, and then rattles away in a torrent down the valley. The rock on the left rises perpendicular with stubbed yew-trees and shrubs starting from its side to the height of at least three hundred feet; but those are not the things; it is that to the right under which you stand to see the fall that forms the principal horror of the place. From its very base it begins to slope forward over you in a black and solid mass, without any crevice in its surface, and overshadows half the area below with its dreadful canopy. When I stood at (I believe) full four yards distance from its foot, the drops which perpetually distill from its brow, fell on my head, and in one part of the top more exposed to the weather, there are loose stones that hang in the air, and threaten visibly some idle spectator with instant destruction. It is safer to shelter yourself close to its bottom, and trust the shelter of that enormous mass which nothing but an earthquake can stir. The gloomy uncomfortable day well suited the savage aspect of the place, and made it still more formidable."

"I stayed there (not without shuddering)," Gray adds, "a quarter of an hour, and thought my trouble richly paid, for the impression will last for life."

Or is what most delights us in Gray his sense of humour? A subtle smile seems to play over his letters—a smile which often eludes our vision, and meets us when we least expect to find it. His humour is quiet; but it is singularly free from restraint. There is no subject upon which it may not suddenly perch, with a touch as light as a bird's. The death of Mr. Walpole's cat, and the death of a head of a college from a surfeit of mackerel, equally afford matter for his delicate laughter, just as his own death does. "The spirit of laziness," he writes from Cambridge, "(the spirit of the place) begins to possess even me, that have so long declaimed against it. Yet has it not so prevailed, but that I feel that discontent with myself, that ennui, that ever accompanies it in its beginnings. Time will settle my conscience, time will reconcile my languid companion; we shall smoke, we shall tipple, we shall doze together, we shall have our little jokes, like other people, and our long stories. Brandy will finish what port begun; and a month after the time you will see in some corner of a London Evening Post 'Yesterday died the Rev. Mr. John Grey, Senior-Fellow of Clare Hall, a facetious companion, and well respected by all that knew him. His death is supposed to have been occasioned by a fit of an apoplexy, being found fallen out of bed with his head in a chamber-pot.'" Such was Gray's humour—the humour of the gently ironical suggestion, not the humour of the loud guffaw. The wild hilarity of a Lamb, and the sombre sarcasm of a Swift were alike alien to his spirit. Nor did he know the Shandean giddiness; he never (to quote his own criticism of Sterne) "threw his periwig in the face of his audience"; his was the least ostentatious of wits; it was born to blush unseen.

When we have mentioned Gray's exquisite taste, his wide culture, and his peculiar humour, we have not exhausted the list of qualities which go to make up that charm which we have noticed as distinctively his. There is another quality of even greater importance than these—his melancholy. Gray was never in high spirits; there was always a little sediment of depression lurking at the bottom of his happiest moods. His melancholy was indeed the quintessential part of him—the true substance of his being; and, in his letters, one perceives it, mixing with his other qualities, and giving them a strange significance, like a French horn among a company of strings. Perhaps it is in his letters to Bonstetten that this underlying characteristic of Gray's finds its clearest expression. Gray was nearing the end of his life when the arrival of that vivacious young foreigner in Cambridge seemed to open up to him a vista of delightful hopes. "I never saw such a boy," he wrote to Nicholls; "our breed is not made on this model. He is busy from morning to night, has no other amusement than that of changing one study for another; likes nobody that he sees here; and yet wishes to stay longer, though he has passed a whole fortnight with us already." In the weeks which followed, Gray's affection for Bonstetten steadily deepened; and when at last the latter was obliged to return to Switzerland, his departure left an aching void in Gray's life. "Alas!" Gray wrote to him. "How do I every moment feel the truth of what I have somewhere read,—'Ce n'est pas le voir, que de s'en souvenir';—and yet that remembrance is the only satisfaction I have left. My life now is but a conversation with your shadow—the known sound of your voice still rings in my ears—there, on the corner of the fender you are standing, or tinkling on the pianoforte, or stretched at length on the sofa. . . . I cannot bear this place where I have spent many tedious years in less than a month since you left me." Three weeks later he writes again, after a journey to Suffolk: "The thought that you might have been with me there has embittered all my hours: your letter has made me happy, as happy as so gloomy, so solitary a being as I am, is capable of being made. I know and have too often felt the disadvantages I lay myself under, how much I hurt the little interest I have in you, by this air of sadness so contrary to your nature and present enjoyments; but sure you will forgive though you cannot sympathize with me. . . . All that you say to me, especially on the subject of Switzerland, is infinitely acceptable. It feels too pleasing ever to be fulfilled, and as often as I read over your truly kind letter, written long since from London, I stop at these words: 'La mort qui peut glacer nos bras avant qu'ils soient entrelacés.' "

The same distinction pervades Gray's melancholy as all his other feelings. His grief has in it "no weakness, no contempt, dispraise or blame," there is no high-pitched exclamation in it—there is only a tender regret. The same note is to be heard in the *Elegy* and in the *Sonnet to West*. One is reminded, as one listens to it, of the exquisite emotion of a sonata by Mozart.

It is difficult to believe that Gray could have lived among more appropriate surroundings than those which were actually his. His spirit seems still to hover about Cambridge. Those retired gardens, those cloistered courts, are as fitted now for his footstep and his smile as they were a hundred years ago. It seems hardly rash, when the midnight fire has been piled up, when sleep has descended upon the profane, when a deeper silence has fallen upon the night, when the unsported oak still stands invitingly ajar, to expect—in spite of the impediments of time and of mortality—a visit from Gray.

The letters of Cowper, though they rank high in English literature, do not require much comment. As far as they go, they are perfect, but they hardly go anywhere at all. Their gold is absolutely pure; but it is beaten out into the thinnest leaf conceivable. They are like soap-bubbles—exquisite films surrounding emptiness, and almost too wonderful to be touched.

Cowper had nothing to say, and he said it beautifully; yet it is difficult not to wish that he had had something more to say, even at the expense of expressing it a little less well. His letters are stricken with sterility; they are dried up; they lack the juices of life. In them, the vast and palpitating eighteenth century seems suddenly to dwindle into a quiet and well-appointed grave. The wheel had come full circle: the flute of Addison was echoed at last by the flute of Cowper; perfection had returned upon itself.

The following extract shows the highest point which Cowper's mastery of the art of making bricks without straw ever reached. "My dear Friend, you like to hear from me. This is a very good reason why I should write—but I have nothing to say. This seems equally a good reason why I should not. Yet if you had alighted from your horse at our door this morning, and at this present writing, being five o'clock in the afternoon, had found occasion to say to me—'Mr. Cowper, you have not spoken since I came in, have you resolved never to speak again?' it would be but a poor reply, if in answer I should plead inability as my best and only excuse. And this, by the way, suggests a seasonable piece of instruction, and reminds me of what I am very apt to forget, when I have any epistolary business in hand; that a letter may be written on anything or nothing, just as that anything or nothing happens to occur. A man that has a journey before him twenty miles in length, which he is to perform on foot, will not hesitate, and doubt, whether he shall set out or not, because he does not readily conceive how he shall ever reach the end of it; for he knows, that by the simple operation of moving one foot forward first, and then the other, he shall be sure to accomplish it. So it is in the present case, and so it is in every similar case. A letter is written as a conversation is maintained, or a journey performed, not by preconcerted or premeditated means, a new contrivance, or an invention never heard before; but merely by maintaining a progress, and resolving, as a postillion does, having once set out, never to stop, till we reach the appointed end. If a man may talk without thinking, why may not he write upon the same terms? A grave gentleman of the last century, a tie-wig, square-toe, Steinkirk figure, would say—'My good sir, a man has no right to do either.' But it is to be hoped that the present century . . ." After all, it was only to be expected that, when Cowper set out to write a letter about nothing at all, it would be too long to quote.

6. Byron, Shelley, Keats, and Lamb

THE reader who passes suddenly from the letters of Walpole, Gray, and Cowper to those of Byron, Shelley, and Keats experiences a strange and violent shock. His sensations resemble those of a rower who has been meandering for many days down a broad and quiet river, among fields and gardens and spacious villas, and who, in a moment, finds himself upon the sea. He has left behind him the elegance, the seclusion, the leisure of the eighteenth century; he has embarked upon the untrammelled ocean of a new age, where he will be refreshed, astonished, and delighted, but where he will find no rest. The contrast is so complete that one is tempted to believe that an intelligent reader from another planet might almost, by the aid of these letters alone, infer the French Revolution. Everything has changed; not only the "atmosphere," the general point of view; but the very form and manner of the expressions, the very clothing of the meanest thoughts, have undergone a mysterious transmutation. The old city has been ploughed up, the old landmarks have been thrown down, new streets and buildings obliterate the buried remnants of the past. The inhabitants have new faces, and speak a language which was never heard before.

The letters of Byron are completely typical of the new spirit. In three respects they differ profoundly from all the letters which preceded them. In the first place their extreme vitality makes the most vivacious passages of Walpole and Lady Mary Wortley Montagu seem bloodless in comparison.

It is only possible to appreciate their energy to the full when a great number of them have been read. The cumulative effect of Byron's vigour acts upon the reader like a tonic or a sea-breeze; he himself begins to wish to throw his ink-bottle through the window, to practise pistol-shooting in bed, to scatter his conversation with resounding oaths. The true essence of Byron cannot be distilled into two or three quotations; but the following extract may serve as an instance of the peculiar masculinity of his style. As an example of this particular quality in Byron it is especially applicable for two reasons: it is one of the rare pieces of description in his letters, and is thus comparatively free from other characteristics which will be considered later; and its subject suggests an interesting comparison with a similar passage by Walpole. It will be best to quote Walpole first: "The scaffold was immediately new-strewed with saw-dust, the block new-covered, the executioner new dressed, and a new axe brought. Then came old Balmerino, treading with the air of a general. As soon as he mounted the scaffold, he read the inscription on his coffin, as he did again afterwards: he then surveyed the spectators, who were in amazing numbers, even upon masts of ships in the river; and pulling out his spectacles, read a reasonable speech. . . . He took the axe and felt it, and asked the headsman how many blows he had given Lord Kilmarnock; and gave him three guineas. Two clergymen, who attended him, coming up, he said, 'No, gentlemen, I believe you have already done me all the service you can.' Then he went to the corner of the scaffold, and called very loud for the warder, to give him his periwig, which he took off, and put on a night-cap of Scotch plaid, and then pulled off his coat and waistcoat and lay down; but being told he was on the wrong side, vaulted round, and immediately gave the sign by tossing up his arm, as if he were giving the signal for battle. He received three blows, but the first certainly took away all sensation. . . . Balmerino certainly died with the intrepidity of a hero, but with the insensibility of one too. As he walked from his prison to execution, seeing every window and top of house filled with spectators, he cried out, 'Look, look, how they are all piled up like rotten oranges!' "

Byron, writing sixty years later, gives the following account of a similar incident: "The day before I left Rome I saw three robbers guillotined. The ceremony—including the *masked* priests; the half-naked executioners; the bandaged criminals; the black Christ and his banner; the scaffold; the soldiery; the slow procession, and the quick rattle and heavy fall of the axe; the splash of blood, and the ghastliness of the exposed heads—is altogether more impressive than the vulgar and ungentlemanly dirty 'new drop' and dog-like agony of infliction upon the sufferers of the English sentence. Two of these men behaved calmly enough, but the first of the three died with great terror and reluctance, which was very horrible. He would not lie down; then his neck was too large for the aperture, and the priest was obliged to drown his exclamations by still louder exhortations. The head was off before the eye could trace the blow; but from an attempt to draw back the head, notwithstanding it was held forward by the hair, the first head was cut off close to the ears; the other two were taken off more cleanly. It is better than the oriental way, and (I should think) than the axe of our ancestors. The pain seems little; and yet the effect to the spectator, and the preparation to the criminal, are very striking and chilling. The first turned me quite hot and thirsty, and made me shake so that I could hardly hold the opera-glass (I was close, but determined to see, as one should see everything, once, with attention); the second and third (which shows how dreadfully soon things grow indifferent), I am ashamed to say, had no effect on me as a horror, though I would have saved them if I could."

There are few passages in Byron's letters so elaborate as this; yet it is clear enough that even this was dashed off at white heat. The careful elegance of the eighteenth century was utterly alien to Byron's manner of writing. He is never ingenious, or polished, or ornamental. His nearest approach to an epigram is a bad pun. He rushes on helter-skelter, as the fancy takes him, into postscripts longer than his letters, and post-postscripts longer than all. His vocabulary is often coarse; his constructions are liable to lose themselves in the current of his thoughts; he is always amusing, but he is very rarely polite. "You are to print in what form you please," he writes to Murray on the subject of the publication of *Manfred*—"that is your concern; as far as your connection with myself has gone, you are the best judge how far you have lost or gained—probably sometimes one and sometimes the other, but when you come to me with your *'can'* and talk to me about the copy of Manfred as if the 'force of purchase would no further go—to *make* a book he separates the two,' I say unto you, verily it is not so; or, as the Foreigner said to the Waiter, after asking him to bring a glass of water, to which the man answered, 'I will, sir,'—'you *will!*—God damn, —I say, you *mush!'* "

The Byron of the letters is the Byron of *Don Juan* and *The Vision of Judgment,* not the Byron of *Childe Harold* and *The Corsair.* Hardly a trace is to be found in them of the sentimentalising and philosophising "Pilgrim"; it is the actual living man of the world whom they display. The picture is not only astonishingly vivid, it is astonishingly different from any other picture in the world. Byron's letters bear the impress of a far more distinct and individual personality than any of the letters of his predecessors. It was not that he was greater than they; it was simply that he was differentiated from his contemporaries to a greater degree; he was the first of those dominating and isolated figures which

53

were to be produced in such profusion in the first half of the nineteenth century.

Unfortunately Byron's character was marred by a defect only too common to men of this particular type: he was a complete egoist. And round this fault a multitude of others naturally clustered—narrowness of interests, lack of real enthusiasms, vulgarity, affectation. His letters are concerned with one subject, and one alone—himself. His own actions, his own thoughts, his own books, his own hopes, his own disappointments and regrets—these were the staple topics of his correspondence. Nor was he content with this direct sort of self-appreciation. He was perpetually trying to rake in a little more admiration than even he was willing to admit to be his due. He was an inveterate *poseur;* and his poetry was merely the result of one out of a large number of his poses. He wished to be thought a philosopher, and a man of feeling, and a republican, and a gay dog; he also wished to be thought a poet. That he convinced the world that he was, is doubtless the most striking proof of his genius. Few save Byron could ever have carried the lack of ear, of taste, and of common sense so far, as would have enabled them to commit to paper the hideous balderdash, for instance, which goes by the name of *Cain;* none save Byron could have hypnotised Europe into believing that that work was worthy of the combined efforts of Milton and Aeschylus. It is difficult to decide which was the more amazing achievement. But perhaps after all it is not in his poetry that we find Byron at his worst. It is only necessary to cast one's eye over the blasphemies and obscenities which he poured forth in his letters to Moore upon the author of *Hyperion* to reach the true measure of the depths of degradation to which Byron's taste could sink. It is satisfactory to know that Keats at any rate was under no delusion as to the value of Byron's poetry.

Some recently discovered lines have brought his opinion of
it to light.[1]

Byron as a reckless and amused adventurer is an object
pleasanter to contemplate than Byron as a poet. In the
former capacity, his Venetian letters give a view of him
which is undoubtedly all the more entertaining owing to the
fact that it distinctly oversteps the bounds of propriety.
Many of Byron's most human, vigorous, and entertaining
qualities seem to have been called out in his dealings with
a certain class of women. The story of the "Fornarina"
(Letter to Murray, August 1, 1819) is a piece of racy narrative worthy of Fielding at his best. It is too long to quote,
but the powers of description which it displays make it clear
that the world would have been the gainer if Byron had
written novels instead of poetry.

Trelawney says, in his *Reminiscences,* that Byron, since his
"school hallucinations," had never had a friend. It is certainly true that Byron's letters bear out this statement. Indeed, he was probably incapable of friendship. There was
no give and take about his nature; and his vanity was such
that he preferred to be flattered by an insignificant mind,
like Moore's, to being treated as an equal by a noble one,
like Shelley's. The exception, however, which Trelawney
makes as to his "school hallucinations" suggests that there
may have been a time when it was otherwise with Byron. His
affection for Lord Clare may have been, after all, no "hal-
lucination"; it may have been the one real friendship of his
life. "I never hear the word 'Clare,' " he wrote in his *Detached Thoughts,* in 1821, "without a beating of the heart
even now, and I write it with the feelings of 1803–4–5– ad

[1] "Apollo! faded! O far-flown Apollo!
  Where is thy misty pestilence to creep
  Into the dwellings, through the door-crannies
  Of all mock-lyrists, large self-worshippers,
  And careless Hectorers in proud bad verse?"
                                    (*The Fall of Hyperion.*)

infinitum." A few weeks later it happened that the friends met on the road between Imola and Bologna. "This meeting," Byron wrote, "annihilated for a moment all the years between the present time and the days of Harrow. It was a new and inexplicable feeling, like rising from the grave, to me. . . . We were but five minutes together, and in the public road; but I hardly recollect an hour of my existence which could be weighed against them. . . . Of all I have ever known, he has always been the least altered in every thing from the excellent qualities and kind affections which attached me to him so strongly at school."

One seems to discern, in these few sentences, a warm and genuine feeling struggling out through the cold wrappings with which years and the world and his own self-conceit had involved the soul of Byron. For a moment or two he had been innocent once more.

The few existing letters of Shelley are chiefly remarkable for their exquisite descriptions of Italian scenery, and their criticisms of Italian literature and art. They do not add materially to our knowledge of the man—that "one thing," as a living poet has said, "sweeter than his own songs were"— though they must increase our admiration of the artist. Shelley's prose is, like his poetry, romantic, coloured, and luxuriant, to the highest degree. Two sentences will give a fair example of the fertile imagination of his style: "The handwriting of Ariosto is a small, firm and pointed character, expressing, as I should say, a strong and keen, but circumscribed energy of mind; that of Tasso is large, free, and flowing, except that there is a checked expression in the midst of its flow, which brings the letters into a smaller compass than one expected from the beginning of the word. It is the symbol of an intense and earnest mind, exceeding at times its own depth, and admonished to return by the chillness of the waters of oblivion striking upon its adventurous feet."

Both Byron and Shelley, no less than Keats, were pagans; but Byron's paganism was that of a Roman Emperor, while the two latter poets were pagans of the Athenian mould. Nothing could be in more complete contrast with the vulgar blasphemies of Byron than this passage, written by Shelley after a visit to Pompeii: "I now understand why the Greeks were such great poets; and, above all, I can account, it seems to me, for the harmony, the unity, the perfection, the uniform excellence, of all their works of art. They lived in a perpetual commerce with external nature, and nourished themselves upon the spirit of its forms. Their theatres were all open to the mountains and the sky. Their columns, the ideal types of a sacred forest, with its roof of interwoven tracery, admitted the light and wind; the odour and the freshness of the country penetrated the cities. The temples were mostly upaithric; and the flying clouds, the stars, or the deep sky, were seen above. O, but for that series of wretched wars which terminated in the Roman conquest of the world; but for the Christian religion, which put the finishing stroke on the ancient system; but for those changes that conducted Athens to its ruin,—to what an eminence might not humanity have arrived!"

Before leaving Shelley, it is impossible not to quote one more passage—the pathetic and beautiful description of the Protestant cemetery at Rome: "The English burying-place is a green slope near the walls, under the pyramidal tomb of Cestius, and is, I think, the most beautiful and solemn cemetery I ever beheld. To see the sun shining on its grass, fresh, when we first visited it, with the autumnal dews, and hear the whispering of the wind among the leaves of the trees which have overgrown the tomb of Cestius; and the soil which is stirring in the sun-warm earth, and to mark the

tombs, mostly of women and young people who were buried
there, one might, if one were to die, desire the sleep they
seem to sleep. Such is the human mind, and so it peoples
with its wishes vacancy and oblivion." It is fortunately as
needless as it is impossible to make any comment upon writing such as this.

The letters of Keats throw far more fresh light upon their
writer than those of Shelley. Without them, we should hardly
be aware of even the outlines of the character of that most
impersonal of poets. It is sometimes asserted that Keats was
effeminate and anaemic, that he was a weak voluptuary,
whose interests were bounded by the physical forms of
things; and such a view of his nature might, indeed, be supported with some show of truth by quotations from his
poems. His letters, however, provide a striking illustration
of how erroneous judgments of this kind are liable to be.
Passage after passage in them reveals to us the fact that
Keats's mind was in reality no less remarkable for its intellectual activity and strength than for its love of beauty. His
thought ranged easily from criticism to psychology, from reflexions upon political history to reflexions upon the conduct of life; and his thought was never commonplace, never
superficial, never slipshod, and never at rest. "From the
'Paradise Lost' and other works of Milton," he wrote to
Reynolds in 1818, "I hope it is not too presuming, even between ourselves, to say, that his Philosophy, human and
divine, may be tolerably understood by one not much advanced in years. In his time, Englishmen were just emanci-
pated from a great superstition, and men had got hold of
certain points and resting-places in reasoning which were
too newly born to be doubted, and too much opposed by the
mass of Europe not to be thought ethereal and authentically
divine. Who could gainsay his ideas on virtue, vice, and

chastity, in 'Comus,' just at the time of the dismissal of cod-pieces and a hundred other disgraces? Who would not rest satisfied with his hintings at good and evil in the 'Paradise Lost,' when just free from the Inquisition and burnings in Smithfield? The Reformation produced such immediate and great benefits, that Protestantism was considered under the immediate eye of heaven, and its own remaining dogmas and superstitions, then, as it were, regenerated, constituted those resting-places and seeming sure points of Reasoning from that I have mentioned. Milton, whatever he may have thought in the sequel, appears to have been content with these by his writings. He did not think into the human heart as Wordsworth has done. Yet Milton as a philosopher had sure as great powers as Wordsworth. What is then to be inferred? O, many things. It proves there is really a grand march of intellect, it proves that a mighty Providence subdues the mightiest minds to the service of the time being, whether it be in human knowledge or Religion." With trains of thought such as this the letters are crowded; nothing could be less remote from lasciviousness and morbidity, nor bear more obviously the impress of a bold, original, and ripening, though not yet mature, intelligence. When it is remembered that this passage was written when Keats was twenty-two, that he had enjoyed the most meagre of educations, that the apex of his intellectual surroundings was Leigh Hunt, one cannot doubt that if he had lived his mind would have scaled to heights which none of his contemporaries ever reached. "I will essay to reach to as high a summit in poetry," he wrote, "as the nerve bestowed upon me will suffer. The faint conceptions I have of poems to come bring the blood frequently into my forehead." Keats, at any rate, was by no means unaware of his own powers. Indeed, his extreme consciousness, his acute sensitiveness to every perception, to every feeling, to every stimulus,—this was what

59

lay at the basis of his character. "I carry all matters to an extreme," he says, "so that when I have any little vexation, it grows in five minutes into a theme for Sophocles." A vexation, a train of ideas, a beautiful vision—whatever the stimulus, the same activity of thought and feeling was sure to follow. His love of beauty was intense: "I feel assured I should write from the mere yearning and fondness I have for the beautiful, even if my night's labours should be burnt every morning, and no eye ever shine upon them." But his mind responded no less vividly to very different impressions. "On our return from Belfast, we met a sedan—the Duchess of Dunghill. It is no laughing matter though. Imagine the worst dog-kennel you ever saw, placed upon two poles from a mouldy fencing. In such a wretched thing sat a squalid old woman, squat like an ape half-starved from a scarcity of biscuit in its passage from Madagascar to the Cape, with a pipe in her mouth, and looking out with a round-eyed skinny-lidded inanity; with a sort of horizontal idiotic movement of her head, while two ragged, tattered girls carried her along. What a thing would be a history of her life and sensations!" In Keats's own history it was the violence of his sensations which was the culminating tragedy of his life. His last letters to Fanny Brawne and to Brown, in the intensity of the emotions which they display, are unsurpassed in the whole of literature. The same sacred horror of passion speaks in them as speaks in the lyrics of Catullus and of Heine, and in some of the sonnets of Shakespeare. But it is something of a desecration even to refer to such agonies and such splendours; to cut pieces out of them for notice and for admiration would be almost to commit the unforgivable sin.

It is difficult to believe that the letters of Lamb ever went through the same post as those of Byron and Keats. Indeed, it is difficult to believe that they ever went through the post at all. They are letters which a voyaging angel might write to the City of Heaven; they bear no marks of time or space or such sublunary accidents; one doubts whether it was ever true that they were not. Nothing shows more clearly Lamb's detachment from his age than his attitude towards Nature. "I must confess," he says, "that I am not romance-hit about *Nature*. The earth, and sea, and sky (when all is said) is but as a house to dwell in. . . . Just as important to me (in a sense) is all the furniture of my world; eye-pampering, but satisfies no heart. Streets, streets, streets, streets, markets, theatres, churches, Covent Gardens, shops sparkling with pretty faces of industrious milliners, neat sempstresses, ladies cheapening, gentlemen behind counters lying, authors in the street with spectacles, George Dyers (you may know them by their gait), lamps lit at night, pastry-cooks' and silversmiths' shops, beautiful Quakers of Pentonville, noise of coaches, drowsy cry of mechanic watchmen at night, with rakes reeling home drunk; if you happen to wake at midnight, cries of 'Fire!' and 'Stop, thief!', inns of court, with their learned air, and halls and butteries, just like Cambridge colleges; old bookstalls, 'Jeremy Taylors,' 'Burtons on Melancholy,' and 'Religio Medicis' on every stall. These are thy pleasures, O London! with thy many sins. O City, abounding in w——s, for these may Keswick and her giant brood go hang!"

Though the friend of Wordsworth and Coleridge can hardly be counted as of their generation, his very power of overstepping the limits of time made him a keener admirer of their poetry. "I had rather be a doorkeeper in your margin," he bursts out to Wordsworth, who had been maltreated by the reviewers, "than have their proudest text swelling with my eulogies." Yet his failure to appreciate either Keats or Shelley shows that even Lamb's critical eye might be dazzled by too much radiance. The quality of his imagination was so wholly different from theirs that their

61

speech fell

speech fell upon his ears like a strange language. The images which moved him were neither materially beautiful nor spiritually exalted; they were too human to lose themselves in the tropical luxuriances of *Endymion* or upon the mountain snows of the *Prometheus Unbound*. They remained beside the fire, in the candle-light, among midnight folios and innocent jests. And, in its own way, Lamb's fancy was no less exuberant than that of his great contemporaries. "Why do cats grin in Cheshire?" he exclaims in a sudden parenthesis. "Because it was once a County Palatine, and the cats cannot help laughing whenever they think of it, though I see no great joke in it." But it is in its longer flights that his imagination displays itself in its most fantastic forms. The *Essays of Elia* are, of course, rich in such passages; but the letters occasionally soar off into even more wonderful regions of unrestrained fooling—regions where the absurd and the serious, the jovial and the pathetic, the true and the false, seem to be inextricably fused together to form one enchanting whole. Perhaps the example which exhibits the peculiar quality of Lamb's imagination more admirably than any other is the letter to Manning, written on the eve of the latter's return from China. "Down with the pagodas!" Lamb bursts out. "Down with the idols—Ching-chong-fo—and his foolish priesthood! Come out of Babylon, O my friend! for her time is come. . . . And in sober sense what makes you so long from amongst us, Manning? You must not expect to see the same England again which you left." This is the text of the letter; the rest is commentary. "Empires have been overturned," it goes on, "crowns trodden into dust, the face of the Western world quite changed." (Lamb was writing in Waterloo year, and so far he has truth with him.) "Your friends have all got old," he proceeds—"those you left blooming; myself (who am one of the few that remember you) those golden hairs which you recollect my taking a pride in, turned to silvery and grey." This forms the transition stage from reality to fantasia; with his "golden hairs" Lamb takes a final spring from the earth into the Empyrean: "Mary has been dead and buried many years; she desired to be buried in the silk gown you sent her. Rickman that you remember active and strong, now walks out supported by a servant maid and a stick. Martin Burney is a very old man. The other day an aged woman knocked at my door, and pretended to my acquaintance. It was long before I had the most distant cognition of her; but at last, together, we made her out to be Louisa, the daughter of Mrs. Topham, formerly Mrs. Morton, who had been Mrs. Reynolds, formerly Mrs. Kenney, whose first husband was Holcroft, the dramatic writer of the last century. St. Paul's Church is a heap of ruins; the Monument isn't half so high as you knew it, divers parts being successively taken down which the ravages of time had rendered dangerous; the horse at Charing Cross is gone, no one knows whither; and all this has taken place while you have been settling whether Ho-hing-tong should be spelt with a — or a —."

"Poor Godwin!" the letter continues, piling vision upon vision. "I was passing his tomb the other day in Cripplegate Churchyard. There are some verses upon it written by Miss ——, which if I thought good enough I would send you. He was one of those who would have hailed your return, not with boisterous shouts and clamours, but with the complacent gratulations of a philosopher anxious to promote knowledge as leading to happiness; but his theories are ten feet deep in Cripplegate mould. Coleridge is just dead, having lived just long enough to close the eyes of Wordsworth, who paid the debt to Nature but a week or two before. Poor Col., but two days before he died he wrote to a bookseller proposing an epic poem on the 'Wanderings of Cain' in twenty-four books. It is said he said he has left behind him more than forty thousand treatises in criticism, metaphysics, and divinity, but few of them in a state of completion. They are now destined, perhaps, to wrap up spices. You see what mutations the busy hand of Time has produced."

This is Lamb in his lightest and happiest vein. It is only occasionally that the other side of him—the tragic side—makes its appearance in his letters. When it does, the beauty of the expression is as perfect as ever. "All my strength is gone," he wrote to Miss Wordsworth, during one of his sister's temporary confinements, "and I am like a fool, bereft of her co-operation. I dare not think, lest I should think wrong; so used am I to look up to her in the least and the biggest perplexity. To say all that I know of her would be more than I think anybody could believe, or even understand; and when I hope to have her well again with me, it would be sinning against her feelings to go about to praise her; for I can conceal nothing that I do from her. She is older and wiser and better than I, and all my wretched imperfections I cover to myself by resolutely thinking on her goodness." In the light of such words as these, the words which Coleridge addressed to his friend seem no longer strange to us: "I look upon you as a man called by sorrow and anguish and a strange desolation of hopes into quietness, and a soul set apart and made peculiar to God."

1905.

II

EARLY ESSAYS

1. Two Frenchmen

THE greatest misfortune that can happen to a witty man is to be born out of France. The French tongue is the appointed vehicle of brilliant thought; an Englishman, if he would be polished, pregnant, and concise, must command, like Bacon or like Burke, not only a wit but an inspiration; and it is perhaps as difficult for him to translate a French epigram as to compose an English one. A Frenchman, however, can always sparkle easily, even if he be stupid, and, if he be profound, the aphorism is his instinctive instrument of expression. The aphorism, indeed, dominates the literature of France, as the imagination dominates the literature of England. Even French tragedies are epigrammatic, and in French prose the epigrammatic style is the link which unites minds of such diverse genius as La Rochefoucauld and Vauvenargues, La Bruyère and Saint Simon, Pascal and Voltaire. In coupling together La Bruyère and Vauvenargues for translation into English,[1] Miss Lee has clearly been influenced by the fact that both these masters of aphorism were at the same time writers of "Characters," or short portrait sketches, a form whose genesis is Theophrastus, and best known to English readers in the *Microcosmographie* of Earle. But this seems hardly sufficient reason for a combination which is interesting by virtue neither of resemblance nor of contrast, and Miss Lee, if she could not do with less

[1] *La Bruyère and Vauvenargues: Selections from the Characters, Reflections, and Maxims*. Translated, with Introductory Notes and Memoirs, by Elizabeth Lee. Constable & Co. 1903.

than two authors, would have made, if she had substituted La Rochefoucauld for La Bruyère, a very much better book. For between Vauvenargues and La Rochefoucauld the contrast is complete. Many of Vauvenargues' maxims were written in direct opposition to those of La Rochefoucauld; he left a detailed criticism of the great *Maximes et Réflexions* among his posthumous papers; and, indeed, the casts of mind of the two men were in every respect curiously and radically antipathetic.

La Rochefoucauld, there can be no doubt, was the cleverest duke who ever lived. His brilliant, embittered little book is like a narrow strip of perfectly polished parquet whereon a bored and aristocratic dancer exquisitely moves. Too proud not to be a master of his art, too magnificent to care whether he was or no, he shows, in every line he wrote, that supreme detachment which gives him a place either above or below humanity. When he speaks of love, he is as icy as when he speaks of death; when he speaks of death, it is as if he were already dead. "Vanity of vanities, all is vanity" is his perpetual text (but in a sense different from the Preacher's); and in the safe isolation of this *parti pris*, hedged round by his pride, nourished by his scorn, illuminated by his wit, La Rochefoucauld felt clearly enough how well he could dispense with everything besides—even, perhaps, with the truth itself.

The passionate heart of Vauvenargues revolted against a portrait of humanity restricted and distorted to the extent of being (for all the sobriety of the presentment) really nothing more than a highly ingenious caricature. His mind, so sympathetic as to be often sentimental, so averse from paradox as to be sometimes platitudinous, opposed to La Rochefoucauld's paradoxical cynicism, a profound belief in the simple goodness which resides in the emotions of men. "Le corps a ses grâces," he says, "l'esprit a ses talents; le cœur n'aurait-il que des vices, et l'homme capable de raison serait-il incapable de vertu?" And to La Rochefoucauld's "Nous ne ressentons nos biens et nos maux qu'à proportion de notre amour-propre," he replies with a question which cuts the ground from under the feet of his antagonist: "Est-il contre la raison ou la justice de s'aimer soi-même? Et pourquoi voulons-nous que l'amour-propre soit toujours un vice?"

Vauvenargues, however, needs no foil to make him worthy of study, though perhaps it is difficult to obtain a true view of him through a small selection from his writings. Nor has Miss Lee made up, in her Introduction, for what she cannot give us of Vauvenargues himself. To say that his work betrays no sign of the age in which it was written, shows an entire misconception either of the age or of his work. The truth is, that Vauvenargues was typically eighteenth century; his literary treatment of philosophy, his philosophical treatment of literature, his love of emotion, his sarcasms upon the Church, are almost absurdly characteristic of the period of Voltaire. On every other page of his writings there is a reference to that "Nature" so dear to philosophers from the days of Locke to the days of Rousseau, and so hard for us children of evolution to understand. There is the constant implication that "natural" sentiments must be good; there are the usual contradictory assertions that Racine is too "natural" to write badly, and Shakespeare too "natural" to write well; there is even the conventional "American" who converses philosophically with a Portuguese traveller upon the respective merits of civilisation and the "state of Nature." Such was the intellectual atmosphere which Vauvenargues necessarily breathed. But it was not only in his writings that he was typical of his time; it was in his mind as well. His letters, the letters of Voltaire, and the stray notices of others who knew him, show clearly enough that he possessed that combination of passionate emotions and love of truth which characterises the great Frenchmen of the eighteenth century. That they were sometimes sentimental, these great Frenchmen, and sometimes doctrinaire, cannot be denied; but is this all that can be said (it is too often all that *is* said) of Diderot, of d'Alembert, of Turgot, and of Condorcet? Their defects were the defects of their qualities, and how splendid these qualities were is precisely what the study of Vauvenargues most plainly shows. It shows Voltaire, it shows the "Philosophes," in their true light. "Aimable créature, beau génie!" exclaims the former of Vauvenargues; to how many others of those true Humanists, those worthy heirs of the Renaissance, those noble and charming spirits, might the same words have been addressed!

"Vauvenargues," we find in Miss Lee's Introduction, "understood the art of writing, as an art, scarcely at all." He understood it better than Miss Lee, whose English is never good, and who writes, on p. 135, "Who would believe that others exist who pride themselves in not thinking *like* anyone else thinks?" The actual translation, too, is often unfortunately careless; several times the sense of the original has been quite mistaken; entire phrases have been sometimes omitted without apparent reason; and no effort has been made, by avoiding, for instance, the needless repetition of the same word in the same sentence, to obtain either the ease or the distinction of the original. The style of Vauvenargues is so simple, following, like all eighteenth-century French, almost the precise run of an English sentence, that nothing more was needed than care and a small knowledge of the two languages to have produced an adequate translation. And if Miss Lee has failed with Vauvenargues it was not to be expected that she would succeed with La Bruyère. This would have required a special talent, a fine instinct, and a reverent mind; without these qualities it were better to leave untouched one of the great writers of the world,

whose perfect French it is nothing less than sacrilege to translate into bad English. Why such an attempt as Miss Lee's
should find publicity in print, it is difficult to understand.
For those who cannot read the original it is worse than useless—it is a snare—to represent such a sentence as this—
"Everything they did was suitable to their circumstances,
their expenditure was proportioned to their income, their
liveries, equipages, furniture, table, town, and country
houses were all in proportion to their revenue and circumstances"—as having anything in common with La Bruyère.
It is plain from her Introduction that Miss Lee has no conception of the sanctity upon which she is laying her hands;
and the consequences of this ignorance are, in her translation, even plainer. From the beautiful portrait of Arténice
the charming sentence—"On ne sait si on l'aime ou si on
l'admire"—has been wantonly omitted; and into the very
midst of the exquisite crescendo of the "fleuristes" the hideous phrase "tired with his perambulations" has been inserted, as a translation, one must suppose, of "il se lasse." It
is melancholy to find this shapeless sentence, "A fool is an
automaton, a machine with springs which turn him about
always in one manner and preserve his equilibrium," standing for the mechanical exactitude of "Le sot est automate, il
est machine, il est ressort; le poids l'emporte, le fait mou-
voir, le fait tourner, et toujours, et dans le même sens, et
avec la même égalité." The truth is, that the whole supremacy of La Bruyère's art consists in that absolute precision, that complete finish, that perfect proportion, which
give his Characters the quality of a De Hoogh, and his
aphorisms the brilliant hardness of a Greek gem. Every detail, every rhythm, every word, is essential to the beauty of
the whole; and to destroy a single one of them is to convert
perfection into nothing at all. The connoisseur of fruit, in
Miss Lee's translation, "with much ado gathers the exquisite

plum"; in La Bruyère "il cueille artistement cette prune
exquise": this is exactly how Miss Lee should have treated
her exquisite original.

But La Bruyère was not only a stylist; he was a philosopher. This hardly appears in Miss Lee's selections, which
are confined almost entirely to those "portraits of the more
or less trifling eccentricities of men," which give no true
impression of the width and profundity of La Bruyère's
mind. He was, in fact, a "philosophe" out of water, a
"philosophe" in the *Grand Siècle;* his attitude towards the
old *régime* was almost exactly the eighteenth-century attitude; and his elaborate picture of the Court of Versailles
might have come straight out of the *Lettres Persanes*. Detached enough to recognise the absurdity of rouge and the
injustice of torture, he perceived, perhaps more clearly than
any other Frenchman before the Revolution, the volcano
upon which society reposed. "Quand le peuple est en mouve-
ment," he says, "on ne comprend pas par où le calme peut
y rentrer; et quand il est paisible, on ne voit pas par où le
calme peut en sortir." And he goes on, discussing the general theory of political change, "il y a de certains maux dans
la République qui y sont soufferts parce qu'ils préviennent
ou empêchent de plus grands maux"; he weighs, like Hamlet, these conflicting evils; "les plus sages," he concludes,
"doutent quelquefois s'il est mieux de connâitre ces maux
que de les ignorer."

La Bruyère, however, differed from eighteenth-century
writers in two respects—he was a Roman Catholic and a poet.
His religious bias, which led him to make his one great error
in political judgment—his approval of the Revocation of the
Edict of Nantes—inspires the entire chapter "Des Esprits
Forts," where he confounds atheism, and shows how easy it
is for a great man to be a small metaphysician. His poetry—
that subtle and delicate employment of words, that vivid

imagination, that marvellous command of atmosphere—is scattered all through his book; but it is in the chapters which deal with the intercourse of human beings that it reaches its fullest development. "Il y a du plaisir à rencontrer les yeux de celui à qui l'on vient de donner." Was anything ever written at once so subtle and so simple as that? Or at once so radiant and so intimate as this: "Un beau visage est le plus beau de tous les spectacles, et la plus douce harmonie est le son de voix de celle que l'on aime"? Such sentences are nothing less than prose lyrics, as impossible to translate as the rhymed ones of Heine, and upon these heights it is only natural that Miss Lee should fall behind. "The things we most desire never happen, or if they happen it is neither at the time nor under (*sic*) the circumstances when they would have given most pleasure." This seems to be nothing more than a platitudinous way of saying something that is hardly true. But La Bruyère has in reality expressed in one sentence the whole dismal fatality of things: "Les choses les plus souhaitées n'arrivent point: ou si elles arrivent ce n'est ni dans le temps ni dans les circonstances où elles auraient fait un extrême plaisir." By what magic has he conveyed into these few words the suggestion of his surrender, of his disgust, of his infinite regret?

1903.

2. The Wrong Turning

ENGLISH Men of Letters: Fanny Burney (Madame D'Arblay)." So runs the title of Mr. Dobson's book; [1] and let none but pedants exclaim against a Man of Letters who is a lady, and a lady who is not one lady, but two. For the Fanny Burney of the novels and the Madame D'Arblay of the Diary has each her separate claim to a literary distinction, and memorial beyond the grave. Though *Camilla* has long since faded from the circulating libraries, though Colonel Digby and Mrs. Schwellenberg may only exist for us in an essay of Macaulay, there is yet good reason to remember, now and then, the works that Johnson praised, that Burke sat up all night to finish, that charmed Sir Joshua, that held Gibbon enthralled, and not to forget altogether the girl who scribbled in Newton's Observatory, who grew up amidst the famous circle of "the Club," the friend of Garrick and Warren Hastings and Rogers, who had been paid a compliment by Soame Jenyns and lived long enough to pay one to Walter Scott, the correspondent of "Daddy" Crisp and of Disraeli, who talked scandal with Mrs. Thrale, and wrote plays for Mrs. Siddons, and discussed Shakespeare with George III.

Mr. Dobson has devoted most of his charming volume to the lady of the Diary, though the fifty pages he has given up to the novels contain nothing that is not admirably happy, discriminating, and just. But it is only natural that

[1] *Fanny Burney.* By Austin Dobson. London: Macmillan and Co. 1903.

74

the author of *Beau Brocade* should dwell chiefly upon that side of Fanny Burney's life which brings us most into contact with the delightful and brilliant society of eighteenth-century London; for here his unrivalled knowledge and peculiar sympathy have opened out for him opportunities which he can use to the utmost, with rights and powers all his own. Mr. Dobson, indeed, is himself so much at home in that world "of Drum and Ridotto, of Rake and of Belle," that he succeeds in transferring to the willing reader his own sense of pleasant familiarity and ease. One wanders with him happily from Poland Street to Queen Square, from Bloomsbury to Leicester Fields; one looks in at Portman Square on Mrs. Montagu amid her feathered walls; one catches glimpses of Horace Walpole or Sheridan or Lady Di; one has the *entrée* at Streatham; one visits Brighton, and takes the waters at Bath. Across this past which has become the present there float visions of a remoter past: Sir Isaac walks once more from St. Martin's Street to visit the Princess Caroline at Leicester House; the ghostly chairs of Lady Worsley and Lady Betty Germaine wait still at the narrow approach from the Fields, as they did in the old days when "their mistresses 'disputed Whig and Tory,' with Mrs. Conduit, or were interrupted in a *tête-à-tête* by Gay and the Duchess of Queensberry."

In laying so little stress on Madame D'Arblay's novels, Mr. Dobson has followed the lead of Macaulay, who, in his metallic way, devoted the greater part of an Essay to a description of her life, and reserved only the fag end of it for a discussion of her place in literature. And even then, his criticism amounts to nothing more than saying, with extraordinary cleverness, that her characters were caricatures, and that her style degenerated from Nature to Johnson, and from Johnson to insufferable affectation. Neither Macaulay nor Mr. Dobson has indeed really solved the enigma of why it happened that writings, pronounced immortal by the greatest intellects of their own day, fell almost at once into insignificance, and eventually into nearly complete oblivion. *Evelina* and *Cecilia* were hailed by Johnson, the greatest contemporary critic, as worthy to rank beside the best work of Richardson and Fielding; and *Evelina* is now read only as a quaint example of eighteenth-century literature, while *Cecilia* is not read at all. "Tell them," said Johnson of the latter volume, in a vein of ironic censure, "how little there is in it of human nature, and how well your knowledge of the world enables you to judge of the failings in that book." But the words are ironical in a sense undreamt of by the Doctor; for they exactly express the opinion of the modern reader, who inevitably does find in *Cecilia* very little of human nature, and whose knowledge of the world does enable him to judge quite easily of the failings of "that book." The difference is complete; and a compromise appears to be impossible. If we are right, Johnson must have been wrong; if we are wrong, Johnson must have been right. But we, *ex hypothesi*, are right: how then did it happen—it is the only question left to ask—that Johnson came to be wrong?

There can be no doubt that, during the last quarter of the eighteenth century, the English novel experienced a remarkable eclipse. From the publication of *The Vicar of Wakefield*, in 1766, to the composition of *Pride and Prejudice*, in 1796, for the whole of that period of thirty years, no novel of the first class was produced at all; and few indeed of the novels which were actually written attained the level even of Miss Burney's second-class work. English prose, it is true, had never flourished more gloriously; but it reserved its magnificent outpourings for History, for Philosophy, for Oratory, for Essays, for Memoirs, for Letters, for everything, in fact, except the particular sort of prose romance which is concerned with the portrayal of human nature. Why this was the case, why, between the great constellation of Richardson, Fielding, and Sterne, and the great constellation of Jane Austen and Walter Scott, there should intervene a vast tract of literature illumined only by stars of the third magnitude—this is a mystery perhaps beyond solution, though it would be partly accounted for, if it were true that the direct study of human nature was, for some unknown reason, not interesting to the English of that generation. At any rate, whether they were (to use Johnson's phrase) "character-mongers" or no in actual life, it seems clear that at least in literary criticism they were not. It is a standing proof of their innate incapacity for estimating the true value of the characterisation in a work of fiction, their utter lack of *flair* for portraiture, that they left it to the nineteenth century to discover the fact that what makes Sterne immortal is not his sentiment, nor his indecency, nor his asterisks, but his Mr. Shandy and his Uncle Toby.

It was precisely this quality of literary acumen which her contemporaries brought to bear on the novels of Fanny Burney. "You have," Burke wrote to her, "crowded into a few small volumes an incredible variety of characters; most of them well planned, well supported, and well contrasted with each other"; and it is obvious that by "characters" Burke meant just what he should not have meant—descriptions, that is to say, of persons who might exist. The truth is, that if we had been told that Delvile *père* was ten feet high, and that Mr. Morrice was made of cardboard, we should have had very little reason for astonishment; such peculiarities of form would have been remarkable, no doubt, but not more remarkable than those of their minds, which Burke was so ready to accept as eminently natural. In fact, Miss Burney's characters, to use Macaulay's phrase, are in reality nothing but "humours," and not characters at all;

and immediately this is recognised, immediately "humours"
is substituted for "characters" in Burke's appreciation, what
he says becomes perfectly just. They are indeed, these
humours, "well planned, well supported, and well contrasted
with each other"; Miss Burney displays great cleverness and
admirable care in her arrangement of them; and this Burke,
as well as Macaulay, thoroughly understood. But such, both
for Burke and for his distinguished circle, was the limit of
understanding; outside that limit the God of Convention
reigned triumphant. Conventional feelings, conventional
phrases, conventional situations, conventional oddities, conventional loves,—these were the necessary ingredients of their
perfect novel; and all these. Miss Burney was able, with
supreme correctness, to supply. In the culminating scene of
Cecilia, where the conflicting passions of affection and family
pride at last meet face to face, the dialogue is as wonderfully
finished and as superbly orthodox as the dialogue of a second-
rate French tragedy; one cannot help seeing Cecilia and
Mortimer and Mrs. Delvile, in perruques and togas, deliver-
ing their harangues with appropriate gestures from the front
of a Louis Quinze stage, with Corinthian columns in the
background. Johnson's favourite, the mad philanthropical
Albany, does indeed actually burst sometimes into downright blank verse.

"Poor subterfuge of callous cruelty!"

he suddenly exclaims,

"You cheat yourselves to shun the fraud of others!
 And yet how better do you use the wealth
 So guarded?
 What nobler purpose can it answer to you,
 Than even a chance to snatch some wretch from sinking?
 Think less how *much* ye save, and more for *what;*

"And then consider how thy full coffers may hereafter make reparation for the empty catalogue of thy virtues."

"Anan!" cries Mr. Briggs, in reply to these noble sentiments; and that—whatever it may mean—is perhaps the best rejoinder. ·

But it is to be feared that Miss Burney's friends did worse than misjudge her merits; it seems clear that they encouraged her faults, and turned away her energies from where her true strength lay. For, in her first work, she had succeeded in · depicting one character which, though neither elaborate nor profound, was really convincing—Evelina herself. The refined, over-modest girl, around whose perplexities and sufferings and joys the troupe of usual humours dance and tumble, is delicately brought out by a sympathetic hand. Here at last is something that is more than cleverness—a little spark of genius; and it shows itself most clearly in a few little scenes and conversations, of which the following specimen may be taken as a fair example. Lord Orville, who is in love with Evelina, discovers her in the garden at an early hour, talking intimately to Mr. Macartney. Everything points (wrongly, of course) to an assignation. Evelina, who is in love with Lord Orville, returns with him to the house.

"Determined as I was to act honourably by Mr. Macartney, I yet most anxiously wished to be restored to the good opinion of Lord Orville; but his silence, and the thoughtfulness of his air, discouraged me from speaking.

"My situation soon grew disagreeable and embarrassing; and I resolved to return to my chamber till breakfast was ready. To remain longer, I feared, might seem *asking* for his inquiries; and I was sure it would ill become me to be more eager to speak than he was to hear.

"Just as I reached the door, turning to me hastily, he said, 'Are you going, Miss Anville?'

" 'I am, my lord,' answered I; yet I stopped.

79

" 'Perhaps to return to—but I beg your pardon!' He spoke with a degree of agitation that made me readily comprehend he meant to *the garden;* and I instantly said: 'To my own room, my lord.' And again I would have gone; but, convinced by my answer that I understood him, I believe he was sorry for the insinuation; he approached me with a very serious air, though at the same time he forced a smile, and said: 'I know not what evil genius pursues me this morning, but I seemed destined to do or say something I ought not; I am so much ashamed of myself, that I can scarce solicit your forgiveness.' "

That is a small picture, perhaps, of a small affair; it describes hardly more than a turn to and from a door; but it possesses qualities of beauty, of restraint, of quick imagination, of charming feeling, of real atmosphere, that make it approach, in its tiny way, close to perfection. But this quiet sort of miniature analysis Miss Burney repeated in none of her later books. Cecilia is a burlesque Evelina, a wax figure whose refinement has become a settled affectation, whose modesty is an obsession, who blushes every time her lover's name is mentioned, who is scandalised when he proposes, and is too maidenly to be married. Henceforward Miss Burney had no time for the subtleties of art; at all hazards she must be creating "well supported" characters, and putting them into "well planned" situations; and, her work thus cut out for her, she carried it through with credit. But it is impossible not to think that perhaps, if she had written in a more discriminating age, she would have developed her own peculiar vein as it deserved, instead of working others of inferior ore with implements too heavy for her strength. Fortunately for us indeed, she was left to herself in one domain; for her Diary flourished beyond the reach of criticism, deep-rooted in her own most private nature, and fed with truth. No one can doubt that Mr. Dobson is right to place it high above the novels, and to rank it with the great diaries of literature. It is here that Madame D'Arblay appears at full length; it is here that she shows us her mirror of the world, gives us the relish of real persons, real intimacies, real conversations. Who would not be willing to abolish for ever the whole elaborate waste of *Cecilia,* for the sake of those few pages in the Diary, where, looking down upon the crowded benches of Westminster Hall, we can see distinct before us the pale face of Hastings, and watch the Managers in their box and the Duchesses in their gallery, while we listen alternately to the tedious droning of the lawyers, to the whispered flatteries of Mr. Wyndham, and the stupendous oratory of Burke?

1904.

3. Horace Walpole

LOVERS of Walpole will not fail to welcome the first instalment of Mrs. Toynbee's new edition of the incomparable *Letters*.[1] The Clarendon Press is to be congratulated on the production of these charming and comfortable volumes, which, on the score of form alone, are worthy of precedence over the cumbrous tomes of Peter Cunningham. It is pleasant to think that henceforward it will be possible to read with ease the most readable of books, and that the lightest of writers is no longer too heavy to carry. But the present edition has other claims to superiority: it is far more nearly complete than any of its predecessors; it may be supposed, indeed, to be the penultimate Walpole. Peter Cunningham's nine volumes contain 2654 letters; there will be as many as 3061 in Mrs. Toynbee's sixteen, and, out of this new material, no less than 111 letters have never before been printed. In the volumes at present published, the most interesting additions are some early letters to Charles Lyttelton, afterwards Bishop of Carlisle, among them being the first extant letter of Walpole, written while he was still at Eton. But the most important part of the unprinted matter has yet to appear—seven letters, written in French, to Madame du Deffand. At the death of his "dear old friend," Walpole came into the possession of all her papers; his terror of ridi-

[1] *The Letters of Horace Walpole, Fourth Earl of Orford.* Chronologically arranged and edited, with notes and indices, by Mrs. Paget Toynbee, in sixteen volumes, with portraits and facsimiles. Vols. I-IV. The Oxford University Press. 1903.

cule made him anxious to destroy such evidence as they
contained of the lady's strange attachment and his own bad
French. The forthcoming letters, however, seem to have survived by accident, and are all that remains, on Walpole's
part, of a correspondence of sixteen years.

The excellence of Mrs. Toynbee's work makes it all the
more to be regretted that she has been unable to make use
of some unpublished manuscripts still lying at Holland
House; for, with their addition, none of the known letters
of Walpole would have been absent from her collection.
In one other respect alone the present edition seems to fall
short of the ideal. A great many passages "quite unfit for
publication" have been omitted from the letters to Sir Horace Mann. It is true that these passages have never been
printed before; but it is difficult to believe that there is any
adequate reason for their not being printed now. The *jeune
fille* is certainly not an adequate reason, and, even if she
were, the *jeune fille* does not read Walpole. Whoever does
read him must feel that these constant omissions are so many
blots upon perfection, and distressing relics of an age of
barbarous prudery.

The panorama of the correspondence is so vast, that it is
almost a relief to be able to look at it in sections. Never,
indeed, was such exquisite delicacy combined with such enormous bulk; and there can be no doubt that it is owing to
their mass, as well as to their matter, that the letters hold the
place they do in English literature. No other English letter
writer except Byron—and in fact no other in the world except Voltaire, who stands supreme—ever approached the
productiveness of Walpole. But Byron's exuberance of vitality forms a curious contrast to Walpole's prolific ease. The
former is all vigour and hurry, all chops and changes, all
multitudinous romance; he is salt and breezy and racy as
the sea. Walpole flows like a delightful river through his

endless pages, between shady lawns and luxurious villas, dimpling all the way. One common characteristic, and one alone, unites the two men; they both possess a vivid and peculiar imagination. It is this quality in Walpole, this "ease," to use the words of Macaulay, "with which he yokes together ideas between which there would seem, at first sight, to be no connection," that makes him so distinctively English a writer. His fancy roams, indeed, as constantly as that of Keats, though it roams in a different direction. From the letters of his early Cambridge days to the letters of his extreme old age, there is a perpetual procession of sparkling imagery.

"Youthful passages of life," he writes to Montagu, from King's, "are the chippings of Pitt's diamond, set into little heart-rings with mottoes; the stone itself more worth, the filings more gentle and agreeable."

In the letter he wrote to Lady Ossory six weeks before his death, though the style has reached perfection, it is the same style. She had been praising his letters, and he writes to her:

"Pray send me no more such laurels, which I desire no more than their leaves when decked with a scrap of tinsel, and stuck on Twelfth-cakes that lie on the shopboards of pastrycooks at Christmas. I shall be quite content with a sprig of rosemary thrown after me, when the parson of the parish commits my dust to dust."

This mastery of decoration never deserts him. Whatever his theme—the Opposition, or Madame de Sévigné, or the weather, or nothing at all—he contrives to beautify it in a hundred wonderful ways. His writing, as he might have said himself, is like lace; the material is of very little consequence, the embroidery is all that counts; and it shares with lace the happy faculty of coming out sometimes in yards and yards.

The period covered by the present volumes extends over the twenty years which preceded the death of George II. At the beginning of it, Sir Robert was still in power; at the end of it the triumphant Ministry of Pitt was drawing to its close. The political changes during that interval had been immense: in Asia and in America, as well as in Europe, a vast transformation had taken place; the imperial power of Britain, which had hardly been dreamt of in 1740, had become, in 1760, an established fact. Yet the social change during the same period had been almost equally profound. The accession of George III is the dividing point between two distinct ages: the age of Fielding and Hogarth and War- burton on the one hand, and the age of Sterne and Reynolds . and Hume on the other. The difference is curiously illus- trated by the contrast between Sir Robert Walpole and his son Horace, who each possessed, to a somewhat exag- gerated degree, the peculiar characteristics of his generation. All over England, during these years of transition, coarse and vigorous fathers were being succeeded by refined and sentimental sons; sceptics were everywhere stepping into the shoes of deists; in France the same movement at the same time brought about the triumph of the Encyclopaedia. What- ever may have been the causes of this remarkable revolution, there can be no doubt that the latter half of the eighteenth century attained to a height of civilisation unknown in Eu- rope since the days of Hadrian. Horace Walpole was, in England at any rate, the true prophet of the movement. Al- ready, in his earliest letters, he is over-civilised; he is a dilet- tante, a connoisseur who purchases alabaster gladiators and Domenichinos; he languishes among the boors of Houghton like a creature from another world.

"I literally seem to have murdered a man whose name was Ennui, for his ghost is ever before me," he writes at the age of twenty-six; "I fear 'tis growing old. They say there is no English word for *ennui*," he goes on; "I think you may translate it most literally by what is called 'entertaining people,' and 'doing the honours.' "

Twenty years later he was still "entertaining"; but the "people" were different, and he was no longer bored. "My resolutions of growing old and staid," he writes to Lady Hervey, "are admirable; I wake with a sober plan, and intend to pass the day with my friends—then comes the Duke of Richmond, and hurries me down to Whitehall to dinner —then the Duchess of Grafton sends for me to loo in Upper Grosvenor Street—before I can get thither, I am begged to step to Kensington, to give Mrs. Anne Pitt my opinion about a bow-window—after the loo, I am to march back to Whitehall to supper—and after that, am to walk with Miss Pelham on the terrace till two in the morning, because it is moonlight and her chair is not come. All this does not help my morning laziness; and, by the time I have breakfasted, fed my birds and my squirrels, and dressed, there is an auction ready. In short, Madam, this was my life last week, and is I think every week, with the addition of forty episodes."

Thirty years later still, he was "doing the honours" as happily as ever—to the French *émigrés* at Berkeley Square, to Queen Charlotte at Strawberry Hill: he had come into his kingdom with the new age.

If the contrast is great between the first half of the eighteenth century and the last, it is even greater between the latter and the first half of the nineteenth; and nothing shows this more clearly than the treatment which Walpole received in the *Edinburgh*, hardly forty years after his death, at the hands of Macaulay. The criticism is written in the great reviewer's most trenchant style; it contains passages which stand, for cleverness and brilliancy, on the level of his cleverest and most brilliant work; every other sentence is an epigram, and all the paragraphs go off like Catherine-wheels; everything is present, in fact, that could be desired, except the remotest understanding of the subject. Macaulay, stepping out for a moment from his world of machinery and progress, found himself face to face with a phenomenon which scarcely presented anything to his mind. Here was a writer who was not literary, a member of Parliament who was not a politician, an aristocrat who declared himself a Republican, and a Whig who took more interest in a new snuff-box than in the French Revolution. What could the meaning of this portent possibly be? The solution was only too obvious—the creature must be a mere *poseur*, with an empty head, and an empty heart, and a few tricks to amuse the public. In this case, at any rate, Macaulay employed the very method of portraiture with which he charges Walpole himself:

"He copied from the life only those glaring and obvious peculiarities which could not escape the most superficial observation. The rest of the canvas he filled up, in a careless dashing way, with knave and fool, mixed in such proportions as pleased Heaven."

The accusation most commonly raised against Walpole—that he was devoid of true feeling in his intercourse with others—is of course reiterated by Macaulay, though even he feels obliged to admit parenthetically that to Conway at least Walpole "appears to have been sincerely attached." But the truth seems to be, in spite of "those glaring and obvious peculiarities which could not escape the most superficial observation"—his angry, cutting sentences, his constant mockery of his enemies, his constant quarrels with his friends, and his perpetual reserve—that Walpole's nature was in reality peculiarly affectionate. There can be no doubt that he was sensitive to an extraordinary degree; and it is much more probable that the defects—for defects they certainly were—which he showed in social intercourse, were caused by an excess of this quality of sensitiveness, rather than by a lack of sincere feeling. It is impossible to quarrel with one's friends unless one likes them; and it is impossible to like some people very much without disliking other people a good deal. These elementary considerations are quite enough to account for the vagaries and the malice of Walpole. But there was another element in his character which gave his malice all the appearance of a deep malignity, and made his vagaries seem to be the outcome of a callous nature: it was his pride. At heart he was a complete aristocrat; it was impossible for him to be unreserved. The masks he wore were imposed upon him by his caste, by his breeding, by his own intimate sense of the decencies and proprieties of life; so that his hatreds and loves, so easily aroused and so intensely cherished, were forced to express themselves in spiteful little taunts and in artificial compliments. His letter to Mason is an exquisite proof alike of how much he could feel, and how much he could keep back. The account he gives of his own misconduct is utterly dispassionate and polite; he makes no protestations of affection, he expresses not a word of regret; it is only at last, when he touches upon the feelings of Gray, that the veil seems for a moment to be withdrawn. "I treated him insolently. *He loved me, and I did not think he did.*" One must be very blind indeed to see in such words as those nothing more than a frigid indifference; and one must suffer from a strange obliquity of vision to be able to trace in them a likeness to the ape of Macaulay's caricature, mopping and mowing, spitting and gibbering, dressed out in its master's finery, and keeping an eye upon the looking-glass.

There is a portrait of him, taken in later life, which gives a clearer idea of the real Walpole. He is sitting cross-legged on his chair, with a book open in his hand, and Madame du Deffand's dog beside him; in the background, through the window, one catches a glimpse of the Thames, and a barge sailing past amid the spring foliage. It is a pretty picture; and the thin face, with its high forehead and its tiny nervous mouth, is a curiously kind one. Looking at it, it is easy to return in spirit to that little world of Walpole, that happy society of five hundred personages which seems to move and dance perpetually before our gaze, and yet remains fixed for us for ever in a strange fixity, like a fly in amber. To Macaulay, indeed, fresh and victorious from the great fight of the Reform Bill, that society must have seemed a narrow and a petty one, remote from the realities of life. Yet, after all, what could be more real, for instance, than to sit down to cards with "the Archbishopess of Canterbury and Mr. Gibbon"? Or to entertain the Duchess of Hamilton at Strawberry? Or to write verses in honour of the Princess Amelia? Or to exchange confidences with Madame du Deffand? Or to watch long hours from the bow-window in the great room at Isleworth the ferries passing to and fro across the river? Or to print a new edition of the poems of Mr. Gray? Or to scribble notes to Lady Ossory? Or to spend the evening with Mary Berry over the old Duchess of Queensberry and the old Duchess of Marlborough, till the candles expire in their sockets, and one begins to feel that one is getting old one's self? Are these things really less real, Walpole might have asked, than shouting at elections, and writing articles for the magazines?

"One passes away so soon, and worlds succeed to worlds, in which the occupiers build the same castles in the air. What is ours but the present moment? And how many of mine are gone!"

1904.

4. Versailles

THIS book[1] has been presumably compiled to meet the wants of the traveller who has no time for an elaborate monograph but who aspires after something higher than the ordinary tourist's guide. Mr. Farmer's work makes no pretensions to originality; its merits are of another kind: it is not too bulky, it is easily read, and the text is enlivened by a large number of interesting photographs and plans. Based very largely—somewhat more largely, indeed, than the reader is given to understand—upon the exhaustive and scholarly work of Dussieux, the present volume has all the advantage of a sound foundation of research, while it is free from the stuffy laboriousness of an historical treatise. To these merits it is unfortunate that Mr. Farmer has not been able to add the very important one of a graceful style. The general effect of his language is curiously polyglot; and it is often a little difficult to remember whether one is reading English, American, or French. After becoming habituated to "theaters" and "centers," it is trying to be brought up against "the Grand Commun," and it is perplexing to find oneself among "the terraces, the fountains, and the bosquets," as if all these were words of a single tongue. "The Palatine" is certainly not the English of "La Palatine"; and one cannot help doubting whether "the Grand Monarch" is the equivalent of "le Grand Monarque." Nor is Mr. Farmer

[1] *Versailles and the Court under Louis XIV.* By James Eugene Farmer. London: Eveleigh Nash. 1906.

happy in his translations of Saint Simon, whose *Mémoires*
throw so brilliant, so penetrating, a light upon the Court of
Louis XIV. A book which is so full as this is of extracts
from that wonderful writer ought, one would think, to be
readable on that account alone. But in the present instance
it is precisely the quotations from the *Mémoires* which are
difficult to get through. For who can read Saint Simon in
second-rate English? Who can drink the relics of yesterday's
champagne?

"Versailles," says Mr. Farmer, "was a policy, and a system
of government. Versailles was more than a palace; it was a
world." The observation is just, if a trifle hackneyed. But
indeed it would be unreasonable to expect from a modest
handbook that full disquisition upon the philosophy of
places which would certainly form the preface of an ideal
work upon Versailles. What is it, precisely, that creates the
fascination of a place? What are the relative values of its
physical beauty, its personal associations, its historical importance, and (the word is at once a vague and a distinct one)
its "atmosphere"? What is the fundamental difference between London and the Lakes? Why must everyone love
Florence and only admire Venice? Why is it that I prefer to
go to Oxford, while he prefers to go to Birmingham? These
are questions which, as Sir Thomas Browne expresses it, "admit a wide solution"; and they are but a few out of the
many which must be faced by the conscientious connoisseur
of localities. In the case of Versailles, though the spell which
it casts over the most casual and the most *blasé* of travellers
is doubtless the result of a variety of causes, it is clear enough
that its unique distinction is neither personal nor aesthetic,
but historical. "Versailles was more than a palace; it was a
world." It was not, like Windsor, merely the country house
of Kings; it was the local habitation of a vast and complicated national ideal; it was the central point of a great civi-

lisation. In the category of places it takes rank with Athens and with Rome.

The ideal of which Versailles was the embodiment is dead; and Versailles itself is nothing more than its memorial and its grave. The vast edifice is an image of irrevocable failure —of a failure, too, which, like everything else in that strange cemetery, is invested with a grandeur of its own. For Versailles was, in its essence, an attempt to create the superhuman; and its tragedy is the tragedy of an impossible ideal. When La Bruyère compared the attitude of the courtiers towards the king to that of the saints in heaven towards God, he was drawing no exaggerated picture: he was describing the fundamental fact underlying the ideal of Versailles. The king was, in truth, invested with the attributes of divinity; he assumed the God; he became, in that dazzling world of his creation, divine. The features of Louis XIV, which Mr. Farmer reproduces for us from the waxen portrait of Benoist, bear upon them the marks of this inordinate assumption, grown rigid in their obsession of an arrogance so immense as almost to be what it pretends to be—something more than human. It is easy now to point the obvious moral; it is easy to show, after the manner of Thackeray, the mortal creature beneath the robes of greatness, to preach a sermon over the deity who could not keep his temper, who was swayed by women and by priests, and who always ate too much. All this is easy, and it is also cheap. It is more profitable to try to realise in some measure the thoughts and feelings which enabled a great age to lend itself to so extraordinary an experiment; to think of Versailles, not as an emblem of foolish and degraded snobbery, but as a splendid piece of spiritual *tour de force.*

The spirit is departed, but the mortal part remains. Mr. Farmer's photographs do something towards giving a conception of the palace and the gardens to an untravelled reader, but photographs cannot do much. Those who have not visited Versailles need, to gain acquaintance with its "atmosphere," some more elaborate presentation, such as, for instance, may be found in M. de Nolhac's beautiful reproductions from seventeenth-century prints. But even these can hardly raise more than the ghost of the brilliant reality which, after all, is close at hand. One must go to Versailles— one must go with Mr. Farmer's book—to get a glimpse both of what it was and of what it is. One must linger among the fountains and the oranges, the bronzes and the marble gods; one must look back upon the palace through the great trees with their pale spring foliage; one must walk, in autumn, down the melancholy avenues banked with fallen leaves; one must sit in the summer shade within earshot of dropping water, and dream of vanished glories and beauties, of crowned and desecrated loves.

1906.

5. Mademoiselle de Lespinasse

OH! je m'en vais vous paraître folle: je vais vous parler avec la franchise et l'abandon qu'on aurait, si l'on croyait mourir le lendemain; écoutez-moi donc avec cette indulgence et cet intérêt qu'on a pour les mourants." So wrote Mademoiselle de Lespinasse; and the words might well be taken as a motto for the volume of letters which has made her name imperishable. The book, for all its tenderness and pathos, is in many ways a terrible one; it is gloomy, morbid, and remorseless; after one has read it, it is horrible to think that it is true. Yet it is its truth—its uncompromising truth—which gives it an immense and unique value: it is the most complete analysis the world possesses of a passion which actually existed in a human mind. Thus, when one thinks of Mademoiselle de Lespinasse, it is towards passion, and all the fearful accompaniments of passion, that one's imagination naturally turns. One is apt to forget that she was not merely "une amante insensée," that she was also a brilliant and fascinating woman of the world. The Marquis de Ségur, in the biography of her which he has recently published,[1] has been careful to avoid this error. He has drawn a full-length portrait of Julie de Lespinasse; and he has drawn it with a subtlety and a sympathy which compels a delighted attention. His book is enriched with a great mass of information never before made public; his researches have been rewarded with the discovery of authentic docu-

---

[1] Marquis de Ségur. *Julie de Lespinasse.* Paris: Calmann-Lévy.

ments of the deepest interest; and every reader of the present
volume will await with anxious expectation the publication,
which he promises us, of a new and enlarged edition of the
Letters themselves. One of the most important results of
M. de Ségur's labours is the additional knowledge which
they have given us upon the subject of the Comte de Guibert,
to whom the letters were addressed. This alone would have
made the book indispensable to anyone who is interested
in Mademoiselle de Lespinasse. But it would be idle to attempt to recapitulate all the fresh points of importance
which M. de Ségur has brought out; it were best to go to
the book itself. In the meantime, it may be worth while to
trace, however rapidly and imperfectly, the outline of that
tragical history which M. de Ségur has done so much to put
in its proper light.

Julie de Lespinasse was born at Lyons on November 9,
1732. She was the illegitimate daughter of the Comtesse
d'Albon, a lady of distinguished family, who, some years
earlier, had separated from her husband, and established
herself in the neighbourhood of Lyons in the château of
Avauges. So much is certain; but the obscurity which hung
over Julie's birth has never been completely withdrawn.
Who was her father? According to the orthodox tradition,
she was the child of Cardinal de Tencin, whose sister, the
famous Madame de Tencin, was the mother of d'Alembert.
This story has the advantage of discovering a strange and
concealed connection between two lives which were afterwards to be intimately bound together; but it has the dis-
advantage of not being true. M. de Ségur shows conclusively
that, whoever else may have been the father of Mademoiselle
de Lespinasse, Cardinal de Tencin was not; and he produces
some weighty reasons for believing that Julie was the niece,
not of Madame de Tencin, but of a woman equally remark-

able and equally celebrated—Madame du Deffand. If M. de
Ségur's hypothesis be correct—and the evidence which he
adduces is, I think, conclusive—the true history of Julie's
parentage is even more extraordinary than the orthodox one.
Besides Julie herself, Madame d'Albon had two legitimate
children, one of whom was a daughter; this daughter married, in 1739, the Comte Gaspard de Vichy, the eldest
brother of Madame du Deffand. The Comte de Vichy was
the father of Mademoiselle de Lespinasse. Once or twice,
in her correspondence, she touches upon the strange circumstances of her early life. Her history, she said, outdid the
novels of Prévost and of Richardson; it proved that "le vrai
n'est souvent pas vraisemblable"; it was "un composé de
circonstances funestes," which would produce, in the mind
of her correspondent, "une grande horreur pour l'espèce
humaine." These phrases lose their appearance of exaggeration in the light of the Marquis de Ségur's theory. "Ce sont
des horreurs!" exclaimed Gaspard's son, when his mother
had told him all. Even for the eighteenth century, there was
something horrible in Julie's situation. When, at the age
of sixteen, she lost Madame d'Albon, she was obliged to
take up her abode with her sister and the Comte de Vichy.
They treated her as a dependant, as a governess for their
children, as someone to be made use of and kept in place.
There, in her father's strange old castle, with its towers and
its terraces and its moat, amid the quiet Macon country,
neglected, wretched, alone, Julie de Lespinasse grew up into
womanhood; she was waiting for her fate.

Her fate came in the shape of Madame du Deffand. That
great lady was entering upon the final stage of her long
career. She was beginning to grow old, she was beginning
to grow blind, and, in spite of her glory and her dominion,
she was beginning to grow tired of Paris. Disgusted and ill,
she fled into the depths of the country; she spent a summer

with the Vichys, and became acquainted with Mademoiselle de Lespinasse. The two women seem to have felt almost at once that they were made for one another. Julie was now twenty-one; she was determined to escape at all hazards from an intolerable position; and she confided in the brilliant and affectionate marquise. With all her cynicism and all her icy knowledge of the world, Madame du Deffand was nothing if not impulsive. Julie had every virtue and every accomplishment; she was "ma reine"; with her, it would be once more possible to exist; she must come to Paris; it was the only thing to do. For a year Julie hesitated, and then she took the final plunge. In April, 1754, she went to Paris, to live with Madame du Deffand in her apartments in the Convent of St. Joseph.

The famous salon was now reaching the highest point of its glory. Nowhere else in Paris were the forces of intellect and the forces of the world so completely combined. That was Madame du Deffand's great achievement: she was able to mingle every variety of distinction into an harmonious whole. Her drawing-room was filled with eminent diplomatists, with beautiful women of fashion, with famous men of letters; it was the common meeting-place for great ladies like the Duchesse de Choiseul, for politicians like Turgot, for arbiters of taste like the Maréchale de Luxembourg, for philosophers like d'Alembert. Amid these brilliant assemblies, Mademoiselle de Lespinasse very soon obtained an established place. She possessed all the qualities necessary for success in such a society; she had tact, refinement, wit and penetration; she was animated and she was sympathetic; she could interest and she could charm. Madame du Deffand's experiment seemed to be amply justified by the event. Yet, after ten years, Julie's connection with the Convent of St. Joseph came to a sudden and violent termination. The story of the quarrel is sufficiently well known: the informal and surreptitious gatherings in Julie's private room, the discovery of the secret, the fury of the blind old woman, the cold hostility of the younger one, the eternal separation—these things need no further description here. M. de Ségur dwells on them with his usual insight; and his account is peculiarly valuable because it makes quite clear what had always been ambiguous before—the essential points of the situation. The discovery of the secret salon only brought to a head a profound disagreement which had been gathering strength for years; Julie's flight was not the result of a vulgar squabble, it was the outcome of an inherent antagonism pregnant with inevitable disaster. The two women were too much alike for a tolerable partnership; they were both too clever, too strong, and too fond of their own will. In the drawing-room of St. Joseph it was a necessary condition that Julie should play second fiddle; and how could she do that? She was born—it was clear enough—to be nothing less than the leader of an orchestra. Thus the question at issue was a question of spiritual domination; and the dilemma was a tragic one, because it was insoluble except by force. The struggle—the long, the desperate struggle—centred round d'Alembert, who, supreme alike in genius and in conversation, was the keystone of Madame du Deffand's elaborate triumphal arch. When the time came, it was for him to make the momentous decision. He did not hesitate. He knew well how much he owed to Madame du Deffand—fifteen years of unwavering friendship and his position in the world; but his indebtedness to Julie—her sympathy, her attachment, her affection—these things surpassed his computations; and, in exchange, he had given her his heart. He followed where she led, carrying with him in his defection the whole body of the encyclopaedists. The salon of St. Joseph was shattered; it became a wilderness, and, in the eyes of its ruler, life itself grew waste. To the miserable lady, infinitely disillusioned and eternally alone, it must have seemed that she at any rate had experienced the last humiliation. She was wrong. She was yet to know, in what remained to her of life, a suffering far deeper than any that had gone before. She—but this is not the history of Madame du Deffand.

Julie was victorious and free. Her friends closed round her, gallantly subscribed towards her maintenance, established her in a little set of rooms on the upper storey of a house in the rue Saint-Dominique. The years which followed were the happiest of her life. They passed in a perpetual round of visits and conversations, of theatres and operas, of gaiety and success. Her drawing-room became the intellectual centre of Paris, perhaps of the world. Every evening, from six to ten, there assembled within it a circle of illustrious persons. D'Alembert was always there; Condorcet and Turgot constantly, sometimes Malesherbes and Diderot, often Chastellux and Suard and Marmontel. One might find there the charming Duchesse de Châtillon, and the amazing Comtesse de Boufflers, and even sometimes the great Madame Geoffrin herself. In addition, there were the distinguished strangers—Caraccioli, the Neapolitan ambassador, the witty and inexhaustible Galiani, the penetrating Lord Shelburne, and the potentate of potentates, David Hume. Oh! It was a place worth visiting—the little salon in the due Saint-Dominique. And, if one were privileged to go there often, one found there what one found nowhere else—a sense of freedom and intimacy which was the outcome of a real equality, a real understanding, a real friendship such as have existed, before or since, in few societies indeed. Mademoiselle de Lespinasse, inspiring and absorbing all, was the crowning wonder, the final delight. To watch the moving expressions of her face was to watch the conversation itself, transmuted to a living thing by the glow of an intense intelligence.

"There is a flame within her!" was the common exclamation of her friends. Nor were they mistaken; she burnt with an inward fire. It was a steady flame, giving out a genial warmth, a happy brilliance. What wind could shake it? What sudden gust transform it to an instrument of devastation? whirl it, with horror and with blindness, into the path of death?

About two years after Julie's establishment in the rue Saint-Dominique, the Marquis de Mora, a young Spaniard of rank and fortune, paid a visit to Paris. He was handsome, clever, and *sensible;* he delighted the French *philosophes,* he fascinated the French ladies; among his conquests was Mademoiselle de Lespinasse. He departed, returned two years later, renewed acquaintance with Julie, and, this time, fell deeply in love. All that is known of him goes to show that he was a man of high worth, endowed with genuine talents, and capable of strong and profound emotions. To Julie, then and ever afterwards, he appeared to be a perfect being, a creature of almost superhuman excellence. She returned his passion with all the force of her nature; her energies had suddenly carried her into a new and splendid universe; she loved him with the intensity of a woman who has lost her youth, and loves for the first time. In spite of the disparity of age, of wealth, and of position, Mora had determined upon marriage. There was only one bar to the completion of their happiness—his ill-health, which perpetually harassed him and was beginning to display the symptoms of consumption. At last, after four years of waiting, everything was prepared; they were about to take the final step; and at that very moment Mora was stricken down by a violent attack of illness. He was obliged to depart from Paris, and return to his native air. The separation was terrible. Julie, worn out with anxiety and watching, her nerves shattered, her hopes crushed, was ready to presage the worst. Yet, however dreadful her fears may have been, they fell far short of the event. After a few weeks of collapse, she managed to pull herself together. She dragged herself to a garden party, in the hope of meeting some of her friends. She met the Comte de Guibert, and her fate was sealed.

The Comte de Guibert was at that moment at the height of his celebrity. A wonderful book on military tactics—now, alas! known no more—had made him the fashion; everyone was at his feet; even ladies, in their enthusiasm, read (or pretended to read) his great work. "Oh, M. de Guibert," said one of them, "que votre tic-tac est admirable!" But it was not only his book, it was the compelling charm of his manner and his conversation which secured him his distinguished place in the Parisian world. His talk was copious, brilliant, and extraordinarily impressive; one came away from him wondering what splendid future was in store for so remarkable a man. In addition, he was young, and gallant in every sense of the word. Mademoiselle de Lespinasse, wandering and dejected, came upon him suddenly, and, with a flash of intuition, recognised his qualities as precisely those of which she stood most in need. He seemed to her a tower of strength and sympathy; she felt him to be something she might cling to for support. She showed it, and he was flattered, attracted, at last charmed. They very soon became friends. Before long she had poured out to him the whole history of her agitations and her sorrows; and when, after a few months of constant intercourse, he left Paris to make a tour in Germany, she immediately continued the stream of her confidence in a series of letters. Thus began the famous and terrible correspondence which has made her immortal. The opening letters are charged with dramatic import and premonitions of approaching disaster. They are full of Mora; but, as they succeed one another, it is easy to observe in them a latent uneasiness rising gradually to the surface—a growing, dreadful doubt. As one peers into their depths, one can see,

forming itself ever more and more distinctly, the image of
the absent Guibert, the intruding symbol of a new, inexplicable desire. The mind of Julie, lonely, morbid, and
hysterical, was losing itself among its memories and imaginations and obsessions; it was falling under a spell. "Dites-moi,"
she breaks out at last, "est-ce là le ton de l'amitié? Est-ce celui
de la confiance? Qui est-ce qui m'entraine? Faites-moi con-
naître à moi-même; aidez-moi à me remettre en mesure. Mon
âme est bouleversée; sont-ce mes remords? Est-ce ma faute?
Est-ce vous? Serait-ce votre départ? Qu'est-ce donc qui me
persécute?" Such was her language when Guibert was still
absent; but when he returned, when, triumphant with fresh
laurels, he besieged her, adored her, when she felt the pressure of his presence and heard the music of his voice, then
indeed there was an end of all doubt and hesitation; blinded,
intoxicated, overwhelmed, she forgot what should never be
forgotten, she forgot Mora, she forgot the whole world.

"C'est Vénus tout entière à sa proie attachée!"

By a cruel irony, the one event which, in other circumstances, might have come as a release, proved, in Julie's case,
nothing less than the final misfortune. Mora died, and his
death took away from her for ever all hope of escape from
an intolerable situation. For, in the months which followed,
it became clear enough that Guibert, whatever else he may
have been, was no Mora. Sainte-Beuve, led astray by insufficient knowledge, has painted Guibert as a callous and dun-
derheaded donkey, a half-grotesque figure, dropping love-
letters out of his pockets, and going to the grave without
a notion of the tumult he had created. Such a person could
never have obtained dominion over Julie de Lespinasse. The
truth is that Guibert's character was infinitely better calculated to bring a woman of high intelligence and violent
emotions to disaster and destruction. He was really a clever

man; he was really well-meaning and warm-hearted; but
that was all. He was attractive, affectionate, admirable, everything, in fact, that a man should be; he had, like most men,
his moments of passion; like most men, he was ambitious:
and he looked forward, like most men, to a comfortable and
domestic old age. It is easy to understand how such a character as that worked havoc with Mademoiselle de Lespinasse.
It seemed to offer so much, and, when it came to the point,
it provided so little—and to her, who asked either for nothing or for all! She had swallowed the bait of his charm and
his excellence, and she was hooked with the deadly compromise which they concealed. "Je n'aime rien de ce qui est
à demi," she wrote of herself, "de ce qui est indécis, de ce
qui n'est qu'un peu. Je n'entends pas la langue des gens du
monde: ils s'amusent et ils bâillent; ils ont des amis, et ils
n'aiment rien. Tout cela me paraît déplorable. Oui, j'aime
mieux le tourment qui consume ma vie, que le plaisir qui
engourdit la leur; mais avec cette manière d'être, on n'est
point aimable; eh bien! on s'en passe; non, on n'est point
aimable, mais on est aimé, et cela vaut mille fois mieux que
de plaire." This was written when Mora was still alive; but,
when she had lost him, she discovered soon enough that even
passion might go without its recompense from one who was,
precisely, a man of the world. "Ah! mon ami," she exclaimed
to Guibert, summing up her tragedy in a single sentence,
"mon malheur, c'est que vous n'avez pas besoin d'être aimé
comme je sais aimer." No, assuredly, he was never tempted to
ask for such dangerous delights. "Mon ami," she told him,
"je vous aime, comme il faut aimer, avec excès, avec folie,
transport, et désespoir."

Her complete consciousness of the situation made her position more pitiable, but it did not help her to escape. She
was bound to him by too many ties; and he, youthful and
complaisant, found it beyond his force to break her bondage.

Even when she despised him most, her senses fought against her reason, and she lost herself in shame. The phantom of Mora was perpetually before her eyes, torturing her with vanished happiness and visionary upbraidings. "Oh! Combien j'ai été aimée! une âme de feu, pleine d'énergie, qui avait tout jugé, tout apprécié, et qui, revenue et dégoûtée de tout, s'était abandonnée au besoin et au plaisir d'aimer: mon ami, voilà comme j'étais aimée. Plusieurs années s'étaient écoulées, remplies du charme et de la douleur inséparables d'une passion aussi forte que profonde, lorsque vous êtes venu verser du poison dans mon cœur, ravager mon âme par le trouble et le remords. Mon Dieu! que ne m'avez-vous point fait souffrir! Vous m'arrachiez à mon sentiment, et je voyais que vous n'étiez pas à moi: comprenez-vous toute l'horreur de cette situation? comment trouve-t-on encore de la douceur à dire: mon ami, je vous aime, mais avec tant de vérité et de tendresse qu'il n'est pas possible que votre âme soit froide en m'écoutant?"

His unfaithfulness and his marriage were, after all, little more than incidents in her anguish; they were the symptoms of an incurable disease. They stimulated her to fresh efforts towards detachment, but it was in vain. She was a wild animal struggling in a net, involving herself, with every twist and every convulsion, more and more inextricably in the toils. Sometimes she sank into a torpor; existence became a weariness; she drugged herself with opium to escape a pain which was too great to bear. Evening after evening she spent at the opera, drinking in the music of Orpheus, the divine melodies of Gluck. "Il n'y a qu'une chose dans le monde," she wrote, "qui me fasse du bien, c'est la musique, mais c'est un bien qu'on appelerait douleur. Je voudrais entendre dix fois par jour cet air qui me déchire, et qui me fait jouir de tout ce que je regrette: *J'ai perdu mon Euridice.*" But she could never shake off her nightmare. Among her friends, in her charming salon, she would suddenly be overcome with tears, and forced to hurry from the room. Every knock upon the door brought desire and terror to her heart. The postman was a minister of death. "Non, les effets de la passion ou de la raison (car je ne sais laquelle m'anime dans ce moment) sont incroyables. Après avoir entendu le facteur avec ce besoin, cette agitation, qui font de l'attente le plus grand tourment, j'en étais malade physiquement: ma toux et ma rage de tête m'en avaient avancée de cinq ou six heures. Et bien! après cet état violent, qui n'est susceptible ni de distraction ni d'adoucissement, le facteur est arrivé, j'ai eu des lettres. Il n'y en avoit point de vous; j'en ai reçu une violente commotion intérieure et extérieure, et puis je ne sais ce qui est arrivé, mais je me suis sentie calmée: il me semble que j'éprouve une sorte de douceur à vous trouver encore plus froid et plus indifférent que vous ne pouvez me trouver bizarre." Who does not discover, beneath these dreadful confidences, a superhuman power moving mysteriously to an appointed doom? a veiled and awful voice of self-immolation?

"Je suis la plaie et le couteau!
Je suis le soufflet et la joue!
Je suis les membres et la roue,
Et la victime et le bourreau!"

Her last letters are one long wail of agony.—"Je ne sais si c'est vous ou la mort que j'implore: j'ai besoin d'être secourue, d'être délivrée du malheur qui me tue."—"Mon ami, *je vous aime*. Quand vous verraije? Voilà le résultat du passé, du présent, et de l'avenir, s'il y a un avenir! Ah! mon ami, que j'ai souffert, que je souffre! Mes maux sont affreux; mais je sens que je vous aime."—"Ah! s'il vous reste quelque bonté, plaignez-moi: je ne sais plus, je ne puis plus vous répondre; mon corps et mon âme sont anéantis. . . . Ah!

Mon Dieu, je ne me connais plus." Yet, in spite of all the pains of her existence, she was glad that she had lived. "J'en mourrai peutêtre," she had written, when she could still hope, "mais cela vaut mieux que de n'avoir jamais vécu"; and, in the depth of her despair, it was still the same.—"Ah! ces souvenirs me tuent! Cependant je voudrais bien pouvoir recommencer, et à des conditions plus cruelles encore." She regretted nothing; she was insatiable. Shattered in body and in mind, she fell at last into complete and irremediable collapse. Guibert, helpless and overwhelmed, hurried to her, declared he could never survive her; she forbade him her presence; the faithful d'Alembert alone watched beside her bed. "Adieu, mon ami," she wrote to Guibert, when the end was approaching. "Si jamais je revenais à la vie, j'aimerais encore à l'employer à vous aimer; mais il n'y a plus de temps." The wretched man, imprisoned in her ante-chamber, awaited the inevitable hour. With a supreme effort, she wrote him her valediction. She implored him to let her die at last.—"Ah! mon ami, faites que je vous doive le repos! Par vertu, soyez cruel une fois." She sank into the arms of d'Alembert, thanking him tenderly for that long kindness, that unalterable devotion; then, begging from him some strange forgiveness, she seemed, for a moment, to be struggling to an avowal of unutterable things. The ghastly secret trembled; but it was too late.

She died on the 22nd of May, 1776, in the forty-fourth year of her life. She was buried quietly in the cemetery of Saint-Sulpice, d'Alembert and Condorcet performing the final rites. For d'Alembert, however, there was one more duty. She had named him her executor; it was his task to examine her papers; and, when he did so, he made a discovery which cut him to the heart. Not a single letter of his own had been preserved among all the multitude; instead, it was Mora, Mora, Mora, and nothing else. He had fondly imagined that, among her friends, his own place had been the first. In his distress, he rushed to Guibert, pouring out his disappointment, his cruel disillusionment: "Oh! we were all of us mistaken; it was Mora that she loved!" Guibert was silent. The tragic irony was complete. A thousand memories besieged him, a thousand thoughts of past delights, of vanished conversations, of delicious annihilated hours; he was stifled by regrets, by remorse, by vain possibilities; he was blinded by endless visions of a pearl richer than all his tribe; a dreadful mist of tears, of desecration, of horror, rose up and clouded him for ever from his agonised and deluded friend.

> "O lasso,
> Quanti dolci pensier, quanto disio
> Menò costoro al doloroso passo!"

1906.

6. The First Earl of Lytton

THE two volumes of letters [1] which Lady Betty Balfour
has put together from the private correspondence of her
father, the late Lord Lytton, cannot fail to appeal to a large
body of readers. The letters themselves are full of interest;
they deal, in a masterly and brilliant way, with a vast variety
of topics; and they are set before the reader with an admirable skill and an unerring sympathy. Lady Betty Balfour
has succeeded not only in the difficult task of selecting and
arranging a mass of material whose very richness was embarrassing; she has invested the whole with a living unity,
and breathed into it a spirit which is the true commentary
of the life which the letters reveal. For there is something
more in these volumes than a succession of good things: there
is also—what is present in every collection of letters worthy
of notice—the portrait of a man. To open the book is to
strike at once into the orbit of a new personality. One feels,
when one has read it, that one has almost made a friend.

A remarkable range of interests and a wide catholicity
of tastes—these are perhaps the most obvious characteristics
of Lord Lytton's correspondence. The letters flow on, naturally and copiously, into a multitude of unbidden channels;
they pass without an effort from poetry to politics, from
hypnotism to Wagner, from a string of anecdotes to reflections upon the destiny of man. Nor is their versatility merely

[1] *Personal and Literary Letters of Robert, First Earl of Lytton*. Edited by
Lady Betty Balfour. In two volumes. Longmans, Green & Co. 1906.

of the dilettante kind; it is the versatility of an enthusiast —of one of those rare enthusiasts whose province is the whole world. *Humani nihil a me alienum puto:* the old sentence, so often thrown out at random, would have been a peculiarly fitting motto for these letters. And the variety of their subject matter is reflected in the diversity of the correspondents to whom they are addressed. Few men of his generation could have had so various an acquaintance as Lord Lytton. He discussed literature with the Brownings, he wrote state papers to Lord Salisbury, he speculated on life and death with Theodore Gomperz, he exchanged epigrams with Lady Dorothy Nevill, he gossiped with Mr. John Morley, and some of his most charming letters are those addressed, when he was Viceroy of India, to the late Queen. He had, too, a genius for friendship, so that his acquaintances very soon became his friends. One of his most intimate correspondents was Sir James Stephen, whom he met for the first time on the eve of his departure to India, and with whom he immediately struck up a lasting friendship. "India," says Lady Betty, "was of course the subject of their talk. Lytton was not more eager to hear than Stephen to tell all that he knew of the conditions of that great empire"; and the two men "did not part till they had spent half the night walking each other home, too absorbed in their subject to feel fatigue or the wish to separate." Stephen went home to write for his new friend a pamphlet on the government of India, which Lord Lytton declared had given him "the master key to the magnificent system of Indian administration." During the four succeeding years Stephen wrote to the Viceroy by every mail. The friendship is remarkable for something more than its swift beginning: it was a mingling of opposites such as it is a rare delight to think upon. Sir James Stephen was eminently unromantic. His qualities were those of solidity and force; he preponderated with a character of formidable grandeur, with a massive and rugged intellectual sanity, a colossal common sense. The contrast is complete between this monolithic nature and the mercurial temperament of Lord Lytton, with his ardent imagination, his easy brilliance, his passionate sympathy, his taste for the elaborate and the coloured and the rococo. Such characteristics offended some of his stiff countrymen; they could not tolerate a man to whom conventions were "incomprehensible things," who felt at home "in the pure light air of foreign life," whose dress "was original, as nearly all about him," and who was not afraid to express his feelings in public. But the great lawyer judged differently. "I never knew a man," he wrote after Lord Lytton's death, "towards whom I felt so warmly and to whom I owed so much. . . . I shall always regard it as one of the most fortunate circumstances of my life that I was for many years one of his most intimate friends."

The story which the letters tell has much of the attractiveness of a romance. But it is one of those romances which state and amplify a problem, only to leave one, at last, still in doubt. Was the hero a statesman of genius whose true faculties the world misunderstood? Or was he a poet, diverted by the pressure of circumstances from a great achievement in art? Different readers will answer the question differently; but, in either case, the reply must involve an admission of failure or perhaps rather of defeat. Lord Lytton's rule in India was at the time the object of unparalleled obloquy, and is now almost forgotten; his poetry blossomed early and blossomed late, but it never bore the fruit which brings immortality. Thus, behind all the sparkling movement of the letters, one may perceive a sense of melancholy, which at moments deepens into the actual expression of gloom. "Whether I look forward or backward, an immense despair always comes over me. If I were younger—but it is all too late now; I know that as a poet I shall never do or be what I feel that I might have done and been." It is difficult to speculate on unfulfilled possibilities; but one may well believe that a writer who trembled so often on the verge of greatness might, if fortune had so willed it, have crossed the perilous line. As it is, one is constantly wondering why Lytton's verse never does quite "soar above the Aonian mount." Was Mrs. Browning right when she told her friend, "You *sympathise* too much"? Perhaps his father came nearer the mark in his protests to John Forster: "He is doing that which the richest mind and the richest soil cannot do long with impunity. He is always taking white crops off his glebe. He never allows poetry to lie fallow." In truth, diamonds are not made in a day; and, though a Shakespeare or a Coleridge may give you, in a moment, a handful of jewels, who knows how many years of superhuman concentration may have gone to the making of them? One may imagine, at Lord Lytton's poetical christening, a bad fairy gliding in among the rest. The good ones were lavish with their gifts of charm, and distinction, and imagination, and humour, and feeling; and then, after them all, came the witch with her deceitful present: "Yes, my dear, and may you always write with ease!" The child grew up endowed with a fatal facility. He could put his thoughts into verse as easily as he could pick pebbles out of a brook. The pebbles, wet and glowing in his hand, were beautiful to look upon; and then in a little while, unaccountably, they seemed to be common stones after all. In this world, a glamour caught too easily fades too soon; it turns out to be an illusion. And an illusion is the one thing that a poet should never have.

A brief note from Disraeli, offering the Viceroyalty of India, dramatically shattered Lord Lytton's dreams of ease and poetry. He accepted the great office with an acute sense of all that it involved. "Oh, the change—the *awful* change!" he exclaims to Forster; and he assured Disraeli "that if, with the certainty of leaving my life behind me in India, I had a reasonable chance of also leaving there a reputation comparable to Lord Mayo's, I would still, without a moment's hesitation, embrace the high destiny you place within my grasp." This is not the place for a discussion of the still controversial questions surrounding Lord Lytton's Indian rule. But no reference to the man or to his life could be even superficially complete without some notice of his political capacity. There is enough in the present volumes—there is far more in Lady Betty Balfour's previous work (*Lord Lytton's Indian Administration*)—to make it clear to the most careless reader· that the popular conception of Lord Lytton as a minor poet masquerading as a Viceroy, who scribbled verses when he should have been composing dispatches, is a glaring travesty of the facts. The antithesis, however, is delightful, like all antitheses; and, in this case, it is supported by that curious English prejudice which has always—since the days when Rochester libelled the most astute of monarchs —refused to allow that a witty man could be a wise one. The ignorance, too, with which the ordinary Englishman habitually seasons his judgments on Indian affairs has done much to obscure the true character of Lytton's statesmanship. Besides the Afghan war, there is one event, and one alone, which "the man in the street" connects with Lytton's Indian administration—the proclamation of the Queen as Empress of India. Important as that event was, it is little short of ludicrous that it should be the one remembered act of the administration which gave free trade to India, which accomplished the great reform of the equalisation of the inland duties on salt, which finally established the grand and far-reaching principle of decentralisation, and which instituted the Famine Insurance Fund. The truth is that Lytton's internal administration must take rank as one of the most pregnant and beneficent known in India since the great Gov-

ernor-Generalship of Dalhousie. It is a curious irony that
the Viceroy who carried, in the face of the opposition of a
majority of his Council, the measure which opened the door
to free trade in India, should labour under the imputation
of political flippancy; but, after all, he was a Viceroy who
had written love-poems, who wore unusual waistcoats, and
who smoked cigarettes. Whether his Afghan policy did or did
not deserve the virulent denunciation which it received is a
question which does not concern us here; what does concern
us is the obvious fact that Lytton's financial and administrative work was the work of a statesman endowed with no
mean share of courage, of wisdom, of energy, and of determination. Unfortunately his opponents failed to notice the
distinction. In the heat of party, he was declared by one
politician to be "everything which a Viceroy ought not to
be"; by a second to be guilty of "financial dishonesty, trick-
ery, treachery, tyranny and cruelty"; by a third to have shown
"a deliberate desire to shed blood, systematic fraud, violence
and inveracity of the vilest kind." Lytton, though it is clear
that he suffered keenly, never let his dignity desert him. To
a friend, who had associated himself with these attacks, he
wrote: "I confess I have sometimes fancied that had our posi-
tions been reversed—you placed in mine, and I in yours—
my confidence in your character and intelligence would have
sufficed to satisfy my judgement that there was more honesty
and wisdom in your action than in the denunciation of it
by persons who could not be fully acquainted with the causes
and conditions of it. But no man dare say of himself how
he would feel, or what he would do, in a position he has
never occupied." Such words as these have something in
them of the old Roman *aequanimitas*—they might have come
from the pen of a Pliny or a Trajan, calm in their great government and their mighty toil. And it was in the same

spirit that, when the time came for relinquishing his task, Lord Lytton wrote to Stephen:

"Were you ever in the Forest of Arden? I have always fancied it must be the most charming place in the world, more especially in summer-time. I shall shortly be on my way to it, I think, and I hasten to give you rendez-vous at the court of the Banished Duke. If you meet our friend, the melancholy Jaques, greet him from me most lovingly, and tell him—Ducdame!—that all the fools are now in the circle and he need pipe to them no more. . . . And tell your own great heart, dear and good friend, that the joy I take from the prospect of seeing you is more precious to me than all that Providence has taken from the fancy prospect I had painted on the blank wall of the Future of bequeathing to India the supremacy of Central Asia and the revenues of a first-class Power."

These are fine words; and, in their wit, their fancy, their ornate elaboration, their half-hidden sadness, their noble wealth of feeling, they are supremely characteristic of their author. One is reminded of the beautiful portrait by Watts, where the rich bright colours—the auburn hair and beard, the blue eyes, the turquoise on the finger—blend so wonderfully into the mysterious melancholy of the face. It is easy to talk of defeat and failure. But if one turns back from the portrait to the book, and then back again from the book to the portrait, if one considers those records of achievement and of thought, one begins to wonder whether such things can be measured by such terms. One seems to discern in them something less unfortunate than failure, and something, perchance, more splendid than success.

1907.

7. Lady Mary Wortley Montagu

IT has often been observed that our virtues and our vices,
no less than our clothes, our furniture, and our fine arts,
are subject to the laws of fashion. The duties of one age
become the temptations of the next; and the historian of
manners might draw up an instructive series of moral
fashion-plates, which would display, for each preceding generation, the good and evil most in vogue. If, not content
with the bare record, he brought to it some touch of inspiration and of art, he would make us, perhaps, begin to feel
at home in those strange worlds which lie so far from us,
across such seas of time. When we open some old book of
memoirs or of letters we are too apt to turn away from
it with the same sort of wondering disgust that fills us when
we contemplate the faded photographs of thirty years ago.
But a Sir Joshua can make even hoops and wigs and powder
seem so natural that the wearers of them are no longer futile
shadows to us, but beautiful human creatures whom we
love. Crinolines and trunk-hose, ruffs and farthingales—these
things are not more out of fashion now than the holiness
of the Middle Ages which embodied itself in prayer, asceti-
cism, and dirt, or the ancient Roman magnanimity whose
highest glory was suicide. To the Italians of the Renaissance
virtue meant self-interested force; to us, it means self-sacrifice. Humanity has come into fashion, and it is hard for us
to recognise the antiquated cold nobilities. Yet, if we would
explore to any purpose the "famous nations of the dead,"

we must leave our insularity behind us. We must descend naked into those abodes, if we would have a wrestling-match with Death.

Lady Mary Wortley Montagu was one of the dominant figures of an epoch which, in its ideals of conduct and of feeling, affords a curious contrast with our own. The greatest intellect of her age was the author of *Gulliver's Travels;* its greatest poet the author of the *Dunciad;* and Lady Mary herself was for many years the most vital force in the mechanism of its social life. She was, like her age, cold and hard; she was infinitely unromantic; she was often cynical, and sometimes gross. "I think there are but two pleasures permitted to mortal man," she wrote at the end of her life— "love and vengeance"; and she used to say that she did not wish her enemies to die: "Oh, no! let them live! let them have the stone, let them have the gout!" She was, in fact, almost devoid of those sympathetic feelings which appear to us to be the essence of all goodness; so that she is read now, when she is read at all, simply for her wit. But, in reality, she was something more than a brilliant letter-writer; she was a moralist. "This is the strength and blood of virtue," says the profound and noble Verulam, "to contemn things that be desired, and to neglect that which is feared." And, judged by that high criterion, Lady Mary's virtue assuredly deserves a crown.

To write of her adequately were a task demanding no small share of sympathy and wisdom; and, unhappily, these qualities are conspicuously absent from the volume on *Lady Mary Wortley Montagu and her Times,*[1] which Mr. George Paston has lately put together. The book, with its slipshod writing, its uninstructed outlook, its utter lack of taste and purpose, is a fair specimen of the kind of biographical work

[1] *Lady Mary Wortley Montagu and her Times.* By George Paston. Methuen & Co.

which seems to give so much satisfaction to large numbers of our reading public. Decidedly, "they order the matter better in France," where such a production could never have appeared. Four-fifths of the book—and it is a bulky one—are devoted to a succession of extracts from Lady Mary's printed correspondence, strung together by feeble paraphrases of passages which have not been quoted, and eked out by a number of tedious and irrelevant letters—hitherto very properly unpublished—concerning the misadventures of Lady Mary's son. Indeed, the volume would be entirely worthless, and undeserving of comment, were it not for the first 150 pages, which contain a series of newly-discovered letters of the deepest interest. Lady Mary's correspondence falls naturally into four sections, determined by four well-marked periods in her life—the letters written to Edward Wortley before her marriage; the letters written during the Embassy to Constantinople; those written while she was reigning in the society of Twickenham and London; and finally those which she wrote during her long retirement in Italy and France. All the new letters of importance belong to the first section of the correspondence. Those in this series which had previously been published indicated clearly enough the main outline of Lady Mary's earliest love-affair—that which ended in her elopement with Edward Wortley; but the new material fills in the details of this remarkable history, and presents us with a picture which is psychologically complete. Unfortunately, however, the compiler has missed his opportunity. He does not print all the letters; he omits portions from those which he does print; and he does not reprint all those which have already been published, so that, in order to follow the whole correspondence, it is necessary to make constant references to the previous editions. He has, moreover, interspersed his quotations with a number of comments which are altogether out of place. If he had been content to collect into one small volume the text—unabridged and unalloyed—of all the existing letters which passed between Lady Mary and her lover, he would have produced something very much more valuable than his present unwieldy and pretentious work.

"L'on n'aime bien," says La Bruyère, "qu'une seule fois, c'est la première; les amours qui suivent sont moins involontaires." That is the key to the part played by Lady Mary in this curious correspondence. When she fell in love with Edward Wortley, she was a girl of twenty, witty, high-spirited, country-bred, and endowed with a taste for serious reading almost unknown among the young ladies of her times. He was twelve years her senior; and he came upon her as a rising man of the world, the intimate of the wits and politicians of London, and the possessor of an intellect, a char-

acter and an experience of... ...her own. She was

fascinated by his strong intelligence, his high accomplishments, above all, perhaps by his over-mastering force of will. "I believe," she wrote to him forty years later, "there are few men in the world (I never knew any) capable of such a strength of resolution as yourself." And he, on his side, found in her the one woman who had ever been able, intellectually, to stand up against him. "There has not yet been," he burst out to her in one of his rare moments of enthusiasm, "there never will be, another Lady Mary." At first sight, it is difficult to understand what impediments there could have been to the marriage of these minds. There was nothing in either to give offence to the other; their tastes were the same; both were sharp-witted, honest, and eminently sensible; and they were in love. Yet for more than two years they hesitated and held back; and, during that time, there was hardly a moment when one or the other was not on the very brink of breaking off for ever. But they were not ordinary lovers; they were intellectual gladiators, and their letters are like the preliminary wary passes of two well-matched wrestlers before they come to grips. If they had been less well-matched, there would have been no such difficulties; but neither could ever be certain that the other was not too strong. She feared that she liked him too much, and he that she liked him too little. "I own I was very uneasy," he wrote to her, "at the beginning of last winter when I saw you and Mr. K. pressing so close upon each other in the Drawing-room, and found that you could not let me speak to you without being overheard by him. What passed between you at the Trial confirmed my suspicions. 'Twould be useless to reckon up all the Passages that gave me pain. The second time I saw you at the Play this year, I was informed of your Passion for him by one that I knew would not conceal it from others. At the Birthnight you remember the many proofs of your affection for him, and cannot have forgot what passed in his favour at the Ball. My observing that you have since been present at the Park, Operas and Assemblies together, and to finish all your contriving, to have him for one of that select number that serenaded you at Acton, and afterwards danced at the Dutchess's—all this had gone a great way in settling my opinion that he and none but he possessed your heart." Did Lady Mary flirt? Perhaps she did. Among her papers she preserved a note from a humble admirer, whose innocent adoration forms a curious contrast to the severity of Mr. Wortley: "Dear Charmer, you are very much in the right to imagine I am in perfect health, for nothing contributes so much to it as your good company and a set of fiddles, and am sorry you made so short a stay at the Ball, for I had not half the satisfaction after you was gone." But the Charmer, though she may have listened for a moment, was soon back again among her arguments and disputations. When Wortley's jealousy had been quieted, there were all her own uneasinesses to be discussed. She speculated on a dozen different subjects—on life in the country, on the ethics of marriage, on poverty and happiness; her anxious spirit surveyed the distant future, and still found matter for doubt. "In my present opinion, I think if I was yours and you used me well, nothing could be added to my misfortune should I lose you. But when I suffer my reason to speak, it tells me that in any circumstance of life (wretched or happy) there is a certain proportion of money, as the world is made, absolutely necessary for the living in it. . . . Should I find myself forty years hence your widow, without a competency to maintain me in a manner suitable in some degree to my education, I shall not then be so old I may not impossibly live twenty years longer without what is requisite to make life easy—happiness is what I should not think of." Sentiments like these from a young lady of twenty-two must have delighted good, careful Mr. Wortley. One is reminded of Professor Raleigh's dictum that in the eighteenth century man lived up to his definition, and was a rational animal; and yet nothing could be further from the truth than to suppose that Lady Mary's financial forethought indicated a coldness of heart. Indeed, precisely the reverse was the case. She was in love for the first time; and she was in love not only involuntarily, but against her will. As her feelings deepened in intensity, she became more and more vehement in her determination not to be carried away by them—to be as dispassionately sensible as a mathematician at work on a theorem. Her logic rose like quicksilver as her heat increased, until at last, when it reached the boiling point, the thermometer burst. In a fine letter, written in reply to the suspicious accusations of her lover, it is easy to trace the process. She begins with wit, she goes on to reasoning, she ends in tears: "The sense of your letter I take to be this. Madam, you are the greatest Coquette I ever knew, and withal very silly; the only happiness you propose to yourself in a Husband is jilting him most abundantly. You must stay till my Lord Hide is a widower or Heaven raises up another Mr. Popham; for my part I know all your tricks. . . . This is the exact miniature of your letter." After this, Lady Mary proceeds to describe her ideal husband: "My first and chiefest wish, if I had a Companion, it should be one (now am I going to make you a picture of my own heart) that I very much loved and that loved me; one that thought that the truest wisdom which most conduced to our happiness, and that it was not below a man of sense to take satisfaction in the conversation of a reasonable woman; one who did not think tenderness a disgrace to his understanding . . . one that would be as willing to be happy as I would be to make him so." And then, suddenly, she breaks out: "After this description of whom I could like, I need not add that it is not you—you who could suspect where you have the least reason, that thinks so wrong of me, as to believe me everything I abhor. . . . I desire you think no more of me. . . . I am heartily glad I can have no answer to this letter, tho' if I could I should now have the courage to return it unopened. You are unjust and I am unhappy—'tis past—I will never think of you more—never." Lady Mary's thermometer had burst.

These strange love-letters are full not only of emotion mixed with common sense, but also of a kind of plain-speaking no less remarkable, and, to modern notions, even more out of place. In a subsequent letter—for of course the thermometer had been repaired—Mr. Wortley, still suspecting a rival, and at the same time determined to make his own position clear, wrote to Lady Mary: "Out of tenderness to you I have forborn to state your case in the plainest light, which is thus. If you have no thoughts of [gallantry] you are mad if you marry him. If you are likely to think of [gallantry] you are mad if you marry me." To the word in brackets the

compiler appends the following note: "Mr. Wortley uses a
word of Elizabethan crudity. In her reply Lady Mary softens
it down to 'gallantry.' Her example is here followed." This
is a piece of unmeaning prudery, but we must be thankful
that the passage, even thus mutilated, has been allowed to
come to light. For Lady Mary did not flinch before the
brutality of her lover; and the reply which she gave to his
sharp questioning was actually her final surrender: "If you
please, I will never see another man. . . . I have examined
my own heart whether I can leave everything for you; I
think I can. If I change my mind, you shall know before
Sunday; after that I will not change my mind."

And, for the first and last time, she did not. In the excitement of the moment, Edward Wortley's usual calm forsook
him, and he despatched a letter full of ecstasy and passion
and protestations of eternal love. "The greatest part of my
life shall be dedicated to you," he wrote. "From everything
that can lessen my passion for you I will fly with as much
speed as from the Plague. I shall sooner chuse to see my
heart torn from my breast than divided from you." The
only difficulties that remained were material ones. Lady
Mary's father had set his heart against the match, and, gain-
ing wind of the intentions of the lovers, carried off his daughter at the last moment to his country seat in Wiltshire.
Mr. Wortley followed in a post-chaise, came up with the
fugitives at an inn on the road, and managed to abstract
the lady. "If we should once get into a coach," he had written a few days earlier, "let us not say one word till we come
before the parson, lest we should engage in fresh disputes."
The advice was excellent, but who can believe that it was
followed? One can imagine the bitter altercations in the
flying carriage, as it swept along between the country hedge-
rows on its way to "the parson." Did Lady Mary put out her

hand, more than once, towards the cord? Ah! how long ago
it is since all that was buried in oblivion!—

> "Ay, ages long ago
> These lovers fled away!" . . .

But, at any rate, they drew up before the church at a happy
moment. For, when they reached the altar, neither the one
nor the other refused to say "I will."

Lady Mary's subsequent history may be briefly told. Her
marriage was a complete failure, and, oddly enough, a failure
of the ordinary kind. There were no exciting ruptures; there
was only a gradual estrangement, ending at last in almost
absolute indifference. Edward Wortley became engrossed in
politics and money-making, while his wife, disillusioned,
reckless, and brilliant, plunged into the vortex of fashionable
London. One day she looked in her looking-glass, and found
she had grown old; upon which she packed her boxes, retired to an Italian villa, and never looked at a looking-glass
again. The last twenty years of her life were spent in that
atmosphere of physical and moral laxity which seems in those
days to have inevitably surrounded the unattached English-
woman who lived abroad. Horace Walpole describes her at
Florence in language of disgusting minuteness, calls her
"Moll Worthless," and declares that she was "so far gone"
in her love for a handsome young gentleman that "she literally took him out to dance country dances last night at a
formal ball, where there was no measure kept in laughing
at her old, foul, tawdry, painted, plastered personage." And,
though Walpole disliked Lady Mary, there can be little
doubt that his account of her represents the superficial truth
about her later years. But there was another side of her,
which neither Walpole nor the majority of her contemporaries had any conception of—the side revealed in the long
series of letters to her daughter, Lady Bute. These letters

contain the last act of Lady Mary's tragedy. That tragedy
began when, in her early days, she became the battlefield
over which her intellect and her emotions furiously fought.
It had been her dream that Edward Wortley would satisfy
both; and he satisfied neither. The battle continued to the
end of her life, and, as she grew older, her emotions became
ever more arbitrary and sterile, her intellect more penetrating and severe. Her dream of perfect love, which Wortley
had shattered, haunted her like a ghost. In her old age she
wrote an essay to disprove the maxim of La Rochefoucauld,
"qu'il y a des mariages commodes mais point de délicieux";
she described the exquisite felicity of "une estime parfaite,
fixée par la reconnaissance, soutenue par l'inclination, et
éveillée par la tendresse de l'amour"; she lingered over "la
joye de voir qu'on fait le bonheur entier de l'objet aimé—
en quel point," she said, "je place la jouissance parfaite."
Alas! in her bedraggled Italian adventures, what kind of
jouissance was it that she found? That she refused to palliate
her situation, that she faced her wretched failure without
flinching and without pretence—there lay the intellectual
eminence which lifts her melancholy history out of the sordid
into the sublime. There is something great, something not
to be forgotten, about the honesty with which she looked
into the worthlessness of things, and the bravery with which
she accepted it. In one of her very latest letters she quoted
a couplet which might well stand as the motto for the book
of her destiny—the summary of what was noblest and most
essential in the spirit of her life—

> "To dare in fields is valour; but how few
> Dare have the real courage to be true?"

1907.

8. *A Simple Story* [1]

A SIMPLE STORY is one of those books which, for some reason or other, have failed to come down to us, as they deserved, along the current of time, but have drifted into a literary backwater where only the professional critic or the curious discoverer can find them out. "The iniquity of oblivion blindly scattereth her poppy"; and nowhere more blindly than in the republic of letters. If we were to inquire how it has happened that the true value of Mrs. Inchbald's achievement has passed out of general recognition, perhaps the answer to our question would be found to lie in the extreme difficulty with which the mass of readers detect and appreciate mere quality in literature. Their judgment is swayed by a hundred side-considerations which have nothing to do with art, but happen easily to impress the imagination, or to fit in with the fashion of the hour. The reputation of Mrs. Inchbald's contemporary, Fanny Burney, is a case in point. Everyone has heard of Fanny Burney's novels, and *Evelina* is still widely read. Yet it is impossible to doubt that so far as quality alone is concerned, *Evelina* deserves to be ranked considerably below *A Simple Story*. But its writer was the familiar friend of the greatest spirits of her age; she was the author of one of the best of diaries; and her work was immediately and immensely popular. Thus it has happened that the name of Fanny Burney has maintained its

[1] Originally published as an introduction to a re-issue of *A Simple Story*. By Mrs. Inchbald. Henry Frowde. 1908.

place upon the roll of English novelists, while that of Mrs. Inchbald is forgotten.

But the obscurity of Mrs. Inchbald's career has not, of course, been the only reason for the neglect of her work. The merits of *A Simple Story* are of a kind peculiarly calculated to escape the notice of a generation of readers brought up on the fiction of the nineteenth century. That fiction, infinitely various as it is, possesses at least one characteristic common to the whole of it—a breadth of outlook upon life, which can be paralleled by no other body of literature in the world save that of the Elizabethans. But the comprehensiveness of view shared by Dickens and Tolstoy, by Balzac and George Eliot, finds no place in Mrs. Inchbald's work. Compared with *A Simple Story* even the narrow canvases of Jane Austen seem spacious pictures of diversified life. Mrs. Inchbald's novel is not concerned with the world at large, or with any section of society, hardly even with the family; its subject is a group of two or three individuals whose interaction forms the whole business of the book. There is no local colour in it, no complexity of detail nor violence of contrast; the atmosphere is vague and neutral, the action passes among ill-defined sitting-rooms, and the most poignant scene in the story takes place upon a staircase which has never been described. Thus the reader of modern novels is inevitably struck, in *A Simple Story,* by a sense of emptiness and thinness, which may well blind him to high intrinsic merits. The spirit of the eighteenth century is certainly present in the book, but it is the eighteenth century of France rather than of England. Mrs. Inchbald no doubt owed much to Richardson; her view of life is the indoor sentimental view of the great author of *Clarissa;* but her treatment of it has very little in common with his method of microscopic analysis and vast accumulation. If she belongs to any school, it is among the followers of the French classical tradition that she must be placed. *A Simple Story* is, in its small way, a descendant of the Tragedies of Racine; and Miss Milner may claim relationship with Madame de Clèves. Besides her narrowness of vision, Mrs. Inchbald possesses another quality, no less characteristic of her French predecessors, and no less rare among the novelists of England. She is essentially a stylist—a writer whose whole conception of her art is dominated by stylistic intention. Her style, it is true, is on the whole poor; it is often heavy and pompous, sometimes clumsy and indistinct; compared with the style of such a master as Thackeray it sinks at once into insignificance. But the interest of her style does not lie in its intrinsic merit so much as in the use to which she puts it. Thackeray's style is mere ornament, existing independently of what he has to say; Mrs. Inchbald's is part and parcel of her matter. The result is that when, in moments of inspiration, she rises to the height of her opportunity, when, mastering her material, she invests her expression with the whole intensity of her feeling and her thought, then she achieves effects of the rarest beauty—effects of a kind for which one may search through Thackeray in vain. The most triumphant of these passages is the scene on the staircase of Elmwood House—a passage which would be spoilt by quotation and which no one who has ever read it could forget. But the same quality is to be found throughout her work. "Oh, Miss Woodley!" exclaims Miss Milner, forced at last to confess to her friend what she feels towards Dorriforth, "I love him with all the passion of a mistress, and with all the tenderness of a wife." No young lady, even in the eighteenth century, ever gave utterance to such a sentence as that. It is the sentence, not of a speaker, but of a writer; and yet, for that very reason, it is delightful, and comes to us charged with a curious sense of emotion, which is none the less real for its elaboration. In *Nature and Art,* Mrs. Inchbald's second novel, the climax of the story is told in a series of short paragraphs, which, for bitterness and concentration of style, are almost reminiscent of Stendhal:

"The jury consulted for a few minutes. The verdict was 'Guilty.'

"She heard it with composure.

"But when William placed the fatal velvet on his head and rose to pronounce sentence, she started with a kind of convulsive motion, retreated a step or two back, and, lifting up her hands with a scream, exclaimed—

" 'Oh, not from *you!*'

"The piercing shriek which accompanied these words prevented their being heard by part of the audience; and those who heard them thought little of their meaning, more than that they expressed her fear of dying.

"Serene and dignified, as if no such exclamation had been uttered, William delivered the fatal speech, ending with 'Dead, dead, dead.'

"She fainted as he closed the period, and was carried back to prison in a swoon; while he adjourned the court to go to dinner."

Here, no doubt, there is a touch of melodrama; but it is the melodrama of a rhetorician, and, in that fine "She heard it with composure," genius has brushed aside the forced and the obvious, to express, with supreme directness, the anguish of a soul.

For, in spite of Mrs. Inchbald's artificialities, in spite of her lack of that kind of realistic description which seems to modern readers the very blood and breath of a good story, she has the power of doing what, after all, only a very few indeed of her fellow-craftsmen have ever been able to do—she can bring into her pages the living pressure of a human passion, she can invest, if not with realism, with something greater than realism—with the sense of reality itself—the

pains, the triumphs, and the agitations of the human heart.
"The heart," to use the old-fashioned phrase—there is Mrs.
Inchbald's empire, there is the sphere of her glory and her
command. Outside of it, her powers are weak and fluctuating. She has no firm grasp of the masculine elements in character: she wishes to draw a rough man, Sandford, and she
draws a rude one; she tries her hand at a hero, Rushbrook,
and she turns out a prig. Her humour is not faulty, but it is
exceedingly slight. What an immortal figure the dim Mrs.
Horton would have become in the hands of Jane Austen!
In *Nature and Art* her attempts at social satire are superficial and overstrained. But weaknesses of this kind—and it
would be easy to prolong the list—are what every reader of
the following pages will notice without difficulty, and what
no wise one will regard. "Il ne faut point juger des hommes
par ce qu'ils ignorent, mais par ce qu'ils savent"; and Mrs.
Inchbald's knowledge was as profound as it was limited. Her
Miss Milner is an original and brilliant creation, compact of
charm and life. She is a flirt, and a flirt not only adorable,
but worthy of adoration. Did Mrs. Inchbald take the suggestion of a heroine with imperfections from the little masterpiece which, on more sides than one, closely touches hers—
Manon Lescaut? Perhaps; and yet, if this was so, the borrow-
ing was of the slightest, for it is only in the fact that she *is*
imperfect that Miss Milner bears to Manon any resemblance
at all. In every other respect the English heroine is the precise contrary of the French one: she is a creature of fiery will,
of high bearing, of noble disposition; and her shortcomings
are born, not of weakness, but of excess of strength. Mrs.
Inchbald has taken this character, she has thrown it under
the influence of a violent and absorbing passion, and, upon
that theme, she has written her delicate, sympathetic, and
artificial book.

As one reads it, one cannot but feel that it is, if not directly and circumstantially, at least in essence, autobiographical. One finds oneself speculating over the author, wondering what was her history, and how much of it was Miss Milner's. Unfortunately, the greater part of what we should most like to know of Mrs. Inchbald's life has vanished beyond recovery. She wrote her Memoirs, and she burnt them; and who can tell whether even there we should have found a self-revelation? Confessions are sometimes curiously discreet, and, in the case of Mrs. Inchbald, we may be sure that it is only what was indiscreet that would really be worth the hearing. Yet her life is not devoid of interest. A brief sketch of it may be welcome to her readers.

Elizabeth Inchbald was born on the 15th of October, 1753, at Standingfield, near Bury St. Edmunds in Suffolk,[1] one of the numerous offspring of John and Mary Simpson. The Simpsons, who were Roman Catholics, held a moderate farm in Standingfield, and ranked among the gentry of the neighbourhood. In Elizabeth's eighth year her father died; but the family continued at the farm, the elder daughters marrying and settling in London, while Elizabeth grew up into a beautiful and charming girl. One misfortune, however, interfered with her happiness—a defect of utterance which during her early years rendered her speech so indistinct as to be unintelligible to strangers. She devoted herself to reading and to dreams of the great world. At thirteen, she declared she would rather die than live longer without seeing the world; she longed to go to London; she longed to go upon the stage. When, in 1770, one of her brothers became an actor at Norwich, she wrote secretly to his manager, Mr. Griffith, begging for an engagement. Mr. Griffith was encouraging, and, though no definite steps were taken, she was suffi-

[1] The following account is based upon the *Memoirs of Mrs. Inchbald, including her familiar correspondence with the most distinguished persons of her time*, edited by James Boaden, Esq.—a discursive, vague, and not unamusing book.

ciently charmed with him to write out his name at length in her diary, with the inscription "Each dear letter of thy name is harmony." Was Mr. Griffith the hero of the company as well as its manager? That, at any rate, was clearly Miss Simpson's opinion; but she soon had other distractions. In the following year she paid a visit to her married sisters in London, where she met another actor, Mr. Inchbald, who seems immediately to have fallen in love with her, and to have proposed. She remained cool. "In spite of your eloquent pen," she wrote to him, with a touch of that sharp and almost bitter sense that was always hers, "matrimony still appears to me with less charms than terrors; the bliss arising from it, I doubt not, is superior to any other—but best not to be ventured for (in my opinion), till some little time have proved the emptiness of all other; which it seldom fails to do." Nevertheless, the correspondence continued, and, early in 1772, some entries in her diary give a glimpse of her state of mind:

Jan. 22. Saw Mr. Griffith's picture.
Jan. 28. Stole it.
Jan. 29. Rather disappointed at not receiving a letter from Mr. Inchbald.

A few months later she did the great deed of her life: she stepped secretly into the Norwich coach, and went to London. The days that followed were full of hazard and adventure, but the details of them are uncertain. She was a girl of eighteen, absolutely alone, and astonishingly attractive—"tall," we are told, "slender, straight, of the purest complexion, and most beautiful features; her hair of a golden auburn, her eyes full at once of spirit and sweetness"; and it was only to be expected that, in such circumstances, romance and daring would soon give place to discomfort and alarm. She attempted in vain to obtain a theatrical engagement; she found herself, more than once, obliged to shift her lodging; and at last, after ten days of trepidation, she was reduced to apply for help to her married sisters. This put an end to her difficulties, but, in spite of her efforts to avoid notice, her beauty had already attracted attention, and she had received a letter from a stranger, with whom she immediately entered into correspondence. She had all the boldness of innocence, and, in addition, a force of character which brought her safely through the risks she ran. While she was still in her solitary lodging, a theatrical manager, named Dodd, attempted to use his position as a cover for seduction. She had several interviews with him alone, and the story goes that, in the last, she snatched up a basin of hot water and dashed it in his face. But she was not to go unprotected for long; for within two months of her arrival in London she had married Mr. Inchbald.

The next twelve years of Mrs. Inchbald's life were passed amid the rough-and-tumble of the eighteenth-century stage. Her husband was thirty-seven when she married him, a Roman Catholic like herself, and an actor who depended for his living upon ill-paid and uncertain provincial engagements. Mrs. Inchbald conquered her infirmity of speech and threw herself into her husband's profession. She accompanied him to Bristol, to Scotland, to Liverpool, to Birmingham, appearing in a great variety of rôles, but never with any very conspicuous success. The record of these journeys throws an interesting light upon the conditions of the provincial companies of those days. Mrs. Inchbald and her companions would set out to walk from one Scotch town to another; they would think themselves lucky if they could climb on to a passing cart, to arrive at last, drenched with rain perhaps, at some wretched hostelry. But this kind of barbarism did not stand in the way of an almost childish gaiety. In Yorkshire, we find the Inchbalds, the Siddonses, and Kemble re-

tiring to the moors, in the intervals of business, to play blind
man's buff or puss-in-the-corner. Such were the pastimes of
Mrs. Siddons before the days of her fame. No doubt this kind
of lightheartedness was the best antidote to the experience
of being "saluted with volleys of potatoes and broken bot-
tles," as the Siddonses were by the citizens of Liverpool, for
having ventured to appear on their stage without having ever
played before the King. On this occasion the audience, according to a letter from Kemble to Mrs. Inchbald, "extin-
guished all the lights round the house; then jumped upon
the stage; brushed every lamp out with their hats; took back
their money; left the theatre, and determined themselves to
repeat this till they have another company." These adventures were diversified by a journey to Paris, undertaken in
the hope that Mr. Inchbald, who found himself without
engagements, might pick up a livelihood as a painter of
miniatures. The scheme came to nothing, and the Inchbalds
eventually went to Hull, where they returned to their old
profession. Here, in 1779, suddenly and somewhat mysteriously, Mr. Inchbald died. To his widow the week that followed was one of "grief, horror, and almost despair"; but
soon, with her old pertinacity, she was back at her work,
settling at last in London, and becoming a member of the
Covent Garden company. Here, for the next five years, she
earned for herself a meagre living, until, quite unexpectedly,
deliverance came. In her moments of leisure she had been
trying her hand upon dramatic composition; she had written
some farces, and, in 1784, one of them, *A Mogul Tale*, was
accepted, acted, and obtained a great success. This was the
turning-point of her career. She followed up her farce with
a series of plays, either original or adapted, which, almost
without exception, were well received, so that she was soon
able to retire from the stage with a comfortable competence.
She had succeeded in life; she was happy, respected, free.

Mrs. Inchbald's plays are so bad that it is difficult to believe that they brought her a fortune. But no doubt it was their faults that made them popular—their sentimentalities, their melodramatic absurdities, their strangely false and high-pitched moral tone. They are written in a jargon which resembles, if it resembles anything, an execrable prose translation from very flat French verse. "Ah, Manuel!" exclaims one of her heroines, "I am now amply punished by the Marquis for all my cruelty to Duke Cordunna—he to whom my father in my infancy betrothed me, and to whom I willingly pledged my faith, hoping to wed; till Romono, the Marquis of Romono, came from the field of glory, and with superior claims of person as of fame, seized on my heart by force, and perforce made me feel I had never loved till then." Which is the more surprising—that actors could be found to utter such speeches, or that audiences could be collected to applaud them? Perhaps, for us, the most memorable fact about Mrs. Inchbald's dramatic work is that one of her adaptations (from the German of Kotzebue) was no other than that *Lovers' Vows* which, as everyone knows, was rehearsed so brilliantly at Ecclesford, the seat of the Right Hon. Lord Ravenshaw, in Cornwall, and which, after all, was *not* performed at Sir Thomas Bertram's. But that is an interest *sub specie aeternitatis;* and, from the temporal point of view, Mrs. Inchbald's plays must be regarded merely as means—means towards her own enfranchisement, and that condition of things which made possible *A Simple Story*. That novel had been sketched as early as 1777; but it was not completely written until 1790, and not published until the following year. A second edition was printed immediately, and several more followed; the present reprint is taken from the fourth, published in 1799—but with the addition of the characteristic preface, which, after the second edition, was dropped.

The four small volumes of these early editions, with their
large type, their ample spacing, their charming flavour of
antiquity, delicacy, and rest—may be met with often enough
in secluded corners of second-hand bookshops, or on some
neglected shelf in the library of a country house. For their
own generation, they represented a distinguished title to
fame. Mrs. Inchbald—to use the expression of her biographer
—"was ascertained to be one of the greatest ornaments of her
sex." She was painted by Lawrence, she was eulogised by
Miss Edgeworth, she was complimented by Madame de Staël
herself. She had, indeed, won for herself a position which
can hardly be paralleled among the women of the eighteenth
century—a position of independence and honour, based upon
talent, and upon talent alone. In 1796 she published *Nature
and Art*, and ten years later appeared her last work—a series
of biographical and critical notices prefixed to a large collection of acting plays. During the greater part of the interven-
ing period she lived in lodgings in Leicester Square—or
"Leicester Fields," as the place was still often called—in a
house opposite that of Sir Joshua Reynolds. The economy
which she had learnt in her early days she continued to practise, dressing with extraordinary plainness, and often going
without a fire in winter, so that she was able, through her
self-sacrifice, to keep from want a large band of poor rela-
tives and friends. The society she mixed with was various,
but, for the most part, obscure. There were occasional visits
from the now triumphant Mrs. Siddons; there were inces-
sant propositions—but, alas! they were equivocal—from Sir
Charles Bunbury; for the rest, she passed her life among
actor-managers and humble playwrights and unremembered
medical men. One of her friends was William Godwin, who
described her to Mrs. Shelley as a "piquante mixture between a lady and a milkmaid," and who, it is said, suggested

part of the plot of *A Simple Story*. But she quarrelled with him when he married Mary Wollstonecraft, after whose death she wrote to him thus: "With the most sincere sympathy in all you have suffered—with the most perfect forgiveness of all you have said to me, there must nevertheless be an end to our acquaintance *for ever*. I respect your prejudices, but I also respect my own." Far more intimate were her relations with Dr. Gisborne—a mysterious figure, with whom, in some tragic manner that we can only just discern, was enacted her final romance. His name—often in company with that of another physician, Dr. Warren, for whom, too, she had a passionate affection—occurs frequently among her papers; and her diary for December 17, 1794, has this entry: "Dr. Gisborne drank tea here, and staid very late: he talked seriously of marrying—but not *me*." Many years later, one September, she amused herself by making out a list of all the Septembers since her marriage, with brief notes as to her state of mind during each. The list has fortunately survived, and some of the later entries are as follows:

1791. London; after my novel, *Simple Story* . . . very happy.

1792. London; in Leicester Square . . . cheerful, content, and sometimes rather happy. . . .

1794. Extremely happy, but for poor Debby's death.

1795. My brother George's death, and an intimate acquaintance with Dr. Gisborne—not happy. . . .

1797. After an alteration in my teeth, and the death of Dr. Warren—yet far from unhappy.

1798. Happy, but for suspicion amounting almost to certainty of a rapid appearance of age in my face. . . .

1802. After feeling wholly indifferent about Dr. Gisborne—very happy but for ill health, ill looks, &c.

1803. After quitting Leicester Square probably for ever—
after caring scarce at all or thinking of Dr. Gisborne . . . very happy. . . .

1806. . . . After the death of Dr. Gisborne, too, often
very unhappy, yet mostly cheerful, and on my
return to London nearly happy.

The record, with all its quaintness, produces a curious impression of stoicism—of a certain grim acceptance of the facts
of life. It would have been a pleasure, certainly, but an
alarming pleasure, to have known Mrs. Inchbald.

In the early years of the century she gradually withdrew
from London, establishing herself in suburban boarding-
houses, often among sisters of charity, and devoting her days
to the practice of her religion. In her early and middle life
she had been an indifferent Catholic: "Sunday. Rose late,
dressed, and read in the Bible about David, &c."—this is one
of the very few references in her diary to anything approaching a religious observance during many years. But, in her
old age, her views changed; her devotions increased with
her retirement; and her retirement was at last complete.
She died, in an obscure Kensington boarding-house, on
August 1, 1821. She was buried in Kensington churchyard.
But, if her ghost lingers anywhere, it is not in Kensington:
it is in the heart of the London that she had always loved.
Yet, even there, how much now would she find to recognise?
Mrs. Inchbald's world has passed away from us for ever; and,
as we walk there today amid the press of the living, it is hard
to believe that she too was familiar with Leicester Square.

1908.

9. An Anthology

THE book, if you can get it, is worth reading, not only for its curiosity, but for its beauty and its charm. It was published ten years since, and one would be tempted to say that the poetry in it is the best that this generation has known, save that the greater part of it has been written for the last ten centuries. Yet, though it contains so much that is excellent and old, one might travel far without meeting a single reader who had ever heard of the poets of this anthology. Have they, then, been lately rediscovered, dug up, perhaps, from a buried city, and so, after the lapse of ages, restored to the admiration that is their due? By no means! These poems have been printed in innumerable editions, and the names of their writers are familiar words in the mouths of millions. Here are contradictions enough to perplex the most expert of Hegelians, but they are contradictions which, like those of Hegel, may be synthesised quite comfortably, if only you know the trick. The book is a collection of verse translations by Professor Giles, of Cambridge; and the translations are from the Chinese.

It is a faint and curious tone which reaches us, re-echoed so sympathetically by Professor Giles's gracious art, from those far-off, unfamiliar voices of singers long since dead. The strange vibrations are fitful as summer breezes, and fragmentary as the music of birds. We hear them, and we are ravished; we hear them not, and we are ravished still. But, as in the most fluctuating sounds of birds or breezes,

we can perceive a unity in their enchantment, and, listening
to them, we should guess these songs to be the work of a
single mind, pursuing through a hundred subtle modula-
tions the perfection which this earth has never known. We
should err; for through the long centuries of Chinese civilisation, poet after poet has been content to follow closely in
the footsteps of his predecessors, to handle the very themes
which they had handled, to fit the old music to the old imaginations, to gather none but beloved and familiar flowers.
In their sight a thousand years seem indeed to have been a
moment; the song of the eighteenth century takes up the
burden of the eighth; so that, in this peculiar literature,
antiquity itself has become endowed with everlasting youth.
The lyrics in our anthology, so similar, so faultless, so compact of art, remind one of some collection of Greek statues,
where the masters of many generations have multiplied in
their eternal marbles the unaltering loveliness of the ath-
lete. The spirit is the classical spirit—that in which the
beauties of originality and daring and surprise are made an
easy sacrifice upon the altar of perfection; but the classicism
of China affords, in more than one respect, a curious contrast to that of Greece. The most obvious difference, no
doubt, is the difference in definition. Greek art is, in every
sense of the word, the most finished in the world; it is for
ever seeking to express what it has to express completely
and finally; and, when it has accomplished that, it is content.
Thus the most exquisite of the lyrics in the Greek Anthology
are, fundamentally, epigrams—though they are, of course,
epigrams transfigured by passion and the highest splendours
of art. One reads them, and one is filled, in a glorified and
ethereal manner, with the same kind of satisfaction as that
produced by a delicious mouthful of wine. One has had a
draught of hippocrene, a taste of the consummation of
beauty, and then one turns over the page, and pours out

another glass. Different, indeed, is the effect of the Chinese lyric. It is the very converse of the epigram; it aims at producing an impression which, so far from being final, must be merely the prelude to a long series of visions and of feelings. It hints at wonders; and the revelation which at last it gives us is never a complete one—it is clothed in the indefinability of our subtlest thoughts.

> "A fair girl draws the blind aside
> And sadly sits with drooping head;
> I see the burning tear-drops glide,
> But know not why those tears are shed."

"The words stop," say the Chinese, "but the sense goes on." The blind is drawn aside for a moment, and we catch a glimpse of a vision which starts us off on a mysterious voyage down the widening river of imagination. Many of these poems partake of the nature of the *chose vue;* but they are not photographic records of isolated facts, they are delicate pastel drawings of some intimately seized experience. Whatever sights they show us—a girl gathering flowers while a dragon-fly perches on her comb—a lonely poet singing to his lute in the moonlight—pink cheeks among pink peach blossoms; whatever sounds they make us hear—the nightjar crying through the darkness—the flute and the swish of the swing among summer trees—all these things are presented to us charged with beautiful suggestions and that kind of ulterior significance which, in our moments of imaginative fervour, the most ordinary occurrences possess. Here, for instance, is a description of a sleepless night—a description made up of nothing but a short list of simple facts, and yet so full of the very mystery of one of those half-vague, half-vivid watchings that we feel ourselves the friends of the eleventh-century poet who wrote the lines:

"The incense-stick is burnt to ash, the water-clock is stilled,
The midnight breeze blows sharply by and all around is
    chilled.
Yet I am kept from slumber by the beauty of the spring:
Sweet shapes of flowers across the blind the quivering
    moonbeams fling!"

Sometimes the impression is more particular, as in this
charming verse:

"Shadows of pairing swallows cross his book,
    Of poplar catkins, dropping overhead . . .
The weary student from his window-nook
    Looks up to see that spring is long since dead."

And sometimes it is more general:

"The evening sun slants o'er the village street;
    My griefs, alas! in solitude are borne;
Along the road no wayfarers I meet,—
    Naught but the autumn breeze across the corn."

Here is the essence of loneliness distilled into four simple
lines; they were written, in our eighth century, by Kêng
Wei.

Between these evanescent poems and the lyrics of Europe
there is the same kind of relation as that between a scent
and a taste. Our slightest songs are solid flesh-and-blood
things compared with the hinting verses of the Chinese
poets, which yet possess, like odours, for all their intangi-
bility, the strange compelling powers of suggested reminis-
cence and romance. Whatever their subject, they remain
ethereal. There is much drunkenness in them, much praise
of the wine-cup and the "liquid amber" of the "Lan-ling
wine"; but what a contrast between their tipsiest lyrics and
the debauched exaltation of Anacreon, or the boisterous

jovialities of our Western drinking-songs! The Chinese poet is drunk with the drunkenness of a bee that has sipped too much nectar, and goes skimming vaguely among the flowers. His mind floats off at once through a world of delicate and airy dreams:

> "Oh, the joy of youth spent in a gold-fretted hall,
> In the Crape-flower Pavilion, the fairest of all,
> My tresses for head-dress with gay garlands girt,
> Carnations arranged o'er my jacket and shirt!
> Then to wander away in the soft-scented air,
> And return by the side of his Majesty's chair. . . ."

So wrote the drunken Li Po one summer evening in the imperial garden eleven hundred years ago, on a pink silk screen held up before him by two ladies of the court. This great poet died as he had lived—in a trance of exquisite inebriation. Alone in a pleasure-boat after a night of revelry, he passed the time, as he glided down the river, in writing a poem on himself, his shadow, and the moon:

> "The moon sheds her rays on my goblet and me,
> And my shadow betrays we're a party of three . . .
> See the moon—how she glances response to my song;
> See my shadow—it dances so lightly along!
> While sober I feel, you are both my good friends;
> When drunken I reel, our companionship ends.
> But we'll soon have a greeting without a good-bye,
> At our next merry meeting away in the sky."

He had written so far, when he caught sight of the reflection of the moon in the water, and leant over the side of the boat to embrace it. He was drowned; but the poem came safely to shore in the empty boat; it was his epitaph.

Besides their lightness of touch and their magic of suggestion, these lyrics possess another quality which is no less

obvious—a recurrent and pervading melancholy. Even their
praise of wine is apt to be touched with sadness; it is praise
of the power that brings release and forgetfulness, the subtle
power which, in one small goblet, can drown a thousand
cares. Their melancholy, so delicate and yet so profound,
seems almost to be an essential condition of an art which is
nothing if not fragmentary, allusive, and dreamy. The gaiety
which bubbles over into sudden song finds no place in this
anthology. Its poets are the poets of reflection, preoccupied
with patient beauties and the subtle relationships of simple
things. Thus, from one point of view, they are singularly
modern, and perhaps the Western writer whose manner they
suggest most constantly is Verlaine. Like him, they know the
art of being quiet in verse. Like him, they understand how
the fluctuations of temperament may be reflected and accen-
tuated by such outward circumstances as the weather or the
time of year. In particular, like him, they are never tired of
the rain. They have realised the curious intimacy of its presence, and its pleasures no less than its desolations.

"You ask when I'm coming: alas, not just yet . . .
How the rain filled the pools on that night when we met!
Ah, when shall we ever snuff candles again,
And recall the glad hours of that evening of rain?"

But this kind influence which unites can also be a cruel
destiny which separates, adding a final bitterness to solitude:

" 'Tis the festival of Yellow Plums! the rain unceasing pours,
And croaking bull-frogs hoarsely wake the echoes out of
doors.
I sit and wait for him in vain, while midnight hours go by,
And push about the chessmen till the lamp-wick sinks to
die."

That is the melancholy of absence—a strain which is re-echoed again and again among these pages, so that, as we read, we begin to feel that here, in this sad sense of the fragility of human intercourse, lies the deepest inspiration of the book. Poet after poet writes of the burden of solitary love, of the long days of loneliness, of the long nights of recollection—

> "Is it thy will, thy image should keep open
> My heavy eyelids to the weary night?"

—the lines might have been written in Chinese. Sometimes the theme is varied; thoughts of the beloved lend a sweetness even to absence:

> "In absence lovers grieve that nights should be,
> But all the livelong night I think of thee.
> I blow my lamp out to enjoy this rest,
> And shake the gathering dew-drop from my vest. . . ."

Or the poet remembers that, after all, sleep has its consolations. "Drive the young orioles away!" he exclaims—

> "Their chirping breaks my slumber through,
> And keeps me from my dreams of you."

And then, often enough, it is the thought of home that haunts these tender singers:

> "I wake, and moonbeams play around my bed,
> Glittering like hoar-frost to my wondering eyes;
> Up towards the glorious moon I raise my head,
> Then lay me down—and thoughts of home arise."

The exile can never forget the beauties of his birthplace—

> "Sir, from my dear old home you come,
> And all its glories you can name;

Oh, tell me,—has the winter-plum
Yet blossomed o'er the window-frame?"

And, when at length he is returning, he trembles and dares not ask the news.

Our finest lyrics are for the most part the memorials of passion, or the swift and exquisite expressions of "the tender eye-dawn of aurorean love." In these lyrics of China the stress and the fury of desire are things unknown, and, in their topsy-turvy Oriental fashion, they are concerned far more with memories of love than expectations of it. They look back upon love through a long vista of years which have smoothed away the agitations of romance and have brought with them the calm familiarity of happiness, or the quiet desolation of regret. Thus, while one cannot be certain that this love is not sometimes another name for a sublimated friendship, one can be sure enough that these lovers are always friends. Affection, no doubt, is the word that best describes such feelings; and it is through its mastery of the tones and depths of affection that our anthology holds a unique place in the literature of the world. For this cause, too, its pages, for all their strange antiquity, are fresh to us; their humanity keeps them immortal. The poets who wrote them seem to have come to the end of experience, to have passed long ago through the wonders and the tumults of existence, to have arrived at last in some mysterious haven where they could find repose among memories that were for ever living, and among discoveries that were for ever old. Their poetry is the voice of a civilisation which has returned upon itself, which has achieved, after the revolution of ages, simplicity. It has learnt to say some things so finely that we forget, as we listen to it, that these are not the only things that can be said.

"We parted at the gorge and cried 'Good cheer!'
The sun was setting as I closed my door;
Methought, the spring will come again next year,
But he may come no more."

The words carry with them so much significance, they produce so profound a sense of finality, that they seem to contain within themselves a summary of all that is most important in life. There is something almost cruel in such art as
this; one longs, somehow or other, to shake it; and one feels
that, if one did, one would shake it into ice. Yet, as it is, it
is far from frigid; but it is dry—dry as the heaped rose-leaves
in a porcelain vase, rich with the perfume of how many
summers! The scent transports us to old gardens, to old palaces; we wander incuriously among forsaken groves; we half
expect some wonder, and we know too well that nothing
now will ever come again. Reading this book, we might be
in the alleys of Versailles; and our sensations are those of a
writer whose works, perhaps, are too modern to be included
in Professor Giles's anthology:

"Here in the ancient park I wait alone.
The dried-up fountains sleep in beds of stone;
The paths are still; and up the sweeping sward
No lovely lady passes, no gay lord.

"Why do I linger? Ah! perchance I'll find
Some solace for the desolated mind
In yon green grotto, down the towering glade,
Where the bronze Cupid glimmers in the shade."

1908.

III

1913-1918

1. Avons-nous Changé Tout Cela?

THERE is a certain house in Rome which deserves, perhaps, in its way, as much attention as the more famous monuments of that famous city. It is an old building, with a slab let into the wall, on which is engraved the following inscription: "Here Galileo was imprisoned for saying that the earth goes round the sun." That is all, and it is enough. The sentence stands there, summing up in its laconic irony a long chapter of human folly and human cruelty—a chapter which possibly even now has not quite been closed. Passers-by look up, read, and, as the humour takes them, smile or frown over the old story. But I have seen a band of seminarists go down that street—twenty slow-stepping, black-robed, pious youths—and somehow it happened, as they passed the building, that they . . . did not look upward. Perhaps it was as wise; for such as these there is something decidedly inconvenient about that inscription. I wanted to run up to them and cry out, "Tell me, O ye youthful votaries of the Church Infallible, when was it that the earth *did* begin to go round the sun?" Certainly, so far as the Holy Father was concerned, no efforts were spared to put off that awkward moment for as long as possible. For more than a century after Galileo's death no whisper of his heretical doctrines was heard in Italy. The profane pages of Casanova show us that even in Venice, half-way through the enlightened eighteenth century, educated gentlemen regarded the theory of Copernicus not merely as a questionable error, but as a downright absurdity. However, at last, in 1835, the works of the great Florentine were removed from the Index.

Reflecting on these things—on that age-long struggle between light and darkness, on the martyrdoms and the triumph of human reason, on the humbled pride of religious persecution—one is almost persuaded to be an optimist. Where shall men look for the thumb-screws of the Inquisition? *Où sont les neiges d'antan?* Here, surely, is an achievement for history to point to. One horror, it seems, has been actually abolished from the earth. The fires of Smithfield are out for ever, and the *Origin of Species* can be bought for a shilling at every bookstall. One is tempted to rejoice with Professor Bury, who in his pleasant little book on *The History of Freedom of Thought,* lately published for a shilling too, has painted the picture of Toleration Victorious all *couleur de rose.* Freedom of Thought, he tells us, was established once and for all in the nineteenth century, and we may go on our way congratulating ourselves. Well, that is very nice, very nice indeed—if it is true. But, after all, can we be quite so sure that it *is* true? Is it really credible that the human race should have got along so far as that? That such deeply rooted instincts as the love of persecution and the hatred of heterodoxies should have been dissipated into thin air by the charms of philosophers and the common sense of that remarkable period the nineteenth century? Perhaps it is worth while looking a little closer to make sure that some mistake has not been made. Optimists like Professor Bury point triumphantly to the undoubted fact that religious persecution has come to an end; and thus, they argue, it follows that the principles of toleration are established. But does it follow? May not there be other causes for the cessation of religious persecution besides the triumph of tolerance? For instance, if religious questions came to be taken less seriously by people in general, would not that lead to the same result? And is not this precisely what has happened? In the sixteenth century the question of Transubstantiation was indeed a burning one: it seemed well worth while sending other people to the stake about it, or even, if it came to a pinch, going to the stake oneself. But today we somehow take less interest in the subject; most of us don't know what Transubstantiation is; and so, naturally enough, we are perfectly tolerant, whatever views may be held upon it. But it is not the principles of toleration that make us so—it is mere indifference. We really have no right to pride ourselves upon our love of free thought because, when a man informs us that he believes (or disbelieves) in the Procession of the Holy Ghost, we refrain from forthwith tearing out his tongue with red-hot pincers; or because, when Dr. McTaggart writes a book on Religion and Dogma in which his subtle and exquisite arguments leave the Trinity not a leg to stand on, we make no attempt to have him put upon the rack.

If we do want to test the strength of our convictions in the matter of tolerance, we must choose some opinion or some state of mind the very thought of which seriously disturbs us—something which makes the blood rush to our heads in such an access of fury as, no doubt, attacked the men of the sixteenth century whenever they thought of anyone believing (or disbelieving) in the Procession of the Holy Ghost. For instance, when some deplorable working-man blurts out the very propositions that Dr. McTaggart has so elegantly propounded, but blurts them out with no sign of elegance— in fact, with every sign of vulgarity and coarseness, with a rough directness that unutterably shocks our sense of propriety and ribald commentaries that make our middle-class ears tingle and turn red—what do we do then? Well, then, we discover that, after all, there are Blasphemy Laws upon the Statute Book and, to show our open-mindedness, we send the working-man to prison for six months.

It seems clear that the change that has come over us is not so much a change in our attitude towards persecution in general as a change in the class of subjects which raise our zeal to persecute. What is known as "bad taste," for instance, is certainly persecuted at the present day. The milder transgressions of this nature are punished by private society with extreme severity; the more serious are rigorously dealt with by the State. Again, the conventions connected with apparel fill our minds with feelings of awe and sanctity which our ancestors of the Middle Ages reserved for the articles of their Faith. If a man wears unusual clothes, we hate him with the hatred of a Franciscan for a Dominican in the fourteenth century. If he goes so far as not to wear black clothes at dinner, we are quite certain that he is doomed to eternal perdition; while if he actually ventures to wear no clothes when he bathes, we can stand it no longer and punish him by law. But, of course, the region of thought which, in England at any rate, arouses feelings of intolerance in their acutest and most mediaeval forms is that which is concerned with sexual questions. It is in this direction particularly that the expression of opinion is interfered with both by private conventions and public authority to a degree which makes the happy theory that free thought and free speech came to their own once for all in the golden years of the nineteenth century peculiarly absurd. Our machinery for the suppression of inquiry upon this subject is varied and highly successful. We have an official censorship of the stage directed solely to that end; we have police regulations to prevent the dissemination of such literature—either scientific or artistic— as may appear to the authorities to savour of this taint; we have our unofficial, but none the less extremely effective, Library censorship; and we have the elaborate conspiracy of "respectable" society, not only to taboo the discussion of such questions, but actually to deny that they exist. Here, indeed, we seem to have managed to go one better even than the Middle Ages. Innocent III himself did not forbid heresy as a topic of conversation. But that is just what our modern Innocents have succeeded in doing.

The revenges of Time in the matter of what may and what may not be mentioned are curious to contemplate. Three centuries ago Rabelais, wishing to put forward his unorthodox religious and philosophical opinions, only ventured to do so under a veil of licentious stories and loose jests. If his book were published today in England (not as an expensive classic, but as a cheap new work), its philosophy would hardly arouse the faintest interest, but it would certainly be suppressed as an obscene libel. One can imagine a modern Rabelais reversing the process, and palming off his revolutionary views on the relations between the sexes under cover of an exquisitely refined attack on the doctrines of Christianity. If he were clever enough, the book would cause a little flutter in religious circles, which would sufficiently distract the attention of the guardians of our conventions to allow the powder, so to speak, to go down with the jam. On the whole, it seems as if the modern characteristic of intolerance was its concern with ethics rather than with metaphysics. Whether this is a change for the better or not it is difficult to say. Perhaps, if we must try to suppress our neighbour's opinions in one way or another, we had better do so over questions of actual conduct in the actual world than over the subtleties of metaphysical speculation; for at least it shows a more practical spirit. Yet there is something attractive, something elevated and transcendental, about the bloodthirsty, uncompromising ferocity with which past ages have attempted to unravel the profoundest and the strangest mysteries. Who cannot help, in the bottom of his heart, admiring those ancient Fathers who plunged Europe into civil war and anarchy in order to reject a single mystic letter from

the creed? After that our own wrangling over such questions
as, let us say, whether a play in which an illegal operation
is referred to should or should not be publicly performed,
strikes one as a trifle *terre-à-terre*. The transition from the
metaphysical to the ethical species of persecution may be
observed in the case of Shelley. The public of the time was
uncertain whether it hated Shelley because he was an Atheist
or because he deserted his wife. Nowadays no one would
dream of troubling to call the most abandoned scoundrel an
Atheist. Will the time ever come when it will seem no less
futile to accuse a man of immorality? The spirit of intolerance may be hunted out of ethics as it has been from metaphysics; and then where will it take refuge? Obviously, in
aesthetics; and, indeed, after the late fulminations of Sir
William Richmond against Post-Impressionism, nobody
could be very much surprised if a stake were set up tomorrow for Mr. Roger Fry in the courtyard of Burlington
House.

1913.

2. The Old Comedy

THE rises and falls in the stock market of literature deserve more study than they have received. The greater and more obvious fluctuations have, no doubt, come in for a certain amount of attention—the boom in Ovid at the end of the sixteenth century, for instance, or the slump in Pope at the beginning of the nineteenth. But the minor variations are in their way almost as interesting, and they have been little discussed. What were the subtle causes which led, quite lately, to the rise in Donne, after he had lain for two hundred years a drug on the market? He is still rising, and shareholders who picked him up for next to nothing—an old song, one might say—fifteen years ago, are now congratulating themselves. There are many other such curious cases—the inflation, followed by a rapid collapse, in R. L. Stevenson, is one of them. Another case, which shows some sign of proving interesting, is that of the Comedy of the Restoration. I think, from what I know of the state of the market generally, that I might recommend this stock to purchasers who are willing to wait a little. It is true that it cannot be described as a gilt-edged security; in fact, this particular stock will, I fear, always be a trifle risky; and its reputation with the public has been so bad for so long that no immediate recovery is likely. But, of course, investors must not expect everything. Shakespeare is perfectly safe, but there is a glut in Shakespeare—you cannot get rid of him. Wordsworth, too, is a good sound investment, but he only yields 2½ per cent.

It is to those who do not object to an occasional flutter that I recommend the Comedy of the Restoration, which is at present quoted at a very low figure—indeed, it is hardly quoted at all.

Mr. John Palmer's book, *The Comedy of Manners* (Bell & Son), is one of the indications of an approaching change of feeling towards those gay old writers who are perhaps still chiefly familiar to the ordinary reader through the grievous wigging meted out to them by Macaulay more than seventy years since. Mr. Palmer's outspoken and interesting attempt to vindicate the impeached dramatists, and incidentally to administer a wigging to Macaulay in his turn, shows, I think, the way in which the critical wind is beginning to blow. Whether this book does more than this—whether it is likely to add much force to the breeze already blowing—seems less certain, partly because of its very anxiety to do so. Mr. Palmer's attitude is a little too much that of the partisan to be thoroughly convincing. He is too anxious to argue upon every point, and perhaps a shade too clever in his arguments. The truth is that no amount of special pleading, however dexterous, will do away with the plain fact that the dramatists of the Restoration were, in the ordinary sense of the word, indecent. It is simpler to state this at once, for by this means not only will a good deal of misunderstanding be avoided, but the dramatists themselves will be given their true place in the history of literature—in that long line of writers who, from Aristophanes to Anatole France, have taken as the theme for their variations of humour and fancy one of the very few universal elements in the nature of man. Macaulay understood that this was so, and saw that if he were to make good his attack upon Wycherley and Congreve he must bring home to them some more heinous fault than that lack of decency which is common to such a vast number of illustrious writers and which, in fact, forms the very essence of the work of some of the most illustrious of all. He accordingly attempted to show that the Restoration dramatists were indecent in a particularly reprehensible way—that they used, so to speak, a particular brand of indecency which made their works both morally detestable and artistically bad. And this is the real question at issue—not whether Wycherley and his successors were or were not indecent, but whether they were or were not indecent with the particular *nuance* that Macaulay imputes to them. His arguments appear to me unconvincing, and they certainly have not convinced Mr. Palmer; what is more important, both Hazlitt and Lamb take the contrary view. Thackeray and Meredith, however, side with Macaulay. When doctors disagree in this way it seems fair to suppose that the underlying difference is less one of principle than one of personal taste. In such delicate and difficult matters individual variations of temperament and of upbringing—to say nothing of the changes in the moral conventions of different epochs, upon which Mr. Palmer lays so much stress—are really the preponderating elements in any judgment. If your stomach is a queasy one, there are many things in this world which will be distasteful to you—among them the Comedies of the Restoration. But that is no reason why the robust gentleman yonder should not wash down his tripe and onions, if the fancy so takes him, with mulled claret and divert his mind with the rollicking scenes of the *Relapse* or the *Plain Dealer*.

If Mr. Palmer had taken this line of defence, rather than the more unyielding one of theoretic disputation, his book would, I think, have gained from the point of view of literary criticism. As it is, the main interest of it seems to lie in its aesthetic doctrines rather than in its appreciations of actual works of art. This is unfortunate, because a sympathetic exposition of what is truly valuable and interesting in this half-forgotten body of literature would have been of real service to the reading public. For instance, there is one very obvious merit in these old plays which, if it had been properly emphasised by critics, would have done much to help the reader to forget their unsavoury reputation, and look into them for their own sakes. It is one of the curious facts about our literature that such a small proportion of it reflects the dominant characteristics of our race. Its greatest achievements are poetical; and we are a nation of shopkeepers. Nor is our poetry of that sober and solid kind which it might have been expected to be; it is for the most part remarkable either for high fantasy, as in Shelley and the Elizabethan lyrists, or for intellectual subtlety, as in Donne and Browning, or for pure artistry, as in Milton and Keats; the very qualities which the ordinary Englishman notoriously lacks. In prose, no doubt, we have Fielding and Scott; but we have also Sir Thomas Browne, Sterne, Lamb and George Meredith. Either the accepted estimate of our national character is altogether wrong, or the average English reader must be pictured as an unfortunate wanderer among alien and uncongenial spirits. Yet, if he would only turn to the Comedy of the Restoration, he would find there all that his heart most yearns for; and he would find it especially in the pages of that writer whose name is familiar to him at present simply as a byword for disgusting indecorum—Wycherley. Mr. Palmer glances for a moment at Wycherley's relation to Molière, only to dismiss the subject as of small importance. In a sense it is certainly unimportant, for Wycherley's indebtedness to his great French contemporary was purely formal; but, from the point of view of the light which it throws upon Wycherley's art, nothing could be more instructive than a comparison of the two writers. It is not the resemblance, it is the contrast, that is so extraordinarily striking. One only grasps to the full the native vigour of Wycherley's genius when one realises that he has taken

the main situation of Molière's *Misanthrope* and has had
the audacity to use it as the basis for his own *Plain Dealer*.
Surely only an Englishman could have done that—could have
remained so utterly impervious to all those qualities in the
French play which have made it a thing of unique and un-
dying beauty—the refinement of its atmosphere, the concentration of its purpose, the intimate delicacy of its character-
drawing—could have brushed all this aside like so much gos-
samer, and have proceeded to create on its ruins his own
coarse, vivid, solid, rough-and-tumble comedy. He makes his
Alceste a hectoring sea captain, who first comes on to the
stage with a couple of jack tars carrying his luggage. Imagine
an able-bodied seaman in Célimène's drawing-room! Everywhere it is the same: instead of the poignant reserve of
Molière's masterpiece, Wycherley gives us the breadth and
bustle of common life—transports us to Westminster Hall
among lawyers and aldermen, drags in litigious widows and
country bumpkins, or whisks us off to "the Cock in Bow
Street," pouring out upon us all the time his jokes and his
vituperations in alternate bucketfuls. The effect is Hogar-
thian; and the atmosphere is unmistakable—it is that which
can only be produced by the combination of solid British
beef, thick British beer, stout British bodies, and let us
add (for even Mr. Palmer, to his regret, is almost obliged to
confess it) stolid British moralising. The loose jests have
precisely the same quality; and this, no doubt, is why
Wycherley's reputation in this respect is so peculiarly bad;
he was English even there. As a true-born Briton he had
to do his job thoroughly; and so his licentiousness, like English furniture and English cutlery, is the genuine article,
turned out regardless of expense.

It would be pleasant to trace out this English vein in further detail, as it runs through the Comedy of Wycherley's
successors, and especially as it appears in the works of Sir

John Vanbrugh, a writer to whom I think justice has never been done, and who only receives at the hands of Mr. Palmer some rather grudging commendation. What Vanbrugh gives us is not the hot, confused and crowded atmosphere of an English inn, but the jovial, high-hearted gaiety of English outdoor life; in his best scenes one has the sense of being carried off at a gallop after the hounds on a fine morning— so brisk and fresh-humoured are they, so full of the exhilarating spirit of happy improvisation. Vanbrugh was something which has always been more common in England than elsewhere—an amateur of genius. He seems to have been naturally inspired with the capacity for doing with absolute *aplomb* whatever he laid his hand to, from the writing of comedies to the building of castles. Luckily, too, he was able to keep his different talents in separate compartments, for while his architecture (as the famous epitaph declares) was the embodiment of massive grandeur, his drama is all light and air. In the *Relapse* we find him at his best, evoking and combining that jolly company of English humours—Sir Tunbelly Clumsy, Miss Hoyden, Tom Fashion, Parson Bull, and the rest—with the spritely ease of consummate theatrical craftsmanship. "Cod's my life!" exclaims Sir Tunbelly, the portentous country squire, when he finds that he has a lord for a visitor. "I ask your lordship's pardon ten thousand times. [*To a Servant*] Here, run in a-doors quickly. Get a Scotch-coal fire in the great parlour; set all the Turkey-work chairs in their places; get the great brass candlesticks out, and be sure stick the sockets full of laurel, run! My lord, I ask your lordship's pardon. And do you hear, run away to nurse, bid her let Miss Hoyden loose again, and if it was not shifting day, let her put on a clean tucker, quick!" Is not this instinct with an admirable vitality? Then there is Miss Hoyden herself with her "I don't care how often I'm married, not I," and her "I never disobey my father in anything but eating of green gooseberries." And then, among them all, there is the superb figure of Lord Foppington, who, with his delicious absurdities, his preposterous airs and graces, his blood-curdling oaths and lackadaisical pronunciation, yet manages to be incessantly witty, to dominate whatever company he may be in, and, in fact, in some strange way, to be great. Vanbrugh, with true English humour, has resisted the temptation of making an utter fool of his fool, and has shown us, even in that strutting clothes-block, the eminence of the human spirit.

And Congreve? It would be lacking in respect to that great name to let it pass unmentioned in any review, however slight, of the Comedy of the Restoration. But the fag-end of an article is no place for a discussion of so high and potent a genius. I would only say that with him, too, as it seems to me, too little stress has been laid upon the broad, the realistic, the solid qualities of his art. Critics are dazzled by the brilliance of his wit and his marvellous verbal felicity. But, if they looked more closely, they would see, I fancy, that even the ineffable figure of Mistress Millamant is planted firmly upon good English earth.

1913.

3. Bonga-Bonga in Whitehall

A CERTAIN African chief, by name Bonga-Bonga, in the course of a tour through Europe in search of instruction upon the principles of civilisation, paid a visit a few days ago to one of our Government Offices, where he was received by the Minister. Being particularly proud of his knowledge of English, Bonga-Bonga unfortunately refused the services of an interpreter, with the result that his remarks, which would otherwise doubtless have been clothed with grammatical and official propriety, were characterised by a barbaric ingenuousness—one might almost say nudity—which, however natural to the speaker, were in the circumstances decidedly out of place. The conversation was private; but there is reason to believe that the following is an accurate report of what passed.

BONGA-BONGA (*entering the room with many bows and exclamations of "Yah! Yah!"—his native formula for expressing respectful admiration*): Honourable Sir, me very glad to come to England. England very fine place. Black coats, tall hats, much wisdom. Yah! Yah!

THE MINISTER: I am delighted to welcome your Highness to the country which, as you know, has ever led the way in the great movement of humanity towards those two chief blessings of civilisation—if I may so express myself—Liberty and Justice.

B.-B.: Yah!

M.: As a member of a Liberal Government, I may claim,

162

perhaps, to represent in a special degree that noble principle of freedom—Freedom of Thought, Freedom of Speech, Freedom of the Press—which it has always been the peculiar glory of my party to uphold. I am also here as the representative, the not unworthy representative I trust, of English justice.

B.-B.: Me know what justice is. Justice very fine thing. Bad man, whacky-whacky; very bad man, screwy-necky. Yah!

M.: I fear that your Highness's ideas of British justice are —er—hardly up to date. In England we have reached a higher conception of the duties of the State towards the criminal. In England we have done away with barbarous punishments. If a man breaks the law we shave his head, dress him in sack-cloth marked with arrows, feed him on gruel, and place him by himself in a whitewashed cell for five, ten, fifteen, or twenty years, as the case may require.

B.-B.: Ah! how wise are the English! In England no whacky-whacky!

M.: Yes, it has for long been one of the principles of my party that corporal punishment was a mistaken method of treating crime. We have not yet succeeded, however, in abolishing it altogether. Indeed, lately I was obliged—with profound regret, I may say—to pass a Bill authorising a decided increase in the infliction of corporal punishment.

B.-B.: That is great wisdom. Me understand. In England never no whacky-whacky at all—except when there is whacky-whacky. Yah! Yah! And screwy-necky?

M.: We reserve capital punishment for murder. But when a man is convicted of murder on insufficient evidence, we pardon him, and send him to prison for life.

B.-B.: Oh, wisdom! Not sure, locky-uppy for life. But naughty ladies—how you treat them?

M.: I assure your Highness they have nothing to complain of—nothing to complain of at all. If they insist upon starving themselves when they are in prison, it naturally becomes necessary to administer food to them by means of an india-rubber tube inserted through the nose. What else would you have? Are these misguided women to be allowed to defy the law? Are they to be released because they are obstinate? What is your Highness's opinion?

B.-B.: Locky-uppy very good for naughty ladies. Yah! Yah!

M.: Precisely. The majesty of the Law must be maintained at all hazards.

B.-B.: Ah, the majesty of the Law, very fine, very great! But what you do if they never take no food at all? You put tube in nose for ever and ever, amen?

M.: Ah, well, if they persist, it becomes eventually necessary to—er—release them. But the majesty of the Law has been maintained.

B.-B.: Oh, wisdom! Oh, great wisdom! Yah!

M.: I am very glad indeed to have your Highness's support in this matter. But let me pass away from this most unpleasant subject to another, upon which I think I may also count upon your Highness's agreement—the necessity for putting some check upon the publication of pernicious literature. I am doing what I can now, and I intend shortly to introduce a Bill upon the subject. I am sure you will be with me there.

B.-B.: Me understand. Books bad. All books very bad. Burn all books. Oh, that is a wise thing!

M.: Well—er—well, I should not go quite so far as that. Your Highness's views are, I fear, a little reactionary. We in England—the Liberal Party in particular—have long recognised the great principle of the Liberty of the Press. That is most important. But we must distinguish: liberty is not licence. It is one thing to allow the publication of what is good and wholesome, and quite another to stand by while matter, which every respectable person knows to be immoral or unsettling, issues from the Press. For instance, some time ago, a disgusting book, called *Droll Stories*—translated from some French writer—Balzac, I think, was the name—was actually being sold for a shilling. Very properly, the police interfered, and the book was suppressed. It is all very well for people of means and position to read a book like that in the original; but really, to scatter it broadcast among the poor—I ask you, could anything be more deplorable? Then there was another case: a very expensive book, dealing in a distressingly outspoken and scientific manner with certain painful physiological questions, which was also, I am glad to say, suppressed. Imagine a book like that in the hands of a child! Imagine it!

B.-B.: English child very well brought up. English home very goody-goody. Good dull books on table. Bad funny yellow books in cupboard. Oh, great wisdom! But one thing me not understand. One big black book always in English home, on table. Me look in black book, and me find very queer things—very queer things indeed. Me think, if English child looks in big black book, what happen then?

M.: Your Highness must really be careful. Your suggestion appears to me to be most improper, not to say immoral. You are holding up to contempt the religious beliefs of others, and making use of language which is calculated to wound, and indeed can hardly have been uttered without the intention of wounding, the feelings of others. Are you aware that a short time ago an individual was tried, convicted, and sentenced to four months' imprisonment in the third division for that very offence, and that he is undergoing his well-merited punishment at this moment? Freedom of speech and religious toleration are, as I have said, among the great principles of the Liberal Party; but we cannot allow feelings to be wounded. And I regret to say that your Highness has wounded mine.

B.-B. (*prostrating himself*): Oh, pardon, honourable sir, pardon! Me not understand. Me think big black book very holy—very fine indeed. Me not want locky-uppy. Yah! Yah!

M.: Pray be seated, your Highness. I see that your contempt was unintentional, and I am therefore willing to pass it over. Such, your Highness, is the spirit which animates English Justice and English Liberty.

B.-B.: Oh, wisdom! If make angry, locky-uppy. English missionary, he make Bonga-Bonga angry. He says great God Kolly Wobbul very bad Devil. Me locky-uppy English missionary. Yah!

M.: I fear your Highness has misunderstood the nature of our Blasphemy Laws, which are designed, of course, only to protect *right* feelings—the feelings of those who understand that certain matters should not be discussed, and who believe in the Christian religion as by Law established. Your Highness surely would not have us give equal protection to everybody's feelings. That would be absurd. We might as well have no Blasphemy Laws at all. It is, of course, as I have said, a matter of fundamental principle with the Liberal Party to protect and encourage Freedom of Speech. But we recognise, at the same time, that it is our duty to see that freedom is used in the right way. We must protect the true interests of the working classes. But perhaps your Highness will excuse me if I bring this interesting interview to a close. I am due in a few moments at a complimentary luncheon to M. Anatole France.

B.-B.: Honourable sir, me remember all you say. Me forget never-never. Oh, wisdom! England all over free justice, all bang through. Very fine indeed! English bad man, locky-uppy in nice white cell. Never whacky-whacky, oh no, never at all—except when there is whacky-whacky. Oh, wisdom!

English naughty lady, locky-uppy. If still naughty, tube in nose. If still naughty after that, let go. Oh, wisdom! English books never stopped, oh no, never at all—except when stopped. Oh, wisdom! In England, may always make angry, except over big black book, and then locky-uppy. Oh, wisdom! Great thing, liberty all over England, right bang through, everywhere, always, oh yes—except when not. Oh, wisdom! wisdom! wisdom! Yah! Yah!

With these words Bonga-Bonga bowed himself out of the room; but a moment later he reappeared, and with some embarrassment addressed the Minister: "Me very stupid. Me forget one word. Me remember all but name of great party. Me not want forget that. Please tell that word."

"Certainly, your Highness," replied the Minister, with great affability, "*Liberal*—that is the word—*Liberal*."

1914.

4. A Russian Humorist

LOOK well at the face of Dostoïevsky, half a Russian peas-ant's face, half a criminal physiognomy, flat nose, small penetrating eyes beneath lids that quiver with a nervous affection; look at the forehead, lofty, thoroughly well formed; the expressive mouth, eloquent of numberless torments, of abysmal melancholy, of infinite compassion and envy!—An epileptic genius, whose exterior speaks of the mild milk of human kindness, with which his temperament was flooded, and of the depth of an almost maniacal acuteness which mounted to his brain." These words of Dr. Brandes, which occur in a letter to Nietzsche, written in 1888, express with force and precision the view of Dostoïevsky, both as a man and as a writer, which probably every reader of the extraor-dinary works now being translated by Mrs. Garnett [1] would naturally be inclined to take. To the English reader, no less than to the Norwegian critic, what must first be apparent in those works is the strange and poignant mixture which they contain of "an almost maniacal acuteness" with "the mild milk of human kindness"—of the terrible, febrile agitations reflected in those penetrating eyes and their quivering lids, with the serene nobility and "infinite compassion" which left their traces in the expressive mouth and the lofty brow. These conflicting and mingling qualities are, in fact, so ob-vious wherever Dostoïevsky's genius reveals itself in its truly

[1] *The Novels of Fyodor Dostoevsky.* Translated from the Russian by Con-stance Garnett. Vol. II, *The Idiot.* Vol. III, *The Possessed.* London: William Heinemann.

characteristic form, that there is some danger of yet another, and a no less important, element in this complex character escaping the notice which it deserves—the element of humour. That Dostoievsky was a humorist—and a humorist of a remarkable and original type—has not been sufficiently emphasised by critics. Perhaps this may be partly explained by the fact that his most famous and widely read work, *Crime and Punishment,* happens to contain less of this particular quality than any of his other books. But to conclude from a perusal of *Crime and Punishment* that Dostoievsky had no humour would be as fallacious as to suppose that Shakespeare had none because he had written *Othello.* Indeed, just as a perspicacious reader, unacquainted with the rest of Shakespeare, might infer from the massive breadth and the penetrating vision of *Othello* the possibility of the early comedies, so the amazing psychological sympathy of *Crime and Punishment* almost suggests a similar phase of work in Dostoievsky. And, as a matter of fact, such work exists. The group of novels (not at present translated into English) of which *Uncle's Dream, The Eternal Husband,* and *Another's* are typical examples show Dostoievsky in a mood of wild gaiety, sometimes plunging into sheer farce, but more often reminiscent of the Molière of *Le Médecin Malgré Lui* and *Georges Dandin,* in the elaborate concentration of his absurdities, the brilliance of his satire, and his odd combination of buffoonery and common sense. This mood of pure comedy disappears in *The Double*—a singular and highly interesting work, containing a study of the growth of madness in a feeble intellect overcome by extreme self-consciousness—where the ridicule is piled up till it seems to topple over upon itself, and the furious laughter ends in a gnashing of teeth. Then we have *Crime and Punishment,* in which the humorous faculty is almost entirely suspended; and at last, in *The Idiot* and *The Possessed* (the two latest volumes of Mrs. Garnett's complete translation), Dostoievsky's humour appears in its final and most characteristic form, in which it dominates and inspires all his other qualities—his almost fiendish insight into the human heart, his delight in the extraordinary and the unexpected, his passionate love of what is noble in man, his immense creative force—and endows them with a new and wonderful significance.

The truth is that it is precisely in such cases as Dostoievsky's that the presence or the absence of humour is of the highest importance. With some writers it hardly occurs to us to consider whether they are humorous or not. It makes very little difference to us, for instance, that Tolstoy should scarcely show any signs of humour at all. And the reason for this is clear. Tolstoy is one of those writers who present their imaginary world to us with such calmness, with such exactness, with such an appearance at least of judicial impartiality, that we are immediately satisfied and ask for nothing more. But the imaginary world of a Dostoievsky strikes our senses in a very different fashion; it comes to us amid terror and exorbitance—not in the clear light of day, but in the ambiguous glare of tossing torches and meteors streaming through the heavens. Now writing of that kind may have many advantages: it may arouse the curiosity, the excitement, and the enthusiasm of the reader to a high degree; but there is one great risk that it runs—the risk of unreality. The beckoning lights may turn out to be will-o'-the-wisps, the mysterious landscape nothing but pasteboard scenery. And against that risk the only really satisfactory safeguard is a sense of humour. An author with a sense of humour puts, as it were, a stiff, stout walking-stick into the hand of his reader, and bids him lean on that, and, when he is in doubt of the way he is going, feel with it the solid earth under his feet. Balzac is a case in point. He had wit, but no humour; his readers are without that invaluable walking-stick, and the consequence is that they are constantly being tripped up by pieces of stage carpentry, or plunging up to their necks in the bogs of melodrama. If Dostoievsky had been simply what Dr. Brandes describes and nothing more—a genius of excessive acuteness and excessive sensibility—we should have been in the same predicament in his pages. But it was not so. He had humour; and so it happens that, by virtue of that magic power, his wildest fancies have something real and human in them, and his moments of greatest intensity are not melodramatic but tragic. In *The Idiot*, for instance, the unchecked passions of Rogozhin and Nastasya, the morbid agonies of such a figure as Ippolit, the unearthly and ecstatic purity of the Prince—all these things are controlled and balanced by the sheer fun of a hundred incidents, by the ludicrousness of Lebedyev and General Ivolgin, and, above all, by the masterly creation of Madame Epanchin—the sharp-witted, impulsive, irascible old lady, who storms and snorts and domineers through the book with all the vigour of a substantial and familiar reality. Madame Epanchin had many worries, and her daughters were the cause of nearly all of them. Adelaïda, it is true, was engaged to be married, but Alexandra!—

"Sometimes she thought the girl was 'utterly hopeless.' 'She is twenty-five, so she will be an old maid; and with her looks!' Lizaveta Prokofievna positively shed tears at night thinking of her, while Alexandra herself lay sleeping tranquilly. 'What is one to make of her? Is she a Nihilist or simply a fool?' That she was not a fool even Lizaveta Prokofievna had no doubt; she had the greatest respect for Alexandra's judgment and was fond of asking her advice. But that she was a *poule mouillée* she did not doubt for a moment; 'so calm there's no making her out. Though it's true *poules mouillées* are not calm—foo, I am quite muddled over them.'"

The irritatingly phlegmatic Alexandra had a habit which particularly annoyed her mother—she *would* dream the most inept dreams. One day the climax was reached when it transpired that Alexandra had dreamt of nine hens the night before—simply nine hens, and that was all. Madame Epanchin was furious. Such pleasant visions of domestic life are certainly not what one would expect from the inspired epileptic of Dr. Brandes's description; but they are in truth typical of Dostoievsky's art. The thought of those nine hens in Alexandra's dream gives one, somehow, a sense of security amid the storm and darkness of that strange history; one feels that one has one's walking-stick.

But Dostoievsky's humour serves another purpose besides that of being a make-weight to those intense and extreme qualities in his composition which would otherwise have carried him into mere extravagance; it is also the key to his sympathetic treatment of character. There are many ways of laughing at one's fellow-creatures. One may do so with the savage fury of Swift, or the barbed mockery of Voltaire, or the caressing mischief of Jane Austen; but Dostoievsky, in his latest works, uses another sort of laughter—the laughter of lovingkindness. Such laughter is very rare in literature; Shakespeare has some for Falstaff (though there it is complicated by feelings of genuine contempt); it inspired Sterne when he created Uncle Toby, and, of course, there is the classic instance of Don Quixote. Dostoievsky's mastery of this strange power of ridicule, which, instead of debasing, actually ennobles and endears the object upon which it falls, is probably the most remarkable of all his characteristics. *The Idiot* is full of it. It falls in gay cataracts over Madame Epanchin; it lends a humanity to the absurd old General, fallen on evil times, whose romancings drift into imbecility, and who remembers at last quite distinctly that he was one of Napoleon's pages in 1814. But the most elaborate use of it occurs in *The Possessed,* where the figure of Stepan Trofimovitch, the old idealistic Liberal who comes to his ruin among the hideous realities of modern Nihilism, is presented to us through an iridescent veil of shimmering laughter and tears. The final passage describing his death inevitably recalls the famous pages of Cervantes; and, while it would be rash to say that the Russian writer surpasses his Spanish predecessor in native force, it cannot be doubted that he is the superior in subtlety. Stepan Trofimovitch is a nineteenth-century Quixote—a complex creature of modern civilisation, in whom the noblest aspirations are intertwined with the pettiest personal vanities, in whom cowardice and heroism, folly and wisdom, are inextricably mixed. So consummate is the portraiture that one seems to see the whole nature of the man spread out before one like a piece of shot silk, shifting every moment from silliness to saintliness, from meanness to dignity, from egoism to abnegation. This marvellous synthesis is the work of humour, but of humour which has almost transcended itself—a smile felt so profoundly that it is only shown in the eyes.

1914.

5. A Victorian Critic

TO the cold and youthful observer there is a strange fascination about the Age of Victoria. It has the odd attractiveness of something which is at once very near and very far off; it is like one of those queer fishes that one sees behind glass at an aquarium, before whose grotesque proportions and sombre menacing agilities one hardly knows whether to laugh or to shudder; when once it has caught one's eye, one cannot tear oneself away. Probably its reputation will always be worse than it deserves. Reputations, in the case of ages no less than of individuals, depend, in the long run, upon the judgments of artists; and artists will never be fair to the Victorian Age. To them its incoherence, its pretentiousness, and its incurable lack of detachment will always outweigh its genuine qualities of solidity and force. They will laugh and they will shudder, and the world will follow suit. The Age of Victoria was, somehow or other, unaesthetic to its marrow-bones; and so we may be sure it will never loom through history with the glamour that hangs about the Age of Pericles or the brilliance that sparkles round the eighteenth century. But if men of science and men of action were not inarticulate, we should hear a different story.

The case of Matthew Arnold is a case in point. And who has not heard of Matthew Arnold? Certainly, out of every hundred who have, you would not find more than forty who could tell you anything of his contemporary, Lyell, for instance, who revolutionised geology, or more than twenty who would attach any meaning whatever to the name of another of his contemporaries, Dalhousie, who laid the foundations of modern India. Yet, compared to the work of such men as these, how feeble, how insignificant was Matthew Arnold's achievement! But he was a literary man; he wrote poetry, and he wrote essays discussing other poets and dabbling in general reflections. And so his fame has gone out to the ends of the earth, and now the Clarendon Press have done him the honour of bringing out a cheap collection of his essays,[1] so that even the working-man may read him and find out the heights that could be reached, in the way of criticism, during the golden years of the 'sixties. Surely, before it is too late, a club should be started—an Old Victorian Club—the business of whose members would be to protect the reputation of their Age and give it a fair chance with the public. Perhaps such a club exists already—in some quiet corner of Pimlico; but if so, it has sadly neglected one of its most pressing duties —the hushing-up of Matthew Arnold.

For here in this collection of essays there lies revealed what was really the essential and fatal weakness of the Victorian Age—its incapability of criticism. If we look at its criticism of literature alone, was there ever a time when the critic's functions were more grievously and shamelessly mishandled? When Dryden or Johnson wrote of literature, they wrote of it as an art; but the Victorian critic had a different notion of his business. To him literature was always an excuse for talking about something else. From Macaulay, who used it as a convenient peg for historical and moral disquisitions, to Leslie Stephen, who frankly despised the whole business, this singular tradition holds good. In what other age would it have been possible for a literary critic to begin an essay on Donne, as Leslie Stephen once did, with the cool observa-

[1] *Essays by Matthew Arnold.* Oxford University Press.

tion that, as he was not interested in Donne's poetry, he would merely discuss his biography? An historian might as well preface an account of Columbus with the remark that, as he was not interested in Columbus's geographical discoveries, he would say nothing about that part of his career. It was their ineradicable Victorian instinct for action and utility which drove these unfortunate writers into so strangely self-contradictory a position. "No one in his senses," they always seem to be saying, "would discuss anything so impalpable and frivolous as a work of art; and yet it is our painful duty to do so; therefore we shall tell you all we can about the moral lessons we can draw from it, and the period at which it was produced, and the curious adventures of the man who produced it; and so, as you must admit, we shall have done our duty like the Englishmen that we are."

This was not quite Matthew Arnold's way; he went about his business with more subtlety. He was a man, so he keeps assuring us, of a refined and even fastidious taste; it was his mission to correct and enlighten the barbarism of his age; he introduced the term "philistine" into England, and laughed at Lord Macaulay. Yet it is curious to observe the flagrant ineptitudes of judgment committed by a writer of his pretensions directly he leaves the broad flat road of traditional appreciation. On that road he is safe enough. He has an unbounded admiration for Shakespeare, Dante, and Sophocles; he considers Virgil a very fine writer, though marred by melancholy; and he has no doubt that Milton was a master of the grand style. But when he begins to wander on to footpaths of his own, how extraordinary are his discoveries! He tells us that Molière was one of the five or six supreme *poets* of the world; that Shelley will be remembered for his essays and letters rather than for his poetry; that Byron was a greater poet than Coleridge or Shelley or Keats; that the French alexandrine is an inefficient poetical instrument; that Heine was an "incomparably more important figure" in European poetry than Victor Hugo. As to his taste, a remarkable instance of it occurs in his Lectures on translating Homer. Describing the Trojan encampments by night on the plains of Troy, with their blazing watch-fires as numerous as the stars, Homer concludes with one of those astonishingly simple touches which, for some inexplicable reason, seem to evoke an immediate vision of thrilling and magical romance: "A thousand fires were kindled in the plain; and by each one there sat fifty men in the light of the blazing fire. And the horses, munching white barley and rye, and standing by the chariots, waited for the bright-throned Morning." Such was Homer's conception—it was the horses who were waiting for the morning. But Matthew Arnold will not have it so. "I want to show you," he says, "that it is possible in a plain passage of this sort to keep Homer's simplicity without being heavy and dull"; and accordingly he renders the passage thus:

"By their chariots stood the steeds, and champ'd the white barley,
While their masters sate by the fire and waited for Morning."

"I prefer," he explains, "to attribute this expectation of Morning to the master and not to the horse." *I prefer!* Surely, if ever the word "philistine" were applicable, this is the occasion for it. And, indeed, Arnold himself seems to have felt a twinge of conscience. "Very likely," he adds, with a charming ingenuousness, "in this particular, as in any other particular, I may be wrong."

One of the surest signs of a man's taste being shaky is his trying to prop it up by artificial supports. Matthew Arnold was always doing this. He had a craving for Academies. He thought that if we could only have a Literary Academy in

England we should all be able to tell what was good and what was bad without any difficulty; for, of course, the Academy would tell us. He had a profound reverence for the French Academy—a body which has consistently ignored every manifestation of original genius; and no doubt the annual exhibitions of the Royal Academy gave him exquisite satisfaction. He even had dreams of a vast international Academy; carried away by the vision, he seemed almost to imagine that it was already in existence. "To be recognised by the verdict of such a confederation," he exclaims, "is indeed glory; a glory which it would be difficult to rate too highly. For what could be more beneficent, more salutary? The world is forwarded by having its attention fixed on the best things; and here is a tribunal, free from all suspicion of national and provincial partiality, putting a stamp on the best things, and recommending them for general honour and acceptance." But, failing this, failing the impartial tribunal which shall put "a stamp on the best things," one can fall back upon other devices. If one is in doubt as to the merit of a writer, the best course one can take is to make him, so to speak, run the gauntlet of "the great masters." We must "lodge well in our minds" lines and expressions of the great masters—"short passages, even single lines will serve our turn quite sufficiently"—and these we shall find "an infallible touchstone" for testing the value of all other poetry. The plan is delightfully simple; there is, indeed, only one small difficulty about it: it cannot come into operation until we have decided the very question which it is intended to solve—namely, who "the great masters" are.

"The world is forwarded by having its attention fixed on the best things." Yes; *the world is forwarded*. Here, plainly enough, is the tip of the Victorian ear peeping forth from under the hide of the aesthetic lion; the phrase might have come straight from Mr. Roebuck or the *Daily Tele-*

graph—those perpetual targets for Matthew Arnold's raillery. But when he proceeds to suggest yet another test for literature, when he asserts that, in order to decide upon the value of any piece of writing, what we must do is to ask ourselves whether or not it is a "Criticism of Life"—then, indeed, all concealment is over; the whole head of the animal is out. There is something pathetic about the eager persistence with which Matthew Arnold enunciates this doctrine. How pleased with himself he must have been when he thought of it! How beautifully it fitted in with all his needs! How wonderfully it smoothed away all the difficulties of his situation! For, of course, he was nothing if not a critic, a man whose nature it was to look at literature from the detached and disinterested standpoint of a refined—a fastidious—aesthetic appreciation; and yet . . . and yet . . . well, after all (but please don't say so), how *could* anyone, at this time of day, in the 'sixties, be expected to take literature seriously, on its own merits, as if it were a thing to be talked about for its own sake? The contradiction was obvious, and it was reconciled by that ingenious godsend, the theory of the Criticism of Life. By means of that theory it became possible to serve God and Mammon at the same time. Life, as everyone knew, was the one serious affair in the world—active, useful life; but then literature, it turned out—or rather, all literature that was worth anything—was a criticism of life; and so, after all, Matthew Arnold was justified in writing about it, and the public were justified in reading what Matthew Arnold wrote, for they were not merely reading about literature—who would do that?—they were reading about the Criticism of Life. And it is singular to see the shifts to which Matthew Arnold was put in order to carry out this theory consistently. He had somehow to bring all "the great masters" into line with it. Shakespeare was easy enough, for he will fit into any theory; and Sophocles, of course, saw life steadily and saw it whole; but Dante and Milton—a queer kind of criticism of life they give us, surely! But they were so elevated, so extremely elevated, that they would pass; as for Sappho and Catullus, it was convenient not to mention them. Of course Matthew Arnold was careful to give no very exact explanation of his famous phrase, and one is always being puzzled by his use of it. Pope, one would have thought, with those palpitating psychological portraits of his, in which are concentrated the experience and passion of one of the sharpest and most sensitive observers who ever lived—Pope might well be considered a critic of life; but for some reason or other Pope would not do. Byron, on the other hand—not the Byron of *Don Juan,* but the Byron of *Childe Harold* and *Manfred*—did very well indeed. But we must remember that Byron was still fashionable in the 'sixties, and that Pope was not.

Certainly it is a curious and instructive case, that of Matthew Arnold: all the more so since no one could suppose that he was a stupid man. On the contrary, his intelligence was above the average, and he could write lucidly, and he got up his subjects with considerable care. Unfortunately, he mistook his vocation. He might, no doubt, if he had chosen, have done some excellent and lasting work upon the movements of glaciers or the fertilisation of plants, or have been quite a satisfactory collector in an up-country district in India. But no; he *would* be a critic.

1914.

6. Mr. Hardy's New Poems

MR. HARDY's new volume of poems [1] is a very interesting, and in some ways a baffling book, which may be recommended particularly to aesthetic theorists and to those dogmatic persons who, ever since the days of Confucius, have laid down definitions upon the function and nature of poetry. The dictum of Confucius is less well known than it ought to be. "Read poetry, oh, my children!" he said, "for it will teach you the divine truths of filial affection, patriotism, and natural history." Here the Chinese sage expressed, with the engaging frankness of his nation, a view of poetry implicitly held by that long succession of earnest critics for whom the real justification of any work of art lies in the edifying nature of the lessons which it instils. Such generalisations upon poetry would be more satisfactory if it were not for the poets. One can never make sure of that inconvenient and unreliable race. The remark of Confucius, for instance, which, one feels, must have been written with a prophetic eye upon the works of Wordsworth, seems absurdly inapplicable to the works of Keats. Then there is Milton's famous "simple, sensuous, and passionate" test—a test which serves admirably for Keats, but which seems in an odd way to exclude the complicated style, the severe temper, and the remote imaginations of Milton himself. Yet another school insists upon the necessity of a certain technical accomplish-

[1] *Satires of Circumstance, Lyrics and Reveries, with Miscellaneous Pieces.* By Thomas Hardy. Macmillan.

ment; beauty is for them, as it was—in a somewhat different connection—for Herbert Spencer, a *"sine quâ non."* Harmony of sound, mastery of rhythm, the exact and exquisite employment of words—in these things, they declare, lies the very soul of poetry, and without them the noblest thoughts and the finest feelings will never rise above the level of tolerable verse. This is the theory which Mr. Hardy's volume seems especially designed to disprove. It is full of poetry; and yet it is also full of ugly and cumbrous expressions, clumsy metres, and flat, prosaic turns of speech. To take a few random examples, in the second of the following lines cacophony is incarnate:

> "Dear ghost, in the past did you ever find
> Me one whom consequence influenced much?"

A curious mixture of the contorted and the jog-trot appears in such a line as:

> "And adumbrates too therewith our unexpected troublous
> case";

while a line like:

> "And the daytime talk of the Roman investigations."

trails along in the manner of an undistinguished phrase in prose. Even Mr. Hardy's grammar is not impeccable. He speaks of one,

> "whom, anon,
> My great deeds done,
> Will be mine alway."

And his vocabulary, though in general it is rich and apt, has occasional significant lapses, as, for instance, in the elegy on Swinburne, where, in the middle of a passage deliberately tuned to a pitch of lyrical resonance not to be found elsewhere in the volume, there occurs the horrid hybrid "naïvely"—a neologism exactly calculated, one would suppose, to make the classic author of *Atalanta* turn in his grave.

It is important to observe such characteristics, because, in Mr. Hardy's case, they are not merely superficial and occasional blemishes; they are in reality an essential ingredient in the very essence of his work. The originality of his poetry lies in the fact that it bears everywhere upon it the impress of a master of prose fiction. Just as the great seventeenth-century writers of prose, such as Sir Thomas Browne and Jeremy Taylor, managed to fill their sentences with the splendour and passion of poetry, while still preserving the texture of an essentially prose style, so Mr. Hardy, by a contrary process, has brought the realism and sobriety of prose into the service of his poetry. The result is a product of a kind very difficult to parallel in our literature. Browning, no doubt, in his intimate and reflective moods—in *By the Fireside* or *Any Wife to Any Husband*—sometimes comes near it; but the full-blooded and romantic optimism of Browning's temper offers a singular contrast to the repressed melancholy of Mr. Hardy's. Browning was too adventurous to be content for long with the plain facts of ordinary existence; he was far more at home with the curiosities and the excitements of life; but what gives Mr. Hardy's poems their unique flavour is precisely their utter lack of romanticism, their common, undecorated presentments of things. They are, in fact, modern as no other poems are. The author of *Jude the Obscure* speaks in them, but with the concentration, the intensity, the subtle disturbing force of poetry. And he speaks; he does not sing. Or rather, he talks—in the quiet voice of a modern man or woman, who finds it difficult, as modern men and women do, to put into words exactly what is in the mind. He is incorrect; but then how unreal and artificial a thing is correctness! He fumbles; but it is that very fumbling that brings him so near to ourselves. In that "me one whom consequence influenced much," does not one seem to catch the very accent of hesitating and half-ironical affection? And in the drab rhythm of that "daytime talk of the Roman investigations," does not all the dreariness of long hours of boredom lie compressed? And who does not feel the perplexity, the discomfort, and the dim agitation in that clumsy collection of vocables—"And adumbrates too therewith our unexpected troublous case"? What a relief such uncertainties and inexpressivenesses are after the delicate exactitudes of our more polished poets! And how mysterious and potent are the forces of inspiration and sincerity! All the taste, all the scholarship, all the art of the Poet Laureate seem only to end in something that is admirable, perhaps, something that is wonderful, but something that is irremediably remote and cold; while the flat, undistinguished poetry of Mr. Hardy has found out the secret of touching our marrow-bones.

It is not only in its style and feeling that this poetry reveals the novelist; it is also in its subject-matter. Many of the poems—and in particular the remarkable group of "fifteen glimpses" which gives its title to the volume—consist of compressed dramatic narratives, of central episodes of passion and circumstance, depicted with extraordinary vividness. A flashlight is turned for a moment upon some scene or upon some character, and in that moment the tragedies of whole lives and the long fatalities of human relationships seem to stand revealed:

" 'My stick!' he says, and turns in the lane
To the house just left, whence a vixen voice
Comes out with the firelight through the pane,
And he sees within that the girl of his choice
Stands rating her mother with eyes aglare
For something said while he was there.

" 'At last I behold her soul undraped!'
Thinks the man who had loved her more than himself. . . ."

It is easy to imagine the scene as the turning-point in a realistic psychological novel; and, indeed, a novelist in want of
plots or incidents might well be tempted to appropriate some
of the marvellously pregnant suggestions with which this
book is crowded. Among these sketches the longest and most
elaborate is the *Conversation at Dawn,* which contains in its
few pages the matter of an entire novel—a remorseless and
terrible novel of modern life. Perhaps the most gruesome is
At the Draper's, in which a dying man tells his wife how he
saw her in a shop, unperceived:

"You were viewing some lovely things. *'Soon required
For a widow, of latest fashion';*
And I knew 'twould upset you to meet the man
Who had to be cold and ashen

"And screwed in a box before they could dress you
'In the last new note of mourning,'
As they defined it. So, not to distress you,
I left you to your adorning."

As these extracts indicate, the prevailing mood in this
volume—as in Mr. Hardy's later novels—is not a cheerful
one. And, in the more reflective and personal pieces, the
melancholy is if anything yet more intense. It is the melancholy of regretful recollection, of bitter speculation, of immortal longings unsatisfied; it is the melancholy of one who
has suffered, in Gibbon's poignant phrase, "the abridgment
of hope." Mortality, and the cruelties of time, and the ironic
irrevocability of things—these are the themes upon which
Mr. Hardy has chosen to weave his grave and moving variations. If there is joy in these pages, it is joy that is long since

dead; and if there are smiles, they are sardonical. The sentimentalist will find very little comfort among them. Sometimes, perhaps, his hopes will rise a little—for the sentimentalist is a hopeful creature; but they will soon be dashed. "Who is digging on my grave?" asks the dead woman, who has been forgotten by her lover and her kinsfolk and even her enemy; since it is none of these, who can it be?

> "O it is I, my mistress dear,
> Your little dog, who still lives near,
> And much I hope my movements here
> Have not disturbed your rest."

"Ah, yes!" murmurs the ghost:

> "*You* dig upon my grave . . .
> Why flashed it not on me
> That one true heart was left behind?
> What feeling do we ever find
> To equal among human kind
> A dog's fidelity?"

And so, with this comforting conclusion, the poem might have ended. But that is not Mr. Hardy's way. "Mistress," comes the reply:

> "I dug upon your grave
> To bury a bone, in case
> I should be hungry near this spot
> When passing on my daily trot,
> I am sorry, but I quite forgot
> It was your resting-place."

That is all; the desolation is complete. And the gloom is not even relieved by a little elegance of diction.

1914.

7. French Poets Through Boston Eyes

THE interactions between the civilisations of France and America are curious, and would make the subject of an interesting book. Mr. Henry James touched upon the matter with his peculiar delicacy and pungency in more than one of his stories; but the theme might be more scientifically elaborated from the historical and social points of view, with instructive results. The literary aspect of it is well illustrated by such a book as Miss Lowell's,[1] which consists of a collection of lectures on some modern French poets, delivered before an audience in Boston. Miss Lowell's lectures perhaps on the whole throw more light on Boston than on the French poets. The judicious reader will, it is true, find in them much information as to the poets' biographies, copious quotations from their works, in the original (but there is a useful crib at the end of the volume), and reproductions of their photographs: but the still more judicious reader will not stop there. It is the revelation of the attitude of mind both of the lecturer and, by implication, of her audience, which is so peculiarly arresting. "You may bet your boots we're a cultured crowd," the fair Chicago lady remarked to a visitor from Europe; but they are not so crude as that in New England. They know better—far better. Nothing could well surpass the patient sympathy with which Miss Lowell scrutinises her poets, her refined enthusiasm for their

---

[1] *Six French Poets. Studies in Contemporary Literature.* By Amy Lowell. New York: The Macmillan Company.

achievements, her enlightened tolerance of their faults. Yet, as one reads, one becomes aware of some kind of subtle and all-pervading dissonance. It is not that Miss Lowell is not doing her very best by M. Francis Jammes, M. Paul Fort, and the rest of them; it is almost, one feels inclined to say, because she so obviously *is* doing it that one cannot help feeling the presence of a great gulf lying between her and them. Her words, in their effort to bridge the gulf, seem only to emphasise it; and her lectures give the impression of being lectures, not on living human beings, but on some queer animals, submarine fishes, perhaps, illustrated by lantern slides. Miss Lowell knows all about these odd products, and explains them with the loving care of a delighted scientific observer. "This interesting little creature," one can almost hear her saying as the poet is flashed upon the screen for us, melancholy and distinguished, or bold and decorative, or thin and exasperated, as the case may be, "this interesting little creature" . . . and then we learn everything about its singular habits and characteristics that there is to know. There is Samain, who "possessed the gift of wonder; an inestimable possession, by the way"; who used to say "quand je me sens devenir pessimiste, je regarde une rose," but about whom it is not known "whether he ever had a definite love story." It seems, as Miss Lowell hastens to add, "hardly possible for him to have escaped such a usual happening"; though "whether it was a particular woman he gave up, or whether he merely resigned himself to bachelorhood in the abstract," she is unable to say. These curious creatures have a way of remaining a little mysterious even to the most ardent investigators. M. de Régnier, too, is not quite all plain-sailing. There are his poems—very delicate poems indeed; but there are also his novels, "in which," Miss Lowell says, "the Rabelaisian humour I have spoken of is most apparent." How it is possible "for a man of De Régnier's

delicacy to be so coarse is a problem for the psychologist."
M. Paul Fort is a more comprehensible phenomenon. This
agreeable organism "is fairly intoxicated with the idea of
liberty . . . exteriorising, full of vitality and vigour, and
la joie de vivre. . . . He positively bounces with delight
through poem after poem. He is intensely interested in everything. . . . He is master of what Matthew Arnold would
have called 'the grand style,' but he is also past-master of a
hail-fellow-well-met diction to sing the preoccupations of
the Breton sailors. Not even Byron has so fine an irony
as he."

Miss Lowell is sympathetic; but there are moments when
she cannot help showing her audience that she is under no
delusions—that neither she nor they could possibly belong
to the same world as the pictures on the screen. "I hardly
believe religion, as we conceive the term, to be possible
to the Latin mind." *As we conceive the term!*—perhaps; but
one thinks of St. Francis and St. Theresa, of Port Royal and
the French cathedrals, and one would like to interrupt the
lecturer with a question or two; but there is no time. "I
only paused here," Miss Lowell adds, "to note a curious
trait in the Latin character, and one which is often misunderstood, and always thoroughly disliked, by Anglo-Saxons,"
and she hurries on to describe the *Symboliste* movement. Yes,
certainly, the creatures do have "curious traits." Another is
their extraordinary interest in metrical questions—"it is very
hard for an English reader not to smile" at this. "We must
constantly remind ourselves that . . . in France there is a
right and a wrong in pronunciation, there is a correct construction of sentences, and, above all, there is an exact system
of versification." It is all very strange—but one gets used to
it. For instance, there is the mute *e*, which a Frenchman
persists not only in counting metrically, but actually sometimes in pronouncing—"drawing it out," as Miss Lowell says,

"in the disagreeable mannerism of the Comédie Française."
And she adds, "The only thing which I can compare this to
in English is the very bad and foolish tradition of singing
English, in which 'wind' is pronounced 'winde.' " Voltaire
was of a different opinion. "C'est précisément dans ces *e*
muets," he says, "que consiste la grande harmonie de notre
prose et de nos vers. . . . Toutes ces désinences heureuses
laissent dans l'oreille un son qui subsiste encore après le mot
prononcé, comme un clavecin qui résonne quand les doigts
ne frappent plus les touches." But at such refinements, "for
one who is not a Frenchman and therefore in love with the
alexandrine," it certainly *is* "very hard not to smile."

However, Miss Lowell on other occasions amply makes
up for these occasional and natural *brusqueries* by the readi-
ness with which she enters into the difficulties and distresses
of the literary career. No one realises more fully the obstacles
which beset the path of genius. In the 'nineties, for instance,
when "talents were rising to the surface every day . . . the
great Parisian public went about its business quite unconscious." But Miss Lowell consoles us with a reflection:
" 'Twas ever thus; and we need not be surprised that Paris,
clever though she be, is not entirely apart from the stream
of common humanity." No, not entirely; and then there is
another consolation: if only the genius "lives to a reasonable
age, the public may come round to him." Great are the
virtues of "a reasonable age"! Besides, "usually, a man would
seem to have only a certain amount in him. Sometimes he
matures slowly. . . . I have heard it said that Shakespeare
was thirty before he began to write, and we know that
the painter Gauguin was forty before he touched a brush.
Daniel Webster, too, was some forty odd before he made a
speech." The perplexing thing is, though, that one can never
be sure where to have a genius; for "the contrary is often
true. . . . Are we so sure that Keats was unlucky to die

young? The dismal and academic *Hyperion*, so praised by the conventional critic, makes us pause and consider the question." Decidedly the creatures are very capricious. Shakespeare, Gauguin, and Daniel Webster might, one would have supposed, have formed in combination a pretty strong precedent; but no; here is Keats, who will go and write *Hyperion*, and make us begin to think he was quite a lucky fellow to have died so young.

1916.

8. A Sidelight on Frederick the Great

THE Memoirs of Henri de Catt have long been familiar to scholars; they were used by Carlyle in his *Life of Friedrich*, and an elaborate edition of the original manuscript forms one of the valuable series of publications issued from the Prussian State Archives. The book is an extremely interesting one, and the present translation,[1] which makes it for the first time accessible to the ordinary English reader, deserves to be widely read. The translation itself is of a decidedly unpretentious kind. Occasionally, it is somewhat misleading. The rendering, for instance, throughout the book, of Frederick's familiar and affectionate *mon cher* by the stiff formality of "my dear sir" gives a seriously false impression of the King's attitude towards his secretary. Stylistically, however, the excellent Catt has nothing to lose from any translation, however pedestrian. It is not as a piece of literature that his work is to be judged. Nor, except incidentally and indirectly, is it of any real importance from the historical and political point of view. The Frederick of history reaches us through other channels, and our estimate of that extraordinary career does not depend upon the kind of information which Catt provides. The interest of his book is entirely personal and psychological. It is like one of those photographs—old-fashioned and faded, perhaps, but still taken *sur le vif*—which one turns to with an eager curi-

[1] *Frederick the Great: the Memoirs of his Reader, Henri de Catt* (1758-1760). Translated by F. S. Flint. With an Introduction by Lord Rosebery. Constable. 2 vols.

osity, of some remarkable and celebrated man. The historian neglects Oliver Cromwell's warts; but it is just such queer details of a physiognomy that the amateur of human nature most delights in. Catt shows us the queer details of Frederick's mental physiognomy, and some of them are very queer indeed.

His portrait has both the merits and the drawbacks of a photograph: it is true, and it is stupid; and its very stupidity is the measure of its truth. There is not a trace of Boswellian artistry about it—of that power of selection and evocation which clothes its object with something of the palpable reality of life. There is hardly even a trace of criticism. "Let me have men about me that are . . . not too clever," must have been Frederick's inward resolution after his disastrous experience with Voltaire; and obviously it was with some such feeling in his mind that, after a chance meeting on a boat in Holland, he engaged as his "reader" the pious, ingenuous, good-natured Swiss young man. The King's choice was amply justified: the young man was certainly not too clever; one gathers that Frederick actually almost liked him; and, though the inevitable rupture came at last, it was delayed for more than twenty years. Catt was indeed the precise antithesis of Voltaire. And his Memoirs are the precise antithesis of Voltaire's famous lampoon. The Frenchman's devastating sketch is painted with such brilliance that nobody can believe in it, and nobody can help believing in the bland acceptance of Catt's photographic plate.

The Memoirs only cover a period of two years, but it so happens that those years contained the crisis of Frederick's life. Between 1758 and 1761 the hideous convulsion of the Seven Years' War reached its culmination. Frederick, attacked simultaneously by France, Austria and Russia, faced his enemies like a bear tied to the stake: disaster after dis-

aster fell upon him; bloody defeats punctuated his ruinous
marches and desperate manoeuvrings; Berlin itself was taken;
for many months it seemed certain that the doom of Prussia
was sealed; more than once the hopeless King was on the
brink of escaping the final humiliation by suicide. Catt, with
a few brief intervals, was in daily intercourse with Frederick
all through this period, and it is against this lurid background of frenzied struggle and accumulating horror that he
shows us his portrait of his master. Every day, whether in
camp under canvas, or in the cramped quarters of some
wretched village, or amid the uncongenial splendours of
some momentarily conquered palace, he was summoned at
about five in the evening to the royal presence, where he
remained, usually for at least two, and sometimes for four
or five hours. His duties as "reader" were of a purely passive
kind: it was his business, not to read, but to listen. And
listen he did, while the King, putting aside at last the labours
and agitations of the day, the coils of strategy and high
politics, relaxed himself in literary chat, French declama-
tions, and philosophical arguments. Clearly enough, these
evening *tête-à-têtes* with Catt were the one vestige left to
him, in his terrible surroundings, of the pleasures of private
life—of the life of intellectual cultivation and unofficial intercourse; and the spectacle of this grim old conqueror seeking out the company of a mediocre young man from Switzerland, with whom to solace himself in rhymes and rhapsodies,
would be pathetic, if such a word were not so totally inapplicable to such a character. No, the spectacle is not pathetic;
it is simply exceedingly curious. For what Catt shows us is a
man for whom literature was not merely a pastime but a
passion, a man of exaggerated sensibilities, a man who would
devote ungrudging hours to the laborious imitation of
French poetry, a man who would pass the evenings of days

spent in scheming and slaughter reading aloud the plays of his favourite dramatist, until at last he would be overcome by emotion, and break down, in floods of tears. Frederick, in fact, appears in Catt's pages as a literary sentimentalist; he weeps at every opportunity, and is never tired of declaiming high sentiments in alexandrine verse. When he is cheerful, he quotes Chaulieu; when he is satirical, he misquotes *Athalie;* when he is defeated in battle and within an ace of utter destruction, he greets his astonished Reader with a long tirade from *Mithridate.* After Frederick himself, Racine is the real hero of these Memoirs. His exquisite, sensuous, and high-resounding oratory flows through them in a perpetual stream. It is a strange triumph for that most refined of poets: the sobs of Burrhus are heard in the ruined hamlets of Saxony, and the agonies of Zorndorf mingle with those of Phèdre.

And after Racine, Voltaire. Again and again, Frederick recurs, in accents of mingled anger and regret, to the Master whose art he worshipped, whose person he had once held in his clutches, and who had now escaped him for ever. Voltaire was a rogue, no doubt, a heartless scoundrel, capable of any villainy—but his genius!—"Si son cœur égalait ses talents, quel homme, mon ami, quel homme! Et comme il nous humilierait tous!" And so Majesty bent once more over the screed of halting verses, struggling to polish them according to the precepts of the Patriarch; and so, when a letter came from Ferney, the royal countenance beamed with pleasure, and soldiers who had pilfered hen-roosts might hope for fewer lashes that day. Sometimes, when Frederick was particularly pleased with his compositions, he ventured to submit them to the critical eye of the great man. "Mon cher, croyez-vous que ma pièce soit assez bonne pour être envoyée au patriarche?" On one occasion he allowed his author's vanity to interfere even with his policy. He had concocted some highly scurrilous verses on Louis XV and Madame de Pompadour, and was so delighted with them that he proposed at once to send them to Ferney. He had never, he told Catt, done anything better; even the Patriarch would be unable to detect a single fault. Catt allowed the excellence of the verses, but sagaciously pointed out the danger of putting them into the hands of Voltaire—that heartless scoundrel, as his Majesty had so constantly remarked, capable of any villainy—at the very moment when the disasters of the campaign made it important to capture, if possible, the good graces of the French Court. Frederick reflected; agreed that Catt was right; and then, in a day or two, unable to resist the temptation, secretly sent off the verses to Voltaire. The inevitable followed. On the receipt of the verses, Voltaire immediately despatched them to the French authorities, while he wrote to Frederick informing him that the royal letter had been apparently opened in the post, and that therefore, if copies had been taken of it and forwarded to certain quarters, he at any rate was not to blame. Frederick at once realised his folly. Voltaire, he declared to Catt, was a monster, a traitor, and an old monkey. A few months later, a copy of *Candide* arrived from the author. Frederick read it; he read it again, and yet again. It was the best novel, he told Catt, that had ever been written, and Voltaire was the greatest man alive.

Never, surely, was the eighteenth-century theory of the "ruling passion" more signally falsified than in the case of Frederick the Great. He was ambitious, no doubt; but ambitious for what? For political power? For military prestige? Or for the glory of satisfying an old monkey at Ferney that he could write a good alexandrine if he tried? The European bandit who sits up all night declaiming the noble sentiments of Racine's heroes, the hardened cynic who weeps for hours over his own elegies, is certainly a puzzling creature, hard to fit into any cut-and-dried system of psychology. So glaring, indeed, are these contradictions that Lord Rosebery, in his Introduction to the present translation, suggests that Frederick posed to his Reader, that the tears and the literary emotions which Catt chronicles were "the result of dramatic art." When, in particular, Frederick expatiates on his desire for a life of retirement, devoted to the delights of friendship and aesthetic cultivation, Lord Rosebery is disposed to agree with the comment of the Swiss young man that "the whole was a little comedy." It may be so; but it is difficult to believe it. It is hard to see what object Frederick could have had in deluding Catt; and it is easier to suppose that a man should contradict himself, both in his thoughts and his feelings, than that he should spend years in keeping up an elaborate mystification with an insignificant secretary, for no apparent purpose. As a whole, the impression, produced by the Memoirs, of Frederick's sincerity is overwhelming. And perhaps the contradictions in his character, extreme as they were, are more apparent than real. Cynicism and sentimentality, so opposite in their effects, share at their root in a certain crudity; and Frederick, intellectually and spiritually, was crude. His ambitions, his scepticisms, his admirations, his tastes—all were crude; on the one side, this underlying quality came out in public Macchiavellisms and private cruelties, and on the other in highfalutin pathos and a schoolgirl's prostration before the literary man. On a smaller scale, such characters are not uncommon; what makes Frederick's case so extraordinary and at first sight so baffling is the extremity of difference to which the opposite tendencies were pushed. The explanation of this no doubt lies in the portentous, the terrific, energy of the man. His vehemence could be content with no ordinary moderation either in the callous or the lachrymose; and the same amazing force which made Prussia a Great Power created, in spite of incredible difficulties, in a foreign idiom, under the bondage of the harshest literary conventions ever known, that vast mass of fifth-rate poetising from which shuddering History averts her face.

1917.

9. An Adolescent

THERE is a story in Hogg's *Life of Shelley* of how the poet went on one occasion to a large dinner-party at Norfolk House. He sat near the bottom of the table, and after a time his neighbour said to him: "Pray, who is that very strange old man at the top of the table, sitting next to His Grace, who talks so much, so loudly, and in so extraordinary a manner, and all about himself?" "He is my father," Shelley replied; "and he is a very strange old man indeed!" Our knowledge of Timothy Shelley has been hitherto mainly based upon Hogg's portrait of him—the portrait certainly of a "very strange old man"—eccentric, capricious, puzzled, blustering, "scolding, crying, swearing, and then weeping again," then bringing out the old port, and assuring everybody at great length that he was highly respected in the House of Commons—"and by the Speaker in particular, who told him they could not get on without him"—and then turning in a breath from some rambling anecdote of poachers in Sussex to a proof of the existence of the Deity, extracted from "Palley's Evidences." ("My father always will call him Palley," the poet complained; "why does he call him so?" "I do not know, unless it be to rhyme to Sally," was Hogg's only suggestion.) And Hogg produces specimens of "the epistles of the beloved Timothy," which, as he says, are "very peculiar letters"—"exactly like letters that had been cut in two, and the pieces afterwards joined at hazard; cross readings, as it were, cross questions

199

and crooked answers." Such is Hogg's portrait. But Hogg was not always accurate; he was capable of rearranging facts for his own purposes; he was even capable of rewriting letters which he alleged he was quoting from the originals. It seemed, therefore, difficult to accept his presentment of "the poor old governor" as literally true; the letters especially looked as if they had been delicately manipulated—even an irate and port-bibbing country gentleman of the time of the Regency could hardly be supposed in sober earnest to have been the author of quite so much incoherence and of quite so little grammar. One guessed that Hogg, with his unscrupulous pen, had been touching things up. But now Mr. Ingpen has discovered and published [1] a collection of documents which give us a great deal of first-hand information upon Sir Timothy and his relations with his son. These documents, drawn principally from the correspondence of the Shelleys' family lawyer, William Whitton, are full of interest; they are concerned with many important incidents in Shelley's career, and they substantiate—in a remarkable way—Hogg's account of Sir Timothy. It becomes clear, in the light of these new and unimpeachable manuscripts, that Hogg's portrait was by no means a fancy one, that "the epistles of the beloved Timothy" were in truth "very peculiar"—illiterate, confused, and hysterical to an extraordinary degree, and that his conduct was of a piece with his correspondence —a singular mixture of futility and queerness. Indeed, if in all the other elements of his character Shelley was the very antithesis of his father, there can be no doubt at all where his eccentricity came from.

Of course, Sir Timothy is only interesting from the accident of his fatherhood. It is one of Fate's little ironies that the poor old governor, who in the natural course of things

[1] *Shelley in England.* New Facts and Letters from the Shelley-Whitton Papers. By Roger Ingpen. Kegan Paul.

would have dropped long since into a deserved and decent oblivion, should still be read about and thought about—that even his notes to his lawyer should be carefully unearthed, elaborately annotated, and published in a large book—for the sake of a boy whom he disliked and disapproved of, whom he did his best to injure while living, and whose very memory he tried hard to suppress. He is immortal, as the French say, *malgré lui*—an unwilling ghost caught up into an everlasting glory. And as to Shelley himself, it may be hoped that Mr. Ingpen's book will lead the way to a clearer vision of a creature who, for all his fame, still stands in need of a little understanding. It is a misfortune that the critics and biographers of poets should be for the most part highly respectable old gentlemen; for poets themselves are apt to be young, and are not apt to be highly respectable. Sometimes the respectable old gentlemen are frankly put out; but sometimes they try to be sympathetic—with results at least equally unfortunate. In Shelley's case it is difficult to decide whether the distressed self-righteousness of Matthew Arnold's famous essay or the solemn adoration of Professor Dowden's standard biography gives the falser impression. Certainly the sympathetic treatment is the more insidious. The bias of Matthew Arnold's attack is obvious; but the process by which, through two fat volumes, Shelley's fire and air have been transmuted into Professor Dowden's cotton-wool and rose-water is a subtler revenge of the world's upon the most radiant of its enemies.

Mr. Ingpen's book deals chiefly with that part of Shelley's life which elapsed between his expulsion from Oxford and his separation from his first wife. It is the most controversial period of Shelley's career—the period particularly selected by Matthew Arnold for his high-toned fleerings and by Professor Dowden for his most ponderous palliations. It is the period of the elopement with Harriet Westbrook, of the sudden flittings and ceaseless wanderings to and fro between Edinburgh, York, Keswick, Wales, Ireland, Devonshire, and London, of the wild Dublin escapade, of the passionate correspondence and furious quarrel with Miss Hitchener, of the composition of *Queen Mab*, and of the elopement with Mary Godwin. The great merit of Mr. Ingpen's new letters is that they show us the Shelley of these three years, neither as the Divine Poet nor as the Outcast from Society, but in the painful and prosaic posture of a son who is on bad terms with his father and wants to get money out of him. Now there is one fact which must immediately strike every reader of this correspondence, and which really affords the clue to the whole queer history: Shelley's extraordinary youthfulness. And it is just this fact which writers on Shelley seem persistently to ignore. It is almost impossible to remember, as one watches their long faces, that the object of all their concern was a youth scarcely out of his teens; that Shelley was eighteen when he was expelled from Oxford, that he was just nineteen when he eloped with Harriet, who was herself sixteen, that he was under twenty-two when he eloped with Mary, while Mary was not seventeen. In reality, Shelley during these years was an adolescent, and an adolescent in whom the ordinary symptoms of that time of life were present in a peculiarly intense form. His restlessness, his crudity of thought and feeling, his violent fluctuations of sentiment, his enthusiasms and exaggerations, his inability to judge correctly either the mental processes of other people or the causal laws which govern the actual world—all these are the familiar phenomena of adolescence; in Shelley's case they happened to be combined with a high intelligence, a determined will, and a wonderful unworldliness; but, none the less, the adolescence was there.

That was the fundamental fact which his father, like his

commentators, failed to realise. He persisted in treating Shelley's behaviour seriously. The leaflet for which Shelley was sent down from Oxford, *The Necessity of Atheism*, signed "Jeremiah Stukeley," and circulated to all the Bishops and Heads of Houses, was obviously little more than a schoolboy's prank; but Atheism happened at that moment to be the bugbear of the governing classes, and Sir Timothy lost his head. Instead of attempting to win over the youth by kindness, instead of sending his mother to him to bring him home, the old man adopted the almost incredible course of refusing to have any communication with his son, save through the family lawyer. And the lawyer, Whitton, was the last man who should have been entrusted with such a task. His letters show him to have been a formal and testy personage, with the disposition, and sometimes the expressions, of a butler. "You care not, you say," he wrote to Shelley, "for Family Pride. Allow me to tell you that the first part of the Family Pride of a Gent is to preserve a propriety of manners and a decency of expression in communication, and your forgetfulness of those qualifications towards me in the letter I have just received induces me to say," etc. "The Gent," Whitton told Sir Timothy, "is very angry, and has thought proper to lecture me on the occasion." "The occasion" was Shelley's innocent suggestion that he should be allowed to resign his inheritance to the family property (worth over £200,000) in return for a settled income of £100 a year. The lawyer was appalled, and easily whipped up Sir Timothy into a hectic fury. "The insulting, ungentlemanly letter to you," wrote the indignant, incoherent parent, "appears the high-toned, self-will'd dictate of the Diabolical Publications which have unluckily fallen in his way, and given this Bias to his mind, that is most singular. To cast off all thoughts of his Maker, to abandon his Parents, to wish to relinquish his Fortune and to court Persecution all seems to arise from the same source. The most mild mode of giving his conduct a thought, it must occur that these sallies of Folly and Madness ought to be restrain'd and kept within bounds. Nothing provokes him so much as civility, he wishes to become what he would term a martyr to his sentiments—nor do I believe he would feel the Horrors of being drawn upon a Hurdle, or the shame of being whirl'd in the Pillory." If with these views Sir Timothy had decided to cut off his son altogether and let him shift for himself, there might have been something to be said for him. But he could not bring himself to do that. Instead, while refusing to allow Shelley to return home, he doled out to him an allowance of £200 a year; and then, when the inevitable happened, and the inflammable youth, lonely in London, fell into the arms of the beautiful Harriet, imagined he was rescuing her from a persecuting family, and married her, the foolish old man cut off the allowance without a word. Shelley's letters to his father at this juncture reveal completely the absurd ingenuousness of his mind. Penniless, married, in a strange town—he had eloped with Harriet to Edinburgh—and altogether dependent upon his father's good will, Shelley brought himself to beg for money, and yet, in the very same breath, could not resist the opportunity of lecturing Sir Timothy upon his duties as a Christian. "Father, are you a Christian? . . . I appeal to your duty to the God whose worship you profess, I appeal to the terrors of that day which you believe to seal the doom of mortals, then clothed with immortality. Father, are you a Christian? Judge not, then, lest you be judged. . . . What! Will you not forgive? How, then, can your boasted professions of Christianity appear to the world," and so on, and so on, through page after page and letter after letter. As Mr. Ingpen says, it is indeed strange that no inkling of the mingled pathos and comedy of these appeals should have touched Sir Timothy. And then when the poor boy was met by nothing but silence, we see him breaking out into ridiculous invective. "You have treated me *ill, vilely*. When I was expelled for Atheism, you wished I had been killed in Spain. . . . If *you* will not hear my name, *I* will pronounce it. Think not I am an insect whom injuries destroy . . . had I money enough I would meet you in London and hollow in your ears Bysshe, Bysshe, Bysshe . . . aye, Bysshe till you're deaf." Had I money enough! Truly, in the circumstances, an exquisite proviso!

These are the central incidents with which Mr. Ingpen's book is concerned; but it is difficult to indicate in a short space the wealth of human interest and curious detail contained in these important letters. They may be recommended alike to the psychologist and the historian, to the reader of Professor Dowden and the admirer of Matthew Arnold. Mr. Ingpen is also able to throw fresh light on some other circumstances of interest: he shows for the first time that Shelley was actually arrested for debt; he gives new documents bearing upon Harriet's suicide; and he reproduces in facsimile extracts from the poet's manuscript note-book, found among the *débris* of the *Ariel*. Not the least amusing part of his book is that in which he traces the relations between Sir Timothy and Mary Shelley, after the tragedy in the Gulf of Spezzia. The epistles of the beloved Timothy retain their character to the end. "To lose an eldest son in his lifetime," he writes to Whitton, "and the unfortunate manner of his losing that life, is truely melancholy to think of, but as it has pleas'd the Great Author of our Being so to dispose of him I must make up my mind with resignation." And Whitton's own style loses nothing of its charm. After Shelley's death, one of his Oxford creditors—a plumber— applied to the lawyer for the payment of a bill. Whitton not only refused to pay, but took the opportunity of pointing the appropriate moral. "The officious interference of you and others," he informed the unfortunate plumber, "did a most serious injury to the Gent that is now no more."

1917.

10. Rabelais

IT is difficult to think of any other among the very great writers of the world who is appreciated in such a variety of degrees, and for such a variety of reasons, as Rabelais. There are those who worship him, there are those who admire him at a distance, there are those who frankly cannot put up with him at all. He is read by many as a great humanist and moral teacher; by many more, probably, as a teller of stories, and in particular of improper stories; others are fascinated by his language, and others by the curious problems—literary, biographical, allegorical—which his book suggests. Mr. W. F. Smith, of St. John's College, Cambridge, belongs to another class—and it is a larger one than might have been expected—the class of those who read Rabelais for the sake of making notes.[1] Mr. Smith, indeed, devotes one of his chapters to "Rabelais as a Humanist," but it principally consists of a series of jottings upon the French printers of the early sixteenth century, introduced by the remark, "We cannot lose sight of the fact that the Renaissance could not have had such far-reaching influence but for the invention of printing." Of Rabelais as a story-teller, Mr. Smith has very little say; an uninformed reader of his book would hardly guess from it that there was anything amusing about Gargantua and Pantagruel; though he would discover (on the last page but one) a pained reference to the author's "out-

[1] *Rabelais in His Writings.* By W. F. Smith, M.A. Cambridge: At the University Press.

spokenness." "Outspokenness generally," Mr. Smith tells us,
"was tolerated and excused more at that time than now";
and he quotes with approval the observation of "a French
writer" who "has asserted bluntly that, as the early part of
Rabelais' life was spent among monks and friars and the
later part in the medical world, it is not surprising that he
fell in with the freedom of speech usual in those professions."
We are left to suppose that if only Rabelais had read for the
Bar, or had gone into the Army, his writings would never
have raised a blush in the most Victorian cheek. As for his
style, Mr. Smith's chapter upon that subject could, one feels,
have originated nowhere but in the University of Cambridge.
Only a member of that learned body would set out to discuss
one of the most marvellous creations of human art by filling
pages with observations on "the decadence of pure Latinity
observable in the writers of the so-called Silver age, as in-
stanced in Juvenal, Persius, Tacitus, and others," on "the
policy pursued by the Romans of sending out colonies of
veterans to garrison their distant conquests," on "the system
of Roman law, as administered by the Praetors," on "the
Vulgate which was used in the Roman Church services"
(with special reference to "St. Jerome's edition"), on "the
study of Aristotle, which was introduced through the Arabic
philosophers and was taken up by Albertus Magnus"—all
leading to the conclusion that Rabelais "seems to have
formed his style, perhaps unconsciously, on the easy-flowing
periods of Herodotus, full as they are of conversations, as
well as on the cynicism of Lucian, from whom he borrows
freely." Decidedly, Mr. Smith is happier in the less ambitious task of taking notes—in compiling a list of the plants
mentioned by Rabelais, or in tracing his medical references
to their sources in Galen, Hipparchus, and Pliny. It is unfortunate, however, that so large a number of his observations should have been culled from the pages of that admi-

rable and learned journal, *La Revue des Etudes Rabelai-
siennes*. The reader finds it difficult to determine how much
of the book is new, and how much is a *réchauffé;* though the
originality of some of Mr. Smith's remarks is obvious. In a
note, for instance, on one of the fantasies of the disputed
Fifth Book—"les chemins qui cheminent"—after quoting a
French editor to the effect that a similar idea occurs in
Pascal's *Pensées*—"les rivières sont des chemins qui marchent"
—Mr. Smith adds that "the suggestion has been carried out
in practice recently in Paris and elsewhere by means of
slopes, etc., moved by machinery to take the place of stair-
cases, etc." This comment, with the charming glimpse it
gives of the groves of Academe, is really after Rabelais' own
heart.

Upon the question of the authenticity of the Fifth Book—
the greatest of all the Rabelais cruxes—Mr. Smith, of course,
has something to say, and inclines, on the whole, to a belief
in its genuineness. But he does not refer to two of the most
serious arguments in favour of the contrary opinion. Neither
the style nor the general tone of the book appears to be that
of the author of the rest of the work. Upon the point of
style, the English reader can only bow to the judgment of
French critics; but it may be noticed that those who are
only acquainted with Rabelais through the translation of
Urquhart and Motteux can hardly escape a false impression
of the literary quality of the original. The splendid genius
of Urquhart seized upon that side of Rabelais' writing which
was congenial to itself, emphasised it, amplified it, and endowed it with a new immortality. But it was not to be expected that even Urquhart's magic could have transmuted
more than a *part* of the glorious gold of the Master. What
he gives us is the superabundance of Rabelais, his gigantic
linguistic facility, his orgiastic love of words. Urquhart, in
fact, actually increases from his own stores the verbal wealth

of the original; he cannot resist enlarging as he translates, and prolonging, in a kind of competitive ardour, even the enormous lengths of the famous Lists and Litanies. The result is something magnificent, but something that is not quite Rabelais, for the final miracle of Rabelais' writing is that, in spite of its extraordinary fecundity, it yet preserves an exquisite measure, a supreme restraint. There is a beautiful quality of elegance, of cleanness, of economy, of what the French call "netteté," in his sentences, which justifies the paradox that he is one of the most concise of writers. His prose, in short, with all its idiosyncrasies, is characteristically French. Now it is precisely this quality of "netteté" which is absent in the Fifth Book. Even an English reader must be struck by the change from the delicious concluding pages of the Fourth Book, where the writing dances along, flashing, with such an easy lightness, such a swift, consummate grace, to the opening of the Fifth, with its heavy, trailing, formless sentences. The hand of the Master has vanished.

In its general tone the Fifth Book seems to be no less unmistakably unrabelaisian. The great Curé of Meudon may perhaps be described as a satirist; but he was certainly the best-natured satirist who ever lived. No doubt, too, he was a reformer—almost a revolutionary; but of all reformers and revolutionaries he was the most genial, the most urbane. In opinions he was doubtless of the school of Voltaire; but his temperament was the rich, full-blooded, Old Tory temperament of Sir Walter Scott. The good-humoured generosity of his hero, Pantagruel, at times almost verges upon a weak complacency. He seems to tolerate not only the scurvy jests of Panurge but the more serious delinquencies of Bridoison, the imbecile old judge. In the Fifth Book all this changes. The *Isle Sonnante* chapters are full of bitterness; in his comments on the "Papegaut," Panurge, besides being heretical, is brutal into the bargain. More remarkable still is the virulence of feeling in the famous description of the *Chats Fourrés* and of Grippeminaud upon the bench. Here the satire is fierce, unrelenting, terrible; there is not a trace of laughter about it; it is a direct and savage attack. The unknown writer rises for a moment to greatness, and seems, after all, in his very different manner, not unworthy of his company. It is perhaps the strangest feature of this strange work that it should have been completed so enigmatically, so incongruously, and with such success. Rabelais, so extraordinary in his nature, was no less extraordinary in his posthumous fate. Of this, the mysterious Fifth Book was the earliest manifestation; the latest is Mr. Smith's volume; but no doubt it will not be the last.

1918.

11. A Statesman: Lord Morley

IT is obvious that this is an interesting book;[1] it is less obvious in what the precise nature of its interest consists. Like most modern biographies, but in a more marked degree, it appeals to two totally distinct kinds of curiosity: on the one hand, it provides the reader with hitherto unpublished documents of first-rate importance; and on the other, it presents a picture of a man and an age. These two threads of discourse have by no means been woven together into a unity. After more than a volume of general reflections and personal reminiscences, Lord Morley suddenly lifts the curtain upon a high political scene, and reveals, through two hundred pages of private correspondence with Lord Minto, the detailed inner workings of a series of transactions which have made an epoch in the history of the English administration of India. Probably it is this portion of the book which will turn out to be of the more enduring value. The letters of a Secretary of State to a Viceroy are bound to contain material which no future student of Imperial politics can afford to neglect. They are bound to contain authentic information upon important facts, and that is a kind of information very much rarer than is generally supposed—so rare, indeed, that whenever it appears, the world will always treasure it. To take a small example, pp. 331 and 333 of Vol. II give us authentic information as to Lord Kitchener and the Governor-Generalship of India. We there learn that

[1] *Recollections.* By John Viscount Morley, O.M. Macmillan.

Lord Kitchener stated to Lord Haldane that he expected the appointment, that Mr. Asquith personally favoured it, that King Edward vehemently supported it, and that Lord Morley was so strongly opposed to it that he was prepared to resign if it should take place. Apart from incidental revelations of this sort, the whole purport of these letters is of singular interest, owing both to the time of peculiar difficulty at which they were written and to the fact that they give expression to a policy—a policy laid down, elaborated, and at last put into execution with consistency and success. It is possible, no doubt, that the changes in our government of India, which were carried out during Lord Morley's tenure of office, were of somewhat less positive consequence than he himself would seem to suggest; that the "historic plunge," of which he speaks with evident complacency, was more of a *beau geste* than one of those great acts of profound reform which affect the fundamentals of national polity; that, in fact, it will be for its *negative* qualities—its allaying of hatreds, its avoidance of extreme measures, its skill in eluding not merely a host of difficulties, but some appalling dangers—that Lord Morley's work will be esteemed by the historian of the future. This may be so; yet it is difficult to read this record without a feeling of pleasure akin to that produced by some admirable example of dramatic art—the situation is so interesting, the developments are so well managed, and the *dénouement* is so satisfactory. The hand of the master is plainly visible throughout. For, though Lord Minto might perhaps be well described as an average Viceroy, Lord Morley was certainly not at all an average Secretary of State.

Indeed, what the reader finally carries away from this part of the book is the impression of a rare political capacity. That Lord Morley possessed the qualities of a strong and skilful ruler was already vaguely realised; it is now made manifest in explicit detail. His attitude towards Lord Minto, for instance, is highly characteristic. Lord Minto had been appointed by a Tory Government, and his opinions were clearly at variance with those of the Secretary of State, upon many vital questions. It is delightful to observe Lord Morley's virtuosity in the treatment of this thorny situation— his gentle persuasions, his tactful acquiescences, the subtle suggestions of his compliments. "You will not suspect me," he remarks on one occasion, "of vulgar flattery." No, certainly not; who would? But the discerning reader (and of course it is of the essence of the situation that Lord Minto himself could hardly be called one) may be pardoned if he puts a delicate emphasis upon the "vulgar." And then, occasionally, amid all the velvet of the correspondence, one catches a glimpse of underlying steel. On one of his visits to Ireland, Lord Morley made the acquaintance of Lord Waterford, who, he was told, was "of a dictatorial turn." "Perhaps," was Lord Morley's comment in his diary, "I don't mind that." One understands very well, after reading the correspondence with Lord Minto, that he would not mind it; he was of a dictatorial turn himself. But with him the determination to have his own way was both veiled and strengthened by an acute perception of the facts with which he had to deal. Thus it is true to say that his policy was that of an opportunist—but an opportunist, not of the school of Walpole, but of the school of Burke. Perhaps the most remarkable feature of these letters is their constant assertion of great principles. They form a running comment, of the highest value, upon the current platitudes of Imperialist doctrine; and will live, if for no other reason, as the exposition of a statesman's handling of the Liberal creed.

The rest of the book is, from some points of view, decidedly disappointing. The recollections of a life passed in familiar intercourse both with the leading men of letters and the leading politicians of the age, a life intimately connected

with some of the most agitated events of English history, a
life of high achievement in literature as well as in action,
could hardly fail, one might have thought, to be exciting.
But "exciting" is really the last word that anyone would
dream of applying to these pages. "And is this all?" is the
question which rises to one's lips at the end of them. To
have been the friend of John Stuart Mill and Gladstone,
to have negotiated with Parnell, to have fought in the fore-
front of the Home Rule battle, to have worked for ten
years in the inner circle of a Cabinet—when all this, and
the rest, is added up, what a curiously tame, what an almost
obvious affair it seems to come to! If one might hazard the
paradox, it is their very lack of interest that makes these
reminiscences so interesting. Once or twice, Lord Morley
seems to hint that he holds a brief for the Victorian Age;
and there can be no doubt that his book is impregnated
with the Victorian spirit. An air of singular solemnity hovers
over it, and its moral tone is of the highest. Only a Victorian,
one feels, would have, on the one hand, allowed Mr. Gladstone to flit like a shadow through his pages, while, on the
other, devoting a whole long chapter to a series of extracts
from the most esteemed authors on the subject of Death.
Only a Victorian, having made his reputation by writing
the lives of Diderot, Rousseau and Voltaire, would, on his
return from a visit to Paris, have thrown, in horror, two
French novels out of the railway-carriage window. Such details, slight as they are, depict a period. The Victorian Age,
great in so many directions, was not great in criticism, in
humour, in the realistic apprehension of life. It was an age
of self-complacency and self-contradiction. Even its atheists
(Lord Morley was one of them) were religious. The religious atmosphere fills his book, and blurs every outline.
We are shown Mr. Gladstone through a haze of reverence,
and Emerson, and Marcus Aurelius. We begin to long for

a little of the cynicism and scepticism of, precisely, the Age
of Diderot, Rousseau and Voltaire. Perhaps—who knows?—
if Lord Morley and his contemporaries had been less completely devoid of those unamiable and unedifying qualities,
the history of the world would have been more fortunate.
The heartless, irreverent, indecent eighteenth century produced the French Revolution. The Age of Victoria produced
—what?

1918.

12. A Diplomatist: Li Hung-Chang

ONE of the favourite dodges of the satirist is the creation of an imaginary world, superficially different from our own, and yet turning out, on further acquaintance, to contain all the familiar vices and follies of humanity. Swift's Lilliput and Brobdingnag are contrived on this principle. The vanity of courtiers, the mischiefs of politicians, the physical degradations of men and women—these things strike upon our minds with a new intensity when they are shown to us as parts of some queer universe, preposterously minute or enormous. We gain a new vision of war and lust when we see the one waged by statesmen six inches high, and the other agitating young ladies of sixty feet. Mr. Bland's book on Li Hung-Chang,[1] with its account of the society and institutions of China, produces—whether consciously or no it is a little difficult to say—very much the same effect. China is still so distant, its language is so incomprehensible, its customs are so singular, its whole civilisation has such an air of topsy-turvydom about it, that our Western intelligence can survey it with a remote disinterestedness hardly less complete than if it were a part of Laputa or the moon. We do so, with Mr. Bland's guidance; and we very soon perceive that China is, after all, only another Europe, with a touch of caricature and exaggeration here and there to give the satire point. Mr. Bland himself, indeed, seems at times to be almost a second Gulliver, such is the apparent ingenuous-

[1] *Li Hung-Chang.* By J. O. P. Bland. Constable.

ness with which he marvels at the strange absurdities of Chinese life. This, however, may be merely a Swiftian subtlety on his part to heighten the effect. For instance, he tells us with great gravity that one of the chief misfortunes from which China suffers is that she is ruled by officials; that whatever changes of government, whatever revolutions may take place, the officials remain undisturbed in power; and that these officials form a close bureaucratic caste, cut off from the world at large, puffed up with petty vanity, and singularly ignorant of the actual facts of life. He then goes on to relate, with amazement, that the official caste is recruited by means of competitive examinations of a literary kind, and that it is possible—and indeed frequent—to obtain the highest places in these examinations merely through a knowledge of the classics. The foundation of Li Hung-Chang's administrative career, for example, was based on his having been able, in reply to one of his examiners, to repeat a celebrated classic not only forwards, but backwards as well. Then Mr. Bland expatiates on the surprising and distressing atmosphere of "make-believe" in China; he points out how it infects and vitiates the whole system of government, how it is even visible in works of history—even in the Press: "They make their dynastic annals," he says, "conform to the official conception of the world-of-things-as-they-should-be, with little or no relation to the world-of-things-as-they-are, and the native Press, served chiefly by writers imbued with the same predilection for solemn make-believe in the discussion of public affairs, affords but little material for checking or amplifying the official annals." It inevitably follows, as Mr. Bland observes, that (in China) it is exceedingly difficult to discover the truth about any public event. Another singular characteristic of the Chinese is their hatred of foreigners. This passion they carry to extraordinary lengths; they are unwilling to believe that anything good ever came from a foreign country; they put high duties upon foreign importations; at moments of excitement the more violent among them clamour to "make an end, once and for all, of all the obnoxious foreigners, whose presence creates grave difficulties and dangers for the Empire." Strange to say, too, it is particularly the caste of officials which is infected by what Mr. Bland calls "this purblind ignorance and pride of race."

Li Hung-Chang, however—the hero of Mr. Bland's well-informed and spirited book—was different. Though a knowledge of the classics was the basis of his fortunes, it was not his only knowledge; though an official—and in many ways a typical official—he yet possessed a perspicacity which was never taken in by official "make-believe"; above all, he understood something of the nature and the powers of foreigners. Mr. Bland calls him a one-eyed man among the blind, and by "the blind" we are to understand the rest of China. But, in truth, the description applies equally well to every leader in thought or action in every community under the sun. In Europe, no less than in China, the vast majority of men are blind—blind through ignorance and superstition and folly and senseless passions; and the statesmen and the thinkers are one-eyed leaders, who see neither very far nor very many objects, but who see what they do see quite clearly. Li Hung-Chang was a leader because he saw quite clearly the nature of China's position in international affairs. But his one-eyedness is amusingly illustrated by the manner in which this perception was originally forced upon his consciousness. It came through the chance of his being thrown together with General Gordon. It was Gordon who gave him his first vision of Europe. Nothing could be more ironical. The half-inspired, half-crazy Englishman, with his romance and his fatalism, his brandy-bottle and his Bible, the irresponsible knight-errant whom his countrymen first laughed at and neglected, then killed and canonised—a figure straying through the perplexed industrialism of the nineteenth century like some lost "natural" from an earlier Age —this was the efficient cause of Li Hung-Chang's illumination, of his comprehension of the significance of Europe, of the whole trend of his long, cynical, successful, worldly-wise career.

It was particularly in diplomacy that that career achieved its most characteristic triumphs. Of all public servants, the diplomatist and the general alone must, if they are to succeed, have a grasp of actual facts. Politicians, lawyers, administrators, financiers even, can pass their lives in a mist of fictions and go down to posterity as great men. But the general who fails to perceive the facts that surround him will inevitably pay the penalty in defeat. The facts with which the diplomatist has to deal are less specialised and immediate, more subtle, indeterminate and diverse than those which confront the general; they are facts the perception of which requires an all-round intelligence; and thus, while it is possible for a great soldier to be a stupid man, a diplomatist who is stupid must be a failure. Li Hung-Chang's perspicacity was precisely of the universal kind; his cold gaze went through everything it met with an equal penetration. He could measure to a nicety all the complicated elements in the diplomatic game—the strength of his opponents, their intentions, their desires, their tenacity, their amenability to pressure, their susceptibility to bluff—and then the elaborate interactions of international forces, and the dubious movements of public opinion, and the curious influences of personal factors. More than this, he possessed a capacity, rare indeed save among the greatest masters of his craft—he could recognise the inevitable. And when that came, he understood the difficult art of bowing to it, as Mr. Bland pithily remarks, "with mental reservations."

His limitations were no less remarkable than his powers. He was never in the slightest danger of believing in a principle, or of allowing his astuteness to degenerate into profundity. His imagination was purely practical, and his whole conception of life was of a perfectly conventional kind. In this he was only carrying out the high diplomatic tradition; he was following in the footsteps of Queen Elizabeth and Richelieu, Metternich and Bismarck. It seems as if the human mind was incapable of changing its focus: it must either apprehend what is near it or what is far off; it cannot combine the two. Of all the great realists of history, the master spirits in the matter-of-fact business of managing mankind, it is difficult to think of more than one or two at most who, in addition, were moved by philosophical ideals towards noble aims.

Another consideration is suggested by Mr. Bland's book. There is something peculiarly fascinating about the diplomatic art. It is delightful to watch a skilled performer like Li Hung-Chang, baffling and befogging the English into humiliation, bluffing all Europe, by means of an imitation navy, into a genuine fear of a "Yellow Peril," and, finally, when all his sins seem to have found him out, when Japan has "seen" him, and his stakes are forfeit, "tirant son épingle du jeu" with such supreme felicity. Certainly, it is a humane and elegant art, essentially intellectual, concerned, too, with momentous issues, and mingling, in a highly agreeable manner, the satisfactions of self-interest and altruism. Yet one cannot help perceiving indications that its days may be numbered. It belongs to a situation of affairs in the world, which there is no reason to suppose will be permanent, and of which the essential condition is the existence of a few strong States, of approximately equal power, interacting in competitive rivalry. This period began with the Renaissance; and it is at least possible that a time may come when it will have ended, and when the diplomatist will appear as romantic and extinct a creature as the mediaeval baron or the Italian *condottiere.* Perhaps—who knows?—the subtle Oriental with the piercing eye may turn out to have been among the very last of the charming race.

1918.

13. Militarism and Theology

ULTIMATELY the world is governed by moderate men. Extremists and fanatics and desperadoes may make a noise or a disturbance, they may even at times appear to control the course of events; but in reality they are always secondary figures—either symptoms or instruments; whatever happens, the great mass of ordinary, stolid, humdrum, respectable persons remains the dominating force in human affairs. For this reason, among others, the book,[1] lately written by Lieutenant-General Baron von Freytag-Loringhoven, and now translated into English, is a distressing book to read. For the Baron, besides being, as we are told, the Deputy-Chief of the General Staff in Germany, is obviously a moderate man. His book is not the work of some hectic fire-eater, but of a judicious, sensible, conservative gentleman; and that is why it strikes a damp upon the heart. Ostensibly a series of "deductions" from the history of the war, it is, in fact, something much more portentous—an *exposé*, a cool, complacent, and eminently moderate *exposé* of the whole militarist point of view. The "deductions" which the baron draws from the events of the last three years are concerned entirely with the machinery of armies, with the details of strategy, with the measures best calculated to bring to perfection the operations of military power. These are the lessons which the war has taught him—lessons about

---

[1] *Deductions from the World War.* By Lieutenant-General Baron von Freytag-Loringhoven. Constable.

trench-fighting and shock tactics, and the value of barbed-
wire entanglements, and the undesirability of democratic
ideas. That any other kind of lesson could possibly be learnt
from it has clearly never occurred to him. Militarism is an
axiom taken for granted by every word in his book—and
taken for granted so completely that it is hardly even discussed; it is simply, everywhere, and always implied. And
this, surely, is a terrible phenomenon. Militarism yelled by
a Reventlow, or a . . . but one need not particularise . . .
is a sufficiently ghastly doctrine; but militarism blandly ex-
pounded by a Baron von Freytag-Loringhoven, with moderation, with little gentle touches of pedantry even, in a
balanced unemotional style—that is a far more profoundly
menacing spectacle. For it is a revelation of the state of mind
of multitudes of ordinary men.

The book suggests a curious analogy. The unquestioning
conviction with which its premises are held, its whole attitude of single-hearted devotion to a great underlying system of belief, reminds one of nothing so much as of a theological treatise. It has the kind of simplicity which one asso-
ciates with religious faith—with the uncontroversial faith of
the Middle Ages, when Catholicism was a fact as solid as the
earth and as ubiquitous as the atmosphere. One can fancy
the Baron as a Grand Inquisitor of those days, a pious and a
moderate man, compiling his manual on the propagation of
the faith, with chapters on the detection of witchcraft and
the suppression of heresy. One can imagine his conscientious
discussions of the most effective methods of obtaining confessions from recalcitrant persons—his nice comparisons of
the rival merits of the thumbscrew and the rack. Instead of
saying, for instance, as he now says, *apropos* of air raids—"In
the course of these raids some unfortified places without
military significance have had to suffer. The bombardment
of these places is in itself objectionable, but the limits of

what is permissible are in this matter in many ways elastic"
—one can picture him pointing out, with the same perfect
reasonableness, the practical difficulties which sometimes
stand in the way of an ideal administration of torture—how
the executioner, with the best will in the world, may be com-
pelled to break the wrists when he only means to dislocate
the shoulders, that this is "in itself objectionable," but that
in such cases "the limits of what is permissible are in many
ways elastic" for the greater glory, not of Germany, but of
God.

That remarkable branch of Theology, known as "apologetic," also has its counterpart in the Baron's book. He devotes a few perfunctory pages to a militarist apologetic, in
which, precisely in the manner of the theologian, he knocks
over a few dummy opponents and advances triumphantly
to a foregone conclusion. It is not that the validity of militarism is for a moment in doubt; it is simply that without
these little dialectical flourishes something might still be
wanting to the perfect realisation of its beauty and its truth.
There is a certain formality in such high matters, which must
be gone through with a fitting solemnity. It would never do
to make no mention of the well-known fact that eternal
peace is a sentimentalist's dream, and of the equally familiar
truths that peace is really not a desirable end, and that, at
the same time, the justification of militarism is that it en-
sures peace (date of writing, A.D. 1917). Above all it is necessary to state that "war has its basis in human nature, and as
long as human nature remains unaltered war will," etc., etc.
—it would be quite improper to leave that out. What, indeed,
could be more self-evident? War has its basis in human nature: it must be so, for the Baron, looking back through history, observes that "war has existed for thousands of years";
and besides—a still more cogent argument—the Baron himself, a moderate man, a representative specimen of human

nature taken in the bulk, feels intimately convinced of the
necessity of war through all eternity. Perhaps! But since the
Baron has appealed to history, to history let us go. Bearing
in mind our theological parallel, let us imagine the Baron
in the last decade of the seventeenth century, surveying the
world with the eye of a moderate and a deeply religious man.
What would he have seen? Undoubtedly that religion was
the dominating factor in human affairs; that religious questions had moulded the whole polity of Europe for the last
1,400 years; that at that moment theological animosity was
as strong as ever it had been—so strong that Louis XIV, by
revoking the Edict of Nantes, had just committed an act of
extraordinary barbarity, alienated half Europe, and dealt a
fatal blow to the prosperity of France, merely in order that
his religious zeal might find satisfaction. Surely the Baron
would have remarked that intolerance had its basis in human
nature, that religious wars were a part of the constitution of
the universe, and would have felt, too, with the enormous
majority of his contemporaries, quite certain that such a
state of things was not only inevitable but, somehow or other,
right. If he had been a Catholic he would have justified the
dragonnades, as Bossuet did in fact justify them—Bossuet, the
moderate man *par excellence* of that period, whose writings,
owing to the accident of a gorgeous prose style, still survive
to reveal to readers of today the singular limitations of average passions and average thoughts. For within a generation
of the time when the excellent bishop was proving in faultless periods the transcendent import of religion in history
and politics, and the necessity of religious persecution and
religious war, the religious motive had quietly slipped away
altogether from the affairs of nations, and the age of toleration had begun. Civilisation, taking a sudden turn round a
corner, had put the theological frenzies of so many centuries
behind it for ever.

How this happened—how it was that the moderate man whose views were expressed by Bossuet, became transformed into the moderate man whose views were expressed by Montesquieu and Hume—is no doubt a "puzzling question"; but, whatever the causes of the change may have been, two things about it are certain—it was radical and it took place very quickly. There was a greater gulf between Montesquieu and Bossuet than between Bossuet and Bernard of Clairvaux; and Montesquieu might have been Bossuet's son. And perhaps in this consideration we may find some comfort when we next open Baron von Freytag-Loringhoven's depressing book. In spite of all the Baron may say, human nature does change, and it changes sometimes with remarkable rapidity. To moderate men like him, it may well be that militarism and the implications of militarism—the struggles and ambitions of opposing States, the desire for national power, the terror of national ruin, the armed organisation of humanity —that all this seems inevitable with the inevitability of a part of the world's very structure; and yet it may well be, too, that they are wrong, that it is not so, that it is the "fabric of a vision" which will melt suddenly and be seen no more. And in that case what will become of the Baron's book? Will it be read in after ages as a curious example of the aberrations of the moderate man? Alas! probably not; for its style, we fancy, is hardly as good as Bossuet's.

1918.

14. The Claims of Patriotism

THERE are various kinds of patriotism: there is the patriotism of a Mazzini, and there is the patriotism of a —well, let us say the patriotism defined by Dr. Johnson as "the last refuge of a scoundrel." Between these two extremes there is an almost infinite series of gradations; and it is precisely owing to this uncertainty in the connotation of the word that discussions upon the subject are apt to be unsatisfactory. Thus when Mr. J. A. R. Marriott, in his new book,[1] tells us that Shakespeare was "nothing if not a patriot," and that he was "keenly sensitive to every beat of the nation's pulse," he really does not tell us very much; the same might be said with equal truth of Joan of Arc and Lord Northcliffe and Kossuth and the Kaiser. The brand of Mr. Marriott's own patriotism, however, is easier to determine. He is clearly one of those who will "stick at nothing"; his love of his country is limited neither by the meagre bounds of the actual nor by the tiresome dictates of common sense. In his new book he emulates the ardour of those zealous patriots who, as we all unfortunately know, despatched the halt and the lame into the army in order to win the war. It suddenly occurred to him that nobody had thought of enlisting Shakespeare (and the omission was indeed a curious one); so now he has put the author of *Hamlet* into khaki; and if we don't win the war after that it will not be the fault of Mr. Marriott. Shakespeare's historical plays

[1] *English History in Shakespeare.* By J. A. R. Marriott. Chapman & Hall.

have, he is convinced, "for England and the English-speaking world, a political message, the significance of which cannot at this moment of our history be over-emphasised." The phraseology reminds us that Mr. Marriott is a Member of Parliament; for all his enthusiasm, he expresses himself with the carefully qualified moderation of a public man. But what precisely *is* the message of Shakespeare's historical plays to England and the English-speaking world? Apparently, it is as follows: "To the safety of the State and the well-being of the Commonwealth the union of all parties and classes is, above all else, essential." Mr. Marriott, for close on three hundred pages, has gone through, one by one, with painful and scrupulous care, the chronicle plays of Shakespeare; and this is the conclusion he arrives at; this is the "message" the "significance of which cannot, at this moment of our history, be over-emphasised."

That Mr. Marriott should have supposed for a moment that such a lame and impotent conclusion was worth—we will not say the paper it was written on—but the trouble, the energy, the effort of scholarship which have gone to the making of this book, is surely very strange; in fact, it is so strange that only patriotism (in one form or another) can account for it. If only the War Office authorities had been a little less patriotic they might have perceived that it was foolish to fill the army with imbeciles and epileptics; and similarly perhaps, if Mr. Marriott had been a little less patriotic, he might have seen that as a political protagonist "at this moment of our history" Shakespeare was really no go; and that Shakespeare's historical plays contain no "message" whatever—no, not even that singularly flat, stale, and unprofitable one which Mr. Marriott, with infinite labour, has dragged out of them. The quality and the quantity of Shakespeare's patriotism might, no doubt, form an interesting sub-

ject for an essay on literary psychology. But such an essay
could not fail to be absurdly superficial, unless it recognised,
what surely must be obvious to everyone after very slight
reflection, that many of the most important of Shakespeare's
so-called historical plays are not, in any true sense of the
word, historical at all. *Richard II* is not a historical play. It is
not concerned with constitutional questions, or with national
questions, or with any attempt to represent a state of society
in a past age. It is a study—a subtle, sympathetic, and exquisitely moving study—of the introspective and morbid temperament of a minor poet who happened also to be a king.
Again, the vital parts of *Henry IV* are by no means historical: they are a presentment of the contemporary tavern
life of Elizabethan London. These scenes, no doubt, are
placed in a setting of events and characters which may be
called by courtesy "historical"; but it is noticeable that, as
the action proceeds, the vividness of this setting steadily
diminishes, until at last, towards the end of the Second Part,
Shakespeare only reverts with difficulty to his King and his
rebellious noblemen, with whom he has grown frankly bored.
The plain truth is that no light whatever can be thrown
upon the nature of Shakespeare's patriotism by the kind of
minute and learned examination which Mr. Marriott has
devoted to such plays as these. The question must be approached from a different angle; and it would be an excellent thing if Mr. Marriott himself were again to try his hand
at it—after the war.

In the meantime, his present book confronts us, telling us
far more about Mr. Marriott's own patriotism than about
Shakespeare's. And perhaps, "at this moment of our history,"
that is as well. Shakespeare can wait. But the kind of patriotism which urges a Member of Parliament to write a
thick, elaborate book in order to prove that Shakespeare was
in favour of national unity is a phenomenon at once so

strange and so full of actuality that it deserves some notice. Nor is this all. Mr. Marriott's historical sense, no less than his literary sense, seems to have become curiously twisted. His book contains a panegyric of the Tudors; the Tudor monarchy was, he tells us, "a dictatorship"; and dictatorships are justified in times of crisis, because they ensure that national unity which is essential to "the safety of the State and the well-being of the Commonwealth." It is difficult to be certain whether the reader is or is not intended to infer from this that, both in Mr. Marriott's opinion and in Shakespeare's, he should refrain from criticising Mr. Lloyd George; but, in any case, it is surely extraordinary that an English Member of Parliament should apparently have forgotten that it was not through national unity but national disunion that the people of England won their liberties. This, however, is the kind of forgetfulness that Mr. Marriott's patriotism leads him to. The disease is common; yet, after all, it is perhaps difficult to say whether the true cause of it is too much patriotism or too little. The lover who loved his mistress with such passionate ecstasy that he would feed her on nothing but moonshine, with disastrous consequences— did he, perhaps, in reality, not love her quite enough? That, certainly, is a possible reading of the story. And it might be as well for patriots of Mr. Marriott's order to reflect occasionally on that sad little apologue, and to remember that nothing sweetens love—even love of one's country—so much as a little common sense—and, one might add, even a little cynicism. Mr. Marriott himself professes a profound admiration for Queen Elizabeth. She had faults, he confesses, but the "saving salt" of her character lay in her love of England. Yes; but surely there was something about her patriotism that would have distressed Mr. Marriott. For it was a patriotism which paid a very strict attention to disagreeable facts; which was never agitated and never sentimental, which did not deal in pompous platitudes; and which—a not unimportant detail—was always ready to explore every avenue to peace.

1918.

IV

LATER ESSAYS

1. Shakespeare at Cambridge

PERHAPS the best way of realising the implications involved in the fact that the war is over is to pay a visit
to one of the Universities. In London the enormous human
mechanism, in the country the inevitable processes of nature,
serve to conceal the depth of the social change. Somehow or
other, in war as in peace, London lives and works and
amuses itself; and the woods grow green, and the rain and
the sun bring in the harvest. But, to the Universities, the
difference between war and peace was literally the difference
between death and life; when the war ended, they went
through a transformation as complete and sudden as that of
a Russian spring; all at once, after the icy season of sterility,
the sap has begun to flow again, and the exuberance of youth
is made manifest. It is delightful—it is almost incredible—to
see college courts with caps and gowns in them, and swishing
boats tearing after one another on academic streams. Among
other symptoms of this rejuvenescence one welcomes with
peculiar pleasure the reappearance at Cambridge of the Marlowe Society which, with unhesitating vigour, has been re-
viving its pre-war traditions by a production of the First
Part of *King Henry IV*. The Marlowe Society is an under-
graduate body, full of the spirit of youth; and it was primarily as a spontaneous expression both of the high purposes
of youth and of youthful delight in beauty that its rendering
of *Henry IV* must have struck the more mature among the
audience. That young men should have come together, so

soon and so eagerly, to enjoy themselves thus—with candour, with painstaking, with geniality—was surely an admirable thing.

Yet it was not merely from the symptomatic point of view that the performance was interesting. The *blasé* critic might naturally have expected that the pleasure of the evening would be found mainly on the other side of the footlights— that on *his* side it would be chiefly of the reflected kind. The play is not an easy one to act. The Falstaff scenes, with their extraordinary mingling of brilliant wit, sheer fun, and psychological profundity, seem to cry out for acting that is something more than passable—for acting that is really great —and, in addition, for that most difficult product of stage artistry—a perfectly manipulated *ensemble*. On the other hand, the "historical" scenes, with their long speeches and sonorous verse, seem to lack action, and, except for the figure of Hotspur, to be too deficient in character to be made much of, save by actors of high accomplishment. The event, however, was full of surprises. The first, instantaneous impression was one of immense relief. The King was speaking. The *blasé* critic might well prick up his ears. How very rarely has a King been heard to speak on any stage! Yet that was what this King, unmistakably, was doing. He was neither mouthing, nor gesticulating, nor rolling his eyes, nor singing, nor chopping his words into mincemeat, nor dragging them out in slow torment up and down the diatonic scale; he was simply speaking; and as he spoke one became conscious of a singular satisfaction—of soothing harmonies, of lovely language flowing in fine cadences, of beautiful images unwinding beautifully, of the subtle union of thought and sound. He ceased, and another speaker followed, and yet another; and the charm remained unbroken. This, then, was the first surprise—the delight of hearing the blank verse of Shakespeare spoken unaffectedly and with the intonation of civilised English; the next was the perception of the fact that, given a good delivery of the verse, the interest of drama and character automatically followed. These scenes, once realised, were something more than mere poetical declamation; for poetical declamation grows dull, and the King, and Worcester, and Westmoreland, and the rest, were never dull for a moment. The words, devised with the supreme skill of Shakespeare's early maturity, required the minimum of acting; all that was needed was their straightforward enunciation by living human beings on a stage; Shakespeare did the rest. Without effort, without fuss, one's imagination was seized and occupied: a few undergraduates became a group of intriguing statesmen, whose minds were full of interest, and whose deliberations were full of moment. Curiously enough, the one character which failed to make an impression was the very one which seemed to offer the easiest opportunity for a success. But here the exception proved the rule; for the part of Hotspur was taken by an actor who had evidently learned to "act." The result was inevitable. A thick veil of all the elocutionary arts and graces—points, gestures, exaggerations, and false emphases—was thrown over the words of Shakespeare, and in the process Hotspur vanished as effectually as if he had been at His Majesty's. In the Falstaff scenes Shakespeare again triumphed. A Prince Hal who is really young, a Poins who really laughs, a Falstaff who is neither inaudible nor inebriated—with such blessings one can put up with a weak *ensemble,* and only momentarily reflect upon the opportunities for great acting.

It is difficult not to wish that all performances of Shakespeare could resemble that of the Marlowe Society. Is it impossible that they should? Clearly, one great difficulty stands in the way. The actors at Cambridge were obviously amateurs in the fullest sense of the term. They had never learned to act, and therefore their acting had the charm of unselfconsciousness—the charm of primitive art and the drawing and poetry of children. But as soon as the amateur becomes the professional—as soon, that is to say, as he makes a serious and continued practice of his art—self-consciousness necessarily arises, and with self-consciousness the way is opened to the preposterous conventions of the modern stage. The young actor begins to "act," and all is over. But is this inevitable? Is there no means of arriving at self-consciousness without the fatal accompaniments of a bad tradition? It is plain that what is needed is a new tradition, and the conclusion suggests itself that the best hope for a new tradition lies in the deliberate development of the instinctive style of the amateur. If the young actor could only be taught that he has to unlearn nothing, that he must preserve at all costs his natural enunciation, his economy of gesture, his sobriety of emotional expression, that it is his business, not to "interpret" Shakespeare's words, but to speak them, that the first rule for acting Shakespeare is to trust him—how incalculable would the improvement be! One can conceive, with a very little direction, a very little imaginative control, the actors of the Marlowe Society evolving a style of Shakespeare acting which would attain to a permanent excellence—which would be classical, like the acting of Molière at the *théâtre français*. But this is still far off. At present, while dreaming of a perfect instrument, one is fortunate to hear, now and then, the breath of Apollo in a reed.

1919.

2. Voltaire

BETWEEN the collapse of the Roman Empire and the
Industrial Revolution three men were the intellectual
masters of Europe—Bernard of Clairvaux, Erasmus, and Voltaire. In Bernard the piety and the superstition of the Middle Ages attained their supreme embodiment; in Erasmus
the learning and the humanity of the Renaissance. But Erasmus was a tragic figure. The great revolution in the human
mind, of which he had been the presiding genius, ended in
failure; he lived to see the tide of barbarism rising once
more over the world; and it was left to Voltaire to carry off
the final victory. By a curious irony, the Renaissance contained within itself the seeds of its ruin. That very enlight-
enment which seemed to be leading the way to the unlimited progress of the race involved Europe in the internecine
struggles of nationalism and religion. England alone, by a
series of accidents, of which the complexion of Anne Boleyn,
a storm in the Channel, and the character of Charles I were
the most important, escaped disaster. There the spirit of
Reason found for itself a not too precarious home; and by
the beginning of the eighteenth century a civilisation had
been evolved which, in essentials, was not very far distant
from the great ideals of the Renaissance. In the meantime
the rest of Europe had relapsed into mediaevalism. If Bernard of Clairvaux had returned to life at the end of the
seventeenth century, he would have been perfectly at home
at Madrid, and not at all uncomfortable at Versailles. At

239

last, in France, the beginnings of a change became dis-
cernible. The incompetence of Louis XIV's government
threw discredit upon the principles of bigotry and ob-
scurantism; with the death of the old King there was a reaction among thinking men towards scepticism and toleration; and the movement was set on foot which ended,
seventy-five years later, in the French Revolution. Of this
movement Voltaire was the master spirit. For a generation he
was the commander-in-chief in the great war against mediaevalism. Eventually, by virtue of his extraordinary literary skill, his incredible energy, and his tremendous force
of character, he dominated Europe, and the victory was won.
The upheaval which followed, though it was perhaps inevitable, would certainly not have pleased him; but the violence of the French Revolution and its disastrous consequences were evils of small magnitude compared with the
new and terrible complication in which, at the very same
moment, mankind became involved. The ironical Fates were
at work again. By a strange chance, no sooner was mediaevalism dead than industrialism was born. The mechanical ingenuity of a young man in Glasgow plunged the world into
a whole series of enormous and utterly unexpected difficulties, which are still clamouring to be solved. Thus the progress which the Renaissance had envisioned, and which had
seemed assured at the end of the eighteenth century, was
once more side-tracked. Yet the work of Voltaire was not
undone. Short of some overwhelming catastrophe, the doctrine which he preached—that life should be ruled, not by
the dictates of tyranny and superstition, but by those of
reason and humanity—can never be obliterated from the
minds of men.

Voltaire's personal history was quite as remarkable as his
public achievement. Sense and sensibility were the two qualities which formed the woof and the warp of his life. Good

sense was the basis of his being—that supreme good sense which shows itself not only in taste and judgment, but in every field of activity—in an agile adaptation of means to ends, in an unerring acumen in the practical affairs of the world; and Voltaire would probably have become a great lawyer, or possibly a great statesman, had not this fundamental characteristic of his been shot through and through by a vehement sensitiveness—a nervous susceptibility of amazing intensity, which impregnated his solidity with a fierce electric fluid, and made him an artist, an egotist, a delirious enthusiast, dancing, screaming, and gesticulating to the last moment of an extreme old age. This latter quality was no doubt largely the product of physical causes—of an overstrung nervous system and a highly capricious digestion. He was in fact an excellent example of his own theory, propounded when he was over eighty in the delicious *Les Oreilles du Comte de Chesterfield*, that the prime factor in the world's history has always been *la chaise percée*. So constituted, it was almost inevitable that he should take to the profession of letters—the obvious career for a lively and intelligent young man—and, in particular, that he should write tragedies, the tragedy holding in those days the place of the novel in our own. Naturally he was precocious; and by the time he was thirty he was a successful dramatist and a fashionable poet, enjoying a royal pension and the flattering attentions of high society. Then there was a catastrophe which changed his whole life. He quarrelled with the Chevalier de Rohan, was beaten by hired roughs, found himself ridiculed and cut by his fine friends, and finally shut up in the Bastille. This was the first of a long chain of circumstances which ultimately made him the champion of liberty in Europe. But for the Chevalier de Rohan he might have been engulfed in the successes and pleasures of the capital. The *coups de bâton* suddenly made him serious: never again was he satisfied with the state of the world.

The importance of his English exile, which followed, has usually been exaggerated. Voltaire did not need to learn infidelity from the English deists, and he never did learn very much about English political institutions. England was not a cause, but a symbol of his discontent. His book upon the subject was his first definite declaration of war upon the old *régime*, and it was burnt accordingly by the common hangman. It might have been supposed that his course was now clear, that he was embarked, once and for all, on a career of struggle and propaganda. But this was not the case. Circumstance intervened once more, in the shape of the eccentric and terrific Madame du Châtelet, who carried him off to her remote country house, and kept him there for fifteen years engaged on scientific experiments. This long period, which filled the middle years of his life (from forty to fifty-five), though it seems at first sight to have been almost wasted, was in reality a blessing in disguise, for it gave him what was absolutely essential for his future work—a European reputation. When Madame du Châtelet died (at exactly the right moment), Voltaire was recognised not merely as the greatest living dramatist and poet, and as a brilliant exponent of new ideas, but as a man of encyclopaedic knowledge, whose claim to rank as a solid and serious thinker it was impossible to dismiss. All that was needed to put the crown upon his celebrity was some piece of resoundingly personal *réclame;* and this was provided by the Berlin episode, with its splendid opening, its preposterous developments, its hectic climax, and its violent close.

At the age of sixty Voltaire was the most famous man in the world. Yet it is strange to think that his fame was founded on achievements that were almost entirely ephemeral, and that if he had died then he would be remembered now

merely as an overrated poet and a very clever man. His first
sixty years were in reality nothing but an apprenticeship for
those that were to follow. Settled down at last at Ferney, on
the borders of France and Switzerland, perfectly independent, with the large fortune which his business shrewdness
had amassed for him, with his colossal reputation, and his
pen, Voltaire began the work of his life. Apart from his personal prowess, most of the elements in the situation were
favourable to him. The time was ripe: the new movement
was like an engine which had slowly risen up a long and
steep ascent, and was standing at the top, waiting for a master hand to propel it forward and downward with irresistible
force. But there were two contingencies, either of which
might at any moment have proved fatal. Everything depended upon Voltaire's continuing at Ferney for a considerable time: it was clearly impossible to *écraser l'infâme* in
a year or so. Yet how many years could he count upon?
With his abominable health, he had very little reason to
hope for a long old age. Nevertheless, a very long old age
was granted him. Incredible as it seemed, he lived to be
eighty-four, maintaining the whole vigour of his extraordinary vitality to the last second of his existence: for a quarter
of a century he worked with his full power. The other danger lay in the curious fact that he himself never quite realised the strength of his position. In his restless egotism he
was perpetually trying to get leave to return to Paris; and
if he had succeeded the greater part of his influence would
almost certainly have disappeared. At Ferney he was his own
master; he was safe from the intrigues of the capital; and his
remoteness invested him and everything about him with the
mysterious grandeur of a myth. If the authorities had had
the slightest foresight, they would have welcomed him with
open arms to Paris, where his time would have been wasted
in society, where his quarrelsomeness would have landed

him sooner or later in some dreadful mess, where, inevitably, the "patriarch" would at last have vanished altogether in the very fallible old gentleman. It was the final stroke of luck in an amazingly lucky life that Voltaire should have been saved from his own folly by the folly of his enemies.

The history of the years at Ferney is written at large in that gigantic correspondence which forms one of the most impressive monuments of human energy known to the world. Besides the vast body of facts which it contains, besides the day-to-day record of a moving and memorable struggle, besides the exquisite beauty, the aesthetic perfection, of its form, there emerges from it, with peculiar distinctness, the vision of a human spirit. It cannot be said that that vision is altogether a pleasing one. There is a natural tendency—visible in England, perhaps, especially—towards the elegant embellishment of great men; and Voltaire has not escaped the process. In Miss Tallentyre's translation, for instance, of a small selection from his letters, with an introduction and notes,[1] Voltaire is presented to us as a kindly, gentle, respectable personage, a tolerant, broad-minded author, who ended his life as a country gentleman much interested in the drama and social reform. Such a picture would be merely ridiculous, if it were not calculated to mislead. The fact that Voltaire devoted his life to one of the noblest of causes must not blind us to another fact—that he was personally a very ugly customer. He was a frantic, desperate fighter, to whom all means were excusable; he was a trickster, a rogue; he lied, he blasphemed, and he was extremely indecent. He was, too, quite devoid of dignity, adopting, whenever he saw fit, the wildest expedients and the most extravagant postures; there was, in fact, a strong element of farce in his character, which he had the wit to exploit for his

[1] *Voltaire in his Letters. Being a Selection from his Correspondence.* Translated with a Preface and Forewords by S. G. Tallentyre. Murray.

own ends. At the same time he was inordinately vain, and mercilessly revengeful; he was as mischievous as a monkey, and as cruel as a cat. At times one fancies him as a puppet on wires, a creature raving in a mechanical frenzy—and then one remembers that lucid, piercing intellect, that overwhelming passion for reason and liberty. The contradiction is strange; but the world is full of strange contradictions; and, on the whole, it is more interesting, and also wiser, to face them than to hush them up.

1919.

3. Walpole's Letters

THESE two long-expected volumes,[1] which complete and perfect Mrs. Paget Toynbee's great edition of Horace Walpole's Letters, will be welcomed by every lover of English scholarship. They contain a hundred and eleven hitherto unpublished letters, of which the most interesting are a series written in Italy to Sir Horace Mann and two childish letters to Lady Walpole, reproduced in facsimile. Among the letters published elsewhere, but not contained in Mrs. Toynbee's edition, are an important group addressed to Henry Fox and all that is still extant of Walpole's part in his correspondence with Madame du Deffand. But the volumes are chiefly valuable for their mass of *corrigenda* and for the new light which they throw upon a multitude of minor matters. This additional information is almost entirely derived from the remarkable and only lately discovered collection of Walpole MSS. in the possession of Sir Wathen Waller—a collection containing, as Mr. Toynbee tells us, "private journals, note-books, and commonplace books of Horace Walpole, together with numerous letters addressed to him, marked 'for illustration,' which had been carefully preserved by Walpole in a series of letter-books, evidently with a view to their eventual utilisation in the annotation of his own letters"; and we are glad to hear that we may look forward to the appearance of "the most interesting portions of this

[1] *Supplement to the Letters of Horace Walpole, Fourth Earl of Orford.* Chronologically arranged and edited, with notes and indices, by Paget Toynbee, D.Litt. 2 vols. Oxford: Clarendon Press.

material in two further supplementary volumes." It would
be impossible to overrate Mr. Toynbee's erudition, industry,
and exactness; owing to his labours and those of the late Mrs.
Toynbee, we now possess an edition of this great classic truly
worthy of its immense and varied interests—historical, biographical, political, psychological—and its potent literary
charm. The reader who merely reads for entertainment will
find a volume of this edition a perfect companion for a holi-
day; while its elaborate apparatus of notes, indices, and ta-
bles will supply the learned inquirer with everything that
his heart can desire. One blemish, and one only, can we discover in it: the omission of numerous passages on the score
of impropriety. Surely, in a work of such serious intention
and such monumental proportions the publication of the
whole of the original material was not only justifiable, but
demanded by the nature of the case.

Good letters are like pearls: they are admirable in themselves, but their value is infinitely enhanced when there is
a string of them. Therefore, to be a really great letter writer
it is not enough to write an occasional excellent letter; it is
necessary to write constantly, indefatigably, with ever-recur-
ring zest; it is almost necessary to live to a good old age.
What makes a correspondence fascinating is the cumulative
effect of slow, gradual, day-to-day development—the long,
leisurely unfolding of a character and a life. The Walpole
correspondence has this merit in a peculiar degree; its enormous progression carries the reader on and on through sixty
years of living. Even if the individual letters had been dull,
and about tedious things, a collection on such a scale would
hardly have failed to be full of interest. But Walpole's letters are far from dull, and, placed as he was in the very centre
of a powerful and brilliant society, during one of the most
attractive epochs of English history, the topics upon which
he writes are very far from tedious. The result is something

that is certainly unique in our literature. Though from the point of view of style, or personal charm, or originality of observation, other letter writers may deserve a place at least on an equality with that of Walpole, it is indisputable that the collected series of his letters forms by far the most important single correspondence in the language.

The achievement was certainly greater than the man. Walpole, in fact, was not great at all; though it would be a mistake to suppose that he was the fluttering popinjay of Macaulay's picture. He had great ability and great industry. Though it amused him to pose as a mere fine gentleman, he was in reality a learned antiquary and a shrewd politician; in the history of taste he is remarkable as one of the originators of the Gothic revival; as a writer, apart from his letters, he is important as the author of a series of memoirs which are both intrinsically interesting and of high value as historical material. Personally, he was, of course, affected and foppish in a variety of ways; he had the narrowness and the self-complacency of an aristocrat; but he also had an aristocrat's distinction and reserve; he could be affectionate in spite of his politeness, and towards the end of his life, in his relations with Miss Berry, he showed himself capable of deep feeling. Nevertheless, compare him with the master-spirits of his generation, and it becomes clear at once that he was second-rate. He was as far removed from the humanity of Johnson as from the passion of Burke and the intellectual grasp of Gibbon. His dealings with Chatterton were not particularly discreditable (though he lied heavily in his subsequent account of them); but, in that odd momentary concatenation, beside the mysterious and tragic figure of the "marvellous boy," the worldly old creature of Strawberry Hill seems to wither away into limbo.

The mediocrity of the man has sometimes—by Macaulay among others—been actually suggested as the cause of the excellence of his letters. But this will not do. There is no necessary connection between second-rateness and good letter-writing. The correspondences of Voltaire and of Keats —to take two extremely dissimilar examples—show that it is possible to write magnificent letters, and also to be a man of genius. Perhaps the really essential element in the letter writer's make-up is a certain strain of femininity. The unmixed male—the great man of action, the solid statesman— does not express himself happily on those little bits of paper that go by the post. The medium is unsuitable. Nobody ever could have expected to get a good letter from Sir Robert Peel. It is true that the Duke of Wellington wrote very good letters; but the Duke, who was an exception to all rules, holds a peculiar place in the craft: he reminds one in his letters of a music-hall comedian who has evolved a single inimitable trick, which has become his very own, which is invariably produced, and as invariably goes down. The female element is obvious in Cicero, the father—or should we say the mother?—of the familiar letter. Among English writers, Swift and Carlyle, both of whom were anxious to be masculine, are disappointing correspondents; Swift's letters are too dry (a bad fault), and Carlyle's are too long (an even worse one). Gray and Cowper, on the other hand, in both of whom many of the qualities of the gentler sex are visible, wrote letters which reached perfection; and in the curious composition of Gibbon (whose admirable correspondence is perhaps less read than it deserves) there was decidedly a touch of the she-cat, the naughty old maid. In Walpole himself it is easy to perceive at once the sinuosity and grace of a fine lady, the pettishness of a dowager, the love of trifles of a maiden aunt, and even, at moments, the sensitiveness of a girl.

Another quality is perhaps equally important: the great letter writer must be an egotist. Only those who are extremely

249

interested in themselves possess the overwhelming pertinacity of the born correspondent. No good letter was ever written to convey information, or to please its recipient: it may achieve both those results incidentally; but its fundamental purpose is to express the personality of the writer. This is true of love-letters no less than of others. A desperate egotism burns through the passionate pages of Mademoiselle de Lespinasse; and it is easy to see, in spite of her adoring protestations, that there was *one* person in the world more interesting to Madame de Sévigné than Madame de Grignan. Walpole's letters, with all their variety of appeal, are certainly a case in point. They may be read for many reasons; but the final, the attaching reason is the revelation which they contain of a human being. It is, indeed, a revelation of a curious kind—an uncertain, ambiguous revelation, shifty, deceptive, for ever incomplete. And there the fascination lies. As one reads, the queer man gets hold of one; one reads on—one cannot help it; the long, alembicated sentences, the jauntiness, the elegance, the faint disdain—one grows familiar with it all—and the glitter of the eyes through the mask. But it is impossible to stop: perhaps, just once—who knows?—when no one else is looking, the mask may be lifted; or there may be another, a subtler, change in the turn of the speech. Until at last one comes to feel that one knows that long-vanished vision as well as a living friend—one of those enigmatical friends about whom one is perpetually in doubt as to whether, in spite of everything, one *does* know them at all.

1919.

4. Dizzy

THE absurd Jew-boy, who set out to conquer the world, reached his destination. It is true that he had gone through a great deal, a very great deal, to get there—four volumes by Mr. Buckle and Mr. Monypenny. But there he was. After a lifetime of relentless determination, infinite perseverance and superhuman egotism, he found himself at last old, hideous, battered, widowed, solitary, diseased, but Prime Minister of England. Mr. Buckle's last two volumes [1] show him to us in this final stage—the stage of attainment. The efflorescent Dizzy, Earl of Beaconsfield and Knight of the Garter, stands before us. It is a full-length portrait: twelve hundred pages tell the story of twelve years. Much is revealed to us—much of the highest interest, both personal and public—the curious details of political complexities, a royal correspondence, the internecine quarrels of cabinets, a strange love affair, the thrilling *peripeteia* of world-shaking negotiations, the outside and the inside of high affairs, and yet—why is it? the revelation seems to be incomplete. Is this really everything, one wonders, or was there something else? *Can* this be everything? Is this, in truth, greatness? Can this, and nothing more, have been the end of all those palpitating struggles, the reward of energies so extraordinary, and capacities so amazing? The sinister, mysterious features return one's stare with their mummy-like inscrutability. "What

[1] *The Life of Benjamin Disraeli, Earl of Beaconsfield.* By George Earle Buckle, in succession to W. F. Monypenny. Vols. V and VI. John Murray.

more do you want to know?" they seem to whisper. "I have conquered the world." "Yes, you have conquered the world —granted," we answer. "But *then—?*" Silence.

A moralist, with the pen of a Thackeray, might, indeed, make great play with these twelve hundred pages. He could compile a very pretty sermon out of them, on the text of the vanity of human ambition. He could draw a striking picture of the aged vainglorious creature, racked by gout and asthma, dyed and corseted, with the curl on his miserable old forehead kept in its place all night by a bandana handkerchief, clutching at power, prostrating himself before royalty, tottering to congresses, wheezing out his last gasps, with indefatigable snobbery, at fashionable dinner-tables; and then, with all his shrewdness and his worldly wisdom, so easily taken in!—a dupe of the glittering outsides of things; a silly, septuagenarian child, keeping itself quiet with a rattle of unrealities, unreal patriotism, and unreal loyalty, and unreal literature, and unreal love. Only, unfortunately, the picture would be a little crude. There would be a considerable degree of truth in it, no doubt, but it would miss the really interesting point. It would be the picture of a remarkable, entertaining, edifying figure, but not an important one —a figure that might, after all, be ignored. And Dizzy could not be ignored. He was formidable—one of the most formidable men who ever lived. His conduct of the European negotiations which reached their climax in the Congress of Berlin—laid before us with illuminating detail by Mr. Buckle—reveals a mind in which all the great qualities of action—strength, courage, decision, foresight—were combined to form an engine of tremendous power. It is clear that Bismarck was right in treating him almost if not quite, as an equal; and to have been almost the equal of Bismarck is to have been something very considerable indeed. Nor, of course, was he merely a man of action. He had the nervous sensibility of an artist, living every moment of his life with acute self-consciousness, and observing the world around him with the quick discrimination of an artist's eye. His letters, like his novels, are full of a curious brilliance—an irony more latent than expressed, an artificiality which, somehow or other, is always to the point; and some of his phrases have probably achieved immortality. The puzzle is that so many varied and splendid qualities should, in the aggregate, leave such an unsatisfying impression upon the mind. The gorgeous sphinx seems to ring hollow after all. Never, one guesses, was so much power combined with so little profundity. The intrepid statesman drifts through politics without a purpose; the veteran man of the world is fascinated by the paraphernalia of smart parties; the author of *Endymion* is more ridiculously ingenuous than the author of *The Young Visiters*. He could not, he said, at the age of seventy-four, "at all agree with the great King that all is vanity." One wonders why. It is certainly very difficult to find anything in these twelve hundred pages which is not vanity—excepting, of course, the approbation of Queen Victoria. The correspondence with Lady Bradford is typical of the whole strange case. To pursue, when one is seventy and Prime Minister, a Countess who is fifty-six and a grandmother, with protestations of eternal passion, appears to have presented itself to Dizzy quite genuinely as the secret culmination of his career. Thus, under the rococo futilities of his adoration, a feeling that is not entirely a simulacrum is perceptible—a feeling, not towards the lady, but towards himself and the romantic, the dazzling, and yet the melancholy circumstances of his life. One perceives that in spite of his years and his experience and his cynicism, he never grew old; under all his trappings the absurd Jew-boy is visible till the very end.

But perhaps, in reality, it is a mistake to look at the matter from the moralist's point of view. Perhaps it is as a history, not of values, but of forces, that this long ambiguous, agitated existence should be considered. One would see it then as a mighty demonstration of energies—energies pitted against enormous obstacles, desperately struggling, miraculously triumphant, and attaining at last the apogee of self-expression, perfect and, from the very beginning, pre-ordained. Perhaps it is useless to enquire the object of it all. "Joy's life lies in the doing." Perhaps! Only, if that is so, joy's life is a singularly insubstantial thing. "Condition de l'homme—inconstance, ennui, inquiétude!" Let us moralise with Pascal, if we must moralise at all. And, in Dizzy's case, those three grim spectres seem always to be crouching behind the painted pasteboard scene. Probably, indeed, he never noticed them; for the old comedian, acting in his own most private theatre, with himself for audience, preferred not to question the solidity of the fairy palaces in which he played his marvellous part. But we, who, thanks to Mr. Buckle and Mr. Monypenny, have been provided with seats in the wings, can see only too clearly what lies on the other side of those flimsy erections. Such is the doom of the egotist. While he is alive, he devours all the happiness about him, like a grub on a leaf; but when he goes, the spectacle is not exhilarating. "Le dernier acte est sanglant, quelque belle que soit la comédie en tout le reste. On jette enfin de la terre sur la tête, et en voilà pour jamais."

1920.

5. Sarah Bernhardt

THERE are many paradoxes in the art of acting. One of them—the discrepancy between the real feelings of the actor and those which he represents—was discussed by Diderot in a famous dialogue. Another—the singular divergence between the art of the stage and the art of the drama—was illustrated very completely by the career of Sarah Bernhardt.

It is clear that the primary business of the actor is to interpret the conception of the dramatist; but it is none the less true that, after a certain degree of excellence has been reached, the merits of an actor have no necessary dependence upon his grasp of the dramatist's meaning. To be a moderately good actor one must understand, more or less, what one's author is up to; but the achievements of Sarah Bernhardt proved conclusively that it was possible to be a very good actor indeed without having the faintest notion, not only of the intentions of particular dramatists, but of the very rudiments of the dramatic art.

No one who saw her in *Hamlet* or in *Lorenzaccio* could doubt that this was so. Her *Hamlet* was a fantastic absurdity which far, far surpassed the permitted limits even of a Gallic miscomprehension of "le grand Will." But perhaps even more remarkable was her treatment of *Lorenzaccio. Hamlet,* after all, from every point of view, is an extremely difficult play; but the main drift of Musset's admirable tragedy is as plain as a pikestaff. It is a study in disillusionment—the disillusionment of a tyrannicide, who finds that the assassination, which he has contrived and executed with infinite hazard, skill, and difficulty, has merely resulted in a state of affairs even worse than before. Sarah Bernhardt, incredible as it may seem, brought down the final curtain on the murder of the tyrant, and thus made the play, as a play, absolutely pointless. What remained was a series of exciting scenes, strung together by the vivid and penetrating art of a marvellous actress. For art it was, and not mere posturing. Nothing could be further from the truth than to suppose that the great Frenchwoman belonged to that futile tribe of empty-headed impersonators, who, since Irving, have been the particular affliction of the English stage. Dazzling divinity though she was, she was also a serious, a laborious worker, incessantly occupied—not with expensive stage properties, elaborate make-up, and historically accurate scenery—but simply with acting. Sir Herbert Tree was ineffective because he neither knew nor cared how to act; he was content to be a clever entertainer. But Sarah Bernhardt's weakness, if weakness it can be called, arose from a precisely contrary reason—from the very plenitude of her power over all the resources of her craft—a mastery over her medium of so overwhelming a kind as to become an obsession.

The result was that this extraordinary genius was really to be seen at her most characteristic in plays of inferior quality. They gave her what she wanted. She did not want—she did not understand—great drama; what she did want were opportunities for acting; and this was the combination which the *Toscas*, the *Camélias*, and the rest of them, so happily provided. In them the whole of her enormous virtuosity in the representation of passion had full play; she could contrive thrill after thrill, she could seize and tear the nerves of her audience, she could touch, she could terrify, to the very top of her astonishing bent. In them, above all, she could ply her personality to the utmost. All acting must be, to some extent, an exploitation of the personality; but in the acting of Sarah Bernhardt that was the dominating quality—the fundamental element of her art. It was there that her strength, and her weakness, lay. During her best years, her personality remained an artistic instrument; but eventually it became too much for her. It absorbed both herself and her audience; the artist became submerged in the divinity; and what was genuine, courageous, and original in her character was lost sight of in oceans of highly advertised and quite indiscriminate applause.

This, no doubt, was partly due to the age she lived in. It is odd but certainly true that the eighteenth century would have been profoundly shocked by the actress who reigned supreme over the nineteenth. The gay and cynical creatures of the *ancien régime,* who tittered over *La Pucelle,* and whose adventures were reflected without exaggeration in the pages of *Les Liaisons Dangereuses,* would have recoiled in horror before what they would have called the "indécence" of one of Sarah Bernhardt's ordinary scenes. Every age has its own way of dealing with these matters; and the nineteenth century made up for the high tone of its literature and the decorum of its behaviour by the luscious intensity of its theatrical displays. Strict husbands in icy shirt-fronts and lovely epitomes of all the domestic virtues in bustles would sit for hours thrilling with frenzied raptures over intimate and elaborate presentments of passion in its most feverish forms. The supply and the demand, interacting upon one another, grew together. But by the end of the century the fashion had begun to change. The star of Eleonora Duse rose upon the horizon; Ibsen became almost popular; the Théâtre Antoine, the Moscow Art Theatre, introduced a new style of tragic acting—a prose style—surprisingly effective and surprisingly quiet, and subtle with the sinuosities of actual life. Already by the beginning of the twentieth century the bravura of Sarah Bernhardt seemed a magnificent relic of the past. And the generation which was to plunge with reckless fanaticism into the gigantic delirium of the war found its pleasures at the theatre in a meticulous imitation of the significant trivialities of middle-class interiors.

Fortunately, however, Sarah Bernhardt's genius did not spend itself entirely in amazing personal triumphs and the satisfaction of the emotional needs of a particular age. Fortunately the mightier genius of Jean Racine was of such a nature that it was able to lift hers on to its own level of the immortal and the universal. In this case there was no need on her part for an intellectual realisation of the dramatist's purpose; Racine had enough intellect for both; all that she had to do was to play the parts he had provided for her to the height of her ability; his supreme art did the rest. Her Hermione was a masterpiece; but certainly the greatest of all her achievements was in *Phèdre*. Tragedy possesses an extraordinary quality, which, perhaps, has given it its traditional place of primacy among all the forms of literature. It is not only immortal; it is also for ever new. There are infinite implications in it which reveal themselves by a mysterious law to each succeeding generation. The *Oedipus* acted yesterday at Cambridge was the identical play that won the prize two thousand years ago; and yet it was a different *Oedipus*, with meanings for the modern audience which were unperceived by the Athenians. The records show conclusively that the *Phèdre* of Bernhardt differed as much from that of Rachel as Rachel's differed from Clairon's, and as Clairon's differed from that of the great actress who created the part under the eyes of Racine. But each was *Phèdre*. Probably the latest of these interpretations was less perfect in all its parts than some of its predecessors; but the

great moments, when they came, could never have been surpassed. All through there were details of such wonderful
beauty that they return again and again upon the memory—
unforgettable delights. The hurried horror of

"Mes yeux le retrouvaient dans les traits de son père";

the slow, expanding, mysterious grandeur of

"Le ciel, tout l'univers, est plein de mes aïeux";

the marvellous gesture with which the words of Oenone,
announcing the approach of Thésée, seemed to be pressed
back into silence down her "ill-uttering throat"—such things,
and a hundred others, could only have been conceived and
executed by a consummate artist in her happiest vein. But
undoubtedly the topmost reach came in the fourth act, when
the Queen, her reason tottering with passion and jealousy,
suddenly turns upon herself in an agony of self-reproach.
Sarah Bernhardt's treatment of this passage was extremely
original, and it is difficult to believe that it was altogether
justified by the text. Racine's words seem to import a violent
directness of statement:

"Chaque mot sur mon front fait dresser mes cheveux";

but it was with hysteric irony, with dreadful, mocking
laughter, that the actress delivered them. The effect was absolutely overwhelming, and Racine himself could only have
bowed to the ground before such a triumphant audacity.
Then there followed the invocation to Minos, culminating
in the stupendous

"Je crois voir de ta main tomber l'urne terrible."

The secret of that astounding utterance baffles the imagination. The words boomed and crashed with a superhuman
resonance which shook the spirit of the hearer like a leaf in

the wind. The *voix d'or* has often been raved over; but in Sarah Bernhardt's voice there was more than gold: there was thunder and lightning; there was Heaven and Hell. But the pitcher is broken at the fountain; that voice is silent now for ever, and the Terror and the Pity that lived in it and purged the souls of mortals have faded into incommunicable dreams.

1923.

6. Pope[1]

AMONG the considerations that might make us rejoice or regret that we did not live in the eighteenth century, there is one that to my mind outbalances all the rest—if we had, we might have known Pope. At any rate, we have escaped that. We may lament that flowered waistcoats are forbidden us, that we shall never ride in a sedan-chair, and that we shall never see good Queen Anne taking tea at Hampton Court: but we can at least congratulate ourselves that we run no danger of waking up one morning to find ourselves exposed, both now and for ever, to the ridicule of the polite world—that we are hanging by the neck, and kicking our legs, on the elegant gibbet that has been put up for us by the little monster of Twit'nam. And, on the other hand, as it is, we are in the happy position of being able, quite imperturbably, to enjoy the fun. There is nothing so shamelessly selfish as posterity. To us, after two centuries, the agonies suffered by the victims of Pope's naughtiness are a matter of indifference; the fate of Pope's own soul leaves us cold. We sit at our ease, reading those *Satires* and *Epistles*, in which the verses, when they were written, resembled nothing so much as spoonfuls of boiling oil, ladled out by a fiendish monkey at an upstairs window upon such of the passers-by whom the wretch had a grudge against—and we are delighted. We would not have it otherwise: whatever is, is right.

[1] The Leslie Stephen Lecture for 1925.

In this there is nothing surprising; but what does seem strange is that Pope's contemporaries should have borne with him as they did. His attacks were by no means limited to Grub Street. He fell upon great lords and great ladies, duchesses and statesmen, noble patrons and beautiful women of fashion, with an equal ferocity; and such persons, in those days, were very well able to defend themselves. In France, the fate suffered by Voltaire, at that very time, and on far less provocation, is enough to convince us that such a portent as Pope would never have been tolerated on the other side of the Channel. The monkey would have been whipped into silence and good manners in double quick time. But in England it was different. Here, though "the Great," as they were called, were all-powerful, they preferred not to use their power against a libellous rhymer, who was physically incapable of protecting himself, and who, as a Roman Catholic, lay particularly open to legal pressure. The warfare between Pope and Lady Mary Wortley Montagu illustrates the state of affairs. The origin of their quarrel is uncertain. According to the lady, it was caused by her bursting into fits of laughter upon a declaration of passion from the poet. Another and perhaps more probable story traces the origin of the discord to a pair of sheets, borrowed by Lady Mary from old Mrs. Pope, the poet's mother, and returned by her ladyship, after a fortnight, unwashed. But whatever may have been the hidden cause of the quarrel, its results were obvious enough. Pope, in one of his *Imitations of Horace*, made a reference to "Sappho," whom all the world knew to be Lady Mary, in a couplet of extraordinary scurrility. Always a master of the art of compression, he asserted, in a single line of ten syllables, that his enemy, besides being a slanderous virago, was a debauched woman afflicted with a disgraceful malady. If, after this, Lady Mary had sent her friends or her footmen to inflict a personal chastisement upon the poet, or if she had used her influence with the government to have him brought to his senses, nobody could have been very much surprised. But she did nothing of the sort. Instead, she consulted with Lord Hervey, whom Pope had also attacked, and the two together decided to pay back their tormentor in his own coin. Accordingly they decocted and published a lampoon, in which they did their best to emulate both the style and the substance of the poet. "None," they declared,

"thy crabbed numbers can endure,
Hard as thy heart, and as thy birth obscure."

It shows, they said,

"the Uniformity of Fate
That one so odious should be born to hate."

And if

"Unwhipt, unblanketed, unkick'd, unslain,
That wretched little carcase you retain,
The reason is, not that the world wants eyes,
But thou'rt so mean, they see and they despise."

After sixty lines of furious abuse, they wound up with a shrug of the shoulders, which was far from convincing.

"You strike unwounding, we unhurt can laugh,"

they asseverated. But for the unhurt this was certainly very odd laughter. It was also quite ineffective. Pope's first reply was a prose pamphlet, in which there is at least one amusing passage—"It is true, my Lord, I am short, not well shaped, generally ill-dressed, if not sometimes dirty. Your Lordship and Ladyship are still in bloom, your figures such as rival the Apollo of Belvedere and the Venus of Medicis, and your faces so finished that neither sickness nor passion can deprive them of colour." But, of course, he reserved his most poisonous shafts for his poetry. Henceforth, his readers might be sure that in any especially unsavoury couplet the name of Sappho would be found immortally embedded; while, as for Lord Hervey, he met his final doom in the Character of Sporus—the most virulent piece of invective in the English language.

Lady Mary and Lord Hervey, clever as they were, had been so senseless as to try to fight Pope on his own ground, and, naturally enough, their failure was dismal. But why had they committed this act of folly? Their own explanation was the exact reverse of the truth. Far from despising the poet, they profoundly admired him. Hypnotised by his greatness, they were unable to prevent themselves from paying him the supreme compliment of an inept and suicidal imitation. And in this they were typical of the society in which they lived. That society was perhaps the most civilised that our history has known. Never, at any rate, before or since, has literature been so respected in England. Prior wrote well, and he became an ambassador. Addison wrote well, and he was made a Secretary of State. The Duke of Wharton gave Young £2000 for having written a poem on the Universal Passion. Alderman Barber's great ambition was to be mentioned favourably by Pope. He let it be understood that he would be willing to part with £4000 if the poet would gratify him; a single couplet was all he asked for; but the Alderman begged in vain. On the other hand, Pope accepted £1000 from the old Duchess of Marlborough in return for the suppression of an attack upon the late Duke. Pope cancelled the lines; but soon afterwards printed an envenomed character of the Duchess. And even the terrific Sarah herself—such was the overwhelming prestige of the potentate of letters—was powerless in face of this affront.

For the first time in our history, a writer, who was a writer and nothing more—Shakespeare was an actor and a theatrical manager—had achieved financial independence. Pope effected this by his translation of Homer, which brought him £9000 —a sum equivalent to about £30,000 today. The immense success of this work was a sign of the times. Homer's reputation was enormous: was he not the father of poetry? The literary snobbery of the age was profoundly impressed by that. Yes, it was snobbery, no doubt; but surely it was a noble snobbery which put Homer so *very* high in the table of precedence—probably immediately after the Archbishop of Canterbury. Yet, there were difficulties. It was not only hard to read Homer, it was positively dangerous. Too close an acquaintance might reveal that the mythical figure sweeping along so grandly in front of the Archbishop of York was something of a blackguard—an alarming barbarian, with shocking tastes, small knowledge of the rules, and altogether far from correct. Pope solved these difficulties in a masterly manner. He supplied exactly what was wanted. He gave the eighteenth century a Homer after its own heart—a Homer who was the father—not quite of poetry, indeed, but of something much more satisfactory—of what the eighteenth century believed poetry to be; and, very properly, it gave him a fortune in return.

The eighteenth century has acquired a reputation for scepticism; but this is a mistake. In truth there has never been a less sceptical age. Its beliefs were rigid, intense, and imperturbable. In literature, as in every other department of life, an unquestioning orthodoxy reigned. It was this extraordinary self-sufficiency that gave the age its force; but the same quality caused the completeness of its downfall. When the reaction came, the absolute certainty of the past epoch seemed to invest it with the maximum degree of odium and absurdity. The romantics were men who had lost their faith; and they rose against the old dispensation with all the zeal of rebels and heretics. Inevitably, their fury fell with peculiar vehemence upon Pope. The great idol was overturned amid shouts of execration and scornful laughter. The writer who, for three generations, had divided with Milton the supreme honour of English poetry, was pronounced to be shallow, pompous, monotonous, meretricious, and not a poet at all.

Now that we have perhaps emerged from romanticism, it is time to consider the master of the eighteenth century with a more impartial eye. This is not altogether an easy task. Though we may be no longer in the least romantic, are we not still—I hesitate to suggest it—are we not still slightly Victorian? Do we not continue to cast glances of furtive admiration towards the pontiffs of that remarkable era, whose figures, on the edge of our horizon, are still visible, so lofty, and so large? We can discount the special pleadings of Wordsworth; but the voice of Matthew Arnold, for instance, still sounds with something like authority upon our ears. Pope, said Matthew Arnold, is not a classic of our poetry, he is a classic of our prose. He was without an "adequate poetic criticism of life"; his criticism of life lacked "high seriousness"; it had neither largeness, freedom, insight, nor benignity. Matthew Arnold was a poet, but his conception of poetry reminds us that he was also an inspector of schools. That the essence of poetry is "high seriousness" is one of those noble platitudes which commend themselves immediately as both obvious and comfortable. But, in reality, obviousness and comfort have very little to do with poetry. It is not the nature of poetry to be what anyone expects; on the contrary, it is its nature to be surprising, to be disturbing, to be impossible. Poetry and high seriousness! Of course, to Dr. Arnold's son, they seemed to be inevitably linked together; and certainly had the world been created by Dr. Arnold they actually would have been. But—perhaps fortunately—it was not. If we look at the facts, where do we find

poetry? In the wild fantasies of Aristophanes, in the sordid
lusts of Baudelaire, in the gentle trivialities of La Fontaine.

"Dreadful was the din
Of hissing through the hall, thick swarming now
With complicated monsters, head and tail,
Scorpion, and asp, and amphisbaena dire,
Cerastes horn'd, hydrus, and ellops drear,
And dipsas—"

That is not high seriousness; it is a catalogue of curious
names; and it is poetry. There is poetry to be found lurking
in the metaphysical system of Epicurus, and in the body of
a flea. And so need we be surprised if it invests a game of
cards, or a gentleman sneezing at Hampton Court?—

"Just where the breath of life his nostrils drew,
A charge of snuff the wily virgin threw;
The gnomes direct, to every atom just,
The pungent grains of titillating dust.
Sudden, with starting tears each eye o'erflows,
And the high dome re-echoes to his nose."

Pope, we are told, was not only without "high seriousness"; he lacked no less an "adequate poetic criticism of
life." What does this mean? The phrase is ambiguous; it sig-
nifies at once too much and too little. If we are to understand—as the context seems to imply—that, in Matthew Arnold's opinion, no poetic criticism of life can be adequate
unless it possesses largeness, freedom, and benignity, we must
certainly agree that Pope's poetic criticism of life was far
from adequate; for his way of writing was neither large nor
free, and there was nothing benignant about him. But the
words will bear another interpretation; and in this sense it
may turn out that Pope's poetic criticism of life was adequate to an extraordinary degree.

Let us examine for a moment the technical instrument which Pope used—I mean the heroic couplet.

When he was a young man, the poet Walsh gave Pope a piece of advice. "We have had great poets," he said, "but never one great poet that was correct. I recommend you to make your leading aim—correctness." Pope took the advice, and became the most correct of poets. This was his chief title to glory in the eighteenth century; it was equally the stick that he was most frequently and rapturously beaten with, in the nineteenth. Macaulay, in his essay on Byron, devotes several pages of his best forensic style to an exposure and denunciation of the absurd futility of the "correctness" of the school of Pope. There is in reality, he declared, "only one kind of correctness in literature—that which "has its foundation in truth and in the principles of human nature." But Pope's so-called correctness was something very different. It consisted simply in a strict obedience to a perfectly arbitrary set of prosodic rules. His couplet was a purely artificial structure—the product of mere convention; and, so far from there being any possible poetic merit in the kind of correctness which it involved, this "correctness" was in fact only "another name for dullness and absurdity." A short time ago, the distinguished poet, M. Paul Valéry, demolished Macaulay's argument—no doubt quite unconsciously—in an essay full of brilliant subtlety and charming wit. He showed conclusively the essentially poetic value of purely arbitrary conventions. But, for our purposes, so drastic a conclusion is unnecessary. For Macaulay was mistaken, not only in his theory, but in his facts. The truth is that the English classical couplet—unlike the French—had nothing conventional about it. On the contrary, it was the inevitable, the logical, the natural outcome of the development of English verse.

The fundamental element in the structure of poetry is rhythmical repetition. In England, the favourite unit of this

268

repetition very early became the ten-syllabled iambic line. Now it is clear that the treatment of this line may be developed in two entirely different directions. The first of these developments is blank verse. Milton's definition of blank verse is well known, and it cannot be bettered: it consists, he says, "in apt numbers, fit quantity of syllables, and the sense variously drawn out from one verse into another." Its essence, in other words, is the combination formed by rhythmical variety playing over an underlying norm; and it is easy to trace the evolution of this wonderful measure from the primitive rigidity of Surrey to the incredible virtuosity of Shakespeare's later plays, where blank verse reaches its furthest point of development—where rhythmical variety is found in unparalleled profusion, while the underlying regularity is just, still, miraculously preserved. After Shakespeare, the combination broke down; the element of variety became so excessive that the underlying norm disappeared, with the result that the blank verse of the latest Elizabethans is virtually indistinguishable from prose.

But suppose the ten-syllabled iambic were treated in precisely the contrary manner. Suppose, instead of developing the element of variety to its maximum, the whole rhythmical emphasis were put upon the element of regularity. What would be the result? This was the problem that presented itself to the poets of the seventeenth century, when it appeared to them that the possibilities of blank verse were played out. (In reality they were not played out, as Milton proved; but Milton was an isolated and unique phenomenon.) Clearly, the most effective method of emphasising regularity is the use of rhyme; and the most regular form of rhyme is the couplet. Already, in the splendid couplets of Marlowe and in the violent couplets of Donne, we can find a foretaste of what the future had in store for the measure. Shakespeare, indeed, as if to show that there were no limits either to his comprehension or to his capacity, threw off a few lines which might have been written by Pope, and stuck them into the middle of *Othello*.[1] But it was not until the collapse of blank verse, about 1630, that the essential characteristics which lay concealed in the couplet began to be exploited. It was Waller who first fully apprehended the implications of regularity; and it is to this fact that his immense reputation during the succeeding hundred years was due. Waller disengaged the heroic couplet from the beautiful vagueness of Elizabethanism. He perceived what logically followed from a rhyme. He saw that regularity implied balance, that balance implied antithesis; he saw that balance also implied simplicity, that simplicity implied clarity and that clarity implied exactitude. The result was a poetical instrument contrary in every particular to blank verse—a form which, instead of being varied, unsymmetrical, fluid, complex, profound and indefinite, was regular, balanced, antithetical, simple, clear, and exact. But, though Waller was its creator, the heroic couplet remained, with him, in an embryonic state. Its evolution was slow; even Dryden did not quite bring it to perfection. That great genius, with all his strength and all his brilliance, lacked one quality without which no mastery of the couplet could be complete—the elegance of perfect finish. This was possessed by Pope. The most correct of poets—Pope was indeed that; it is his true title to glory. But the phrase does not mean that he obeyed more slavishly than anybody else a set of arbitrary rules. No, it means something entirely different: it means that the system of versification of which the principle is regularity reached in Pope's hands the final plenitude of

[1] "She that in wisdom never was so frail
To change the cod's head for the salmon's tail;
She that could think, and ne'er disclose her mind;
See suitors following, and not look behind;
She was a wight, if ever such wight were,
To suckle fools and chronicle small beer."

its nature—its ultimate significance—its supreme consummation.

That Pope's verse is artificial there can be no doubt. But
then there is only one kind of verse that is not artificial, and
that is bad verse. Yet it is true that there is a sense in which
Pope's couplet is more artificial than, let us say, the later
blank verse of Shakespeare—it has less resemblance to nature. It is regular and neat; but nature is "divers et on-
doyant"; and so is blank verse. Nature and blank verse are
complicated; and Pope's couplet is simplicity itself. But what
a profound art underlies that simplicity! Pope's great
achievement in English literature was the triumph of sim-
plification. In one of his earliest works, the *Pastorals*, there
is simplicity and nothing else; Pope had understood that if
he could once attain to a perfect simplicity, all the rest
would follow in good time—

"O deign to visit our forsaken seats,
The mossy fountains, and the green retreats!
Where'er you walk, cool gales shall fan the glade;
Trees, where you sit, shall crowd into a shade;
Where'er you tread, the blushing flow'rs shall rise,
And all things flourish where you turn your eyes."

The lines flow on with the most transparent limpidity—

"But see, the shepherds shun the noon-day heat,
The lowing herds to murm'ring brooks retreat,
To closer shades the panting flocks remove;
Ye Gods! and is there no relief for love?"

Everything is obvious. The diction is a mass of *clichés;* the
epithets are the most commonplace possible; the herds low,
the brooks murmur, the flocks pant and remove, the retreats
are green, and the flowers blush. The rhythm is that of a
rocking-horse; and the sentiment is mere sugar. But what a

relief! What a relief to have escaped for once from *le mot propre*, from subtle elaboration of diction and metre, from complicated states of mind, and all the profound obscurities of Shakespeare and Mr. T. S. Eliot! How delightful to have no trouble at all—to understand so very, very easily every single thing that is said!

This is Pope at his most youthful. As he matured, his verse matured with him. Eventually, his couplets, while retaining to the full their early ease, polish, and lucidity, became charged with an extraordinary weight. He was able to be massive, as no other wielder of the measure has ever been—

> "Lo! thy dread empire, Chaos! is restored;
> Light dies before thy uncreating word;
> Thy hand, great Anarch! lets the curtain fall,
> And universal Darkness buries All."

Here the slow solemnity of the effect is produced by a most learned accumulation of accents and quantities; in some of the lines all the syllables save two are either long or stressed. At other times, he uses a precisely opposite method; in line after line he maintains, almost completely, the regular alternation of accented and unaccented syllables; and so conveys a wonderful impression of solidity and force—

> "Proceed, great days! till learning fly the shore,
> Till Birch shall blush with noble blood no more,
> Till Thames see Eton's sons for ever play,
> Till Westminster's whole year be holiday,
> Till Isis' Elders reel, their pupils' sport,
> And Alma Mater lie dissolved in Port!"

Perhaps the most characteristic of all the elements in the couplet is antithesis. Ordinary regularity demands that the sense should end with every line—that was a prime necessity;

but a more scrupulous symmetry would require something more—a division of the line itself into two halves, whose meanings should correspond. And yet a further refinement was possible: each half might be again divided, and the corresponding divisions in the two halves might be so arranged as to balance each other. The force of neatness could no further go; and thus the most completely evolved type of the heroic line is one composed of four main words arranged in pairs, so as to form a double antithesis.

"Willing to wound, and yet afraid to strike"

is an example of such a line, and Pope's poems are full of them. With astonishing ingenuity he builds up these exquisite structures, in which the parts are so cunningly placed that they seem to interlock spontaneously, and, while they are all formed on a similar model, are yet so subtly adjusted that they produce a fresh pleasure as each one appears. But that is not all. Pope was pre-eminently a satirist. He was naturally drawn to the contemplation of human beings, their conduct in society, their characters, their motives, their destinies; and the feelings which these contemplations habitually aroused in him were those of scorn and hatred. Civilisation illumined by animosity—such was his theme; such was the passionate and complicated material from which he wove his patterns of balanced precision and polished clarity. Antithesis penetrates below the structure; it permeates the whole conception of his work. Fundamental opposites clash, and are reconciled. The profundities of persons, the futilities of existence, the rage and spite of genius—these things are mixed together, and presented to our eyes in the shape of a Chinese box. The essence of all art is the accomplishment of the impossible. This cannot be done, we say; and it *is* done. What has happened? A magician has waved his wand. It is impossible that Pope should convey to us his withering sense of the wretchedness and emptiness of the fate of old women in society, in five lines, each containing four words, arranged in pairs, so as to form a double antithesis. But the magician waves his wand, and there it is—

"See how the world its veterans rewards!
A youth of frolics, an old age of cards;
Fair to no purpose, artful to no end,
Young without lovers, old without a friend,
A fop their passion, and their prize a sot;
Alive ridiculous, and dead forgot!"

And now, perhaps, we have discovered what may truly be said to have been Pope's "poetic criticism of life." His poetic criticism of life was, simply and solely, the heroic couplet.

Pope was pre-eminently a satirist; and so it is only natural that his enemies should take him to task for not being something else. He had no benignity; he had no feeling for sensuous beauty; he took no interest in nature; he was pompous —did he not wear a wig? Possibly; but if one is to judge poets by what they are without, where is one to end? One might point out that Wordsworth had no sense of humour, that Shelley did not understand human beings, that Keats could not read Greek, and that Matthew Arnold did not wear a wig. And, if one looks more closely, one perceives that there were a good many things that Pope could do very well— when he wanted to. Sensuous beauty, for instance—

"Die of a rose in aromatic pain."

If that is not sensuously beautiful, what is? Then, we are told, he did not "compose with his eye on the object." But once Pope looked at a spider, and this was what he composed—

"The spider's touch, how exquisitely fine!
Feels at each thread, and lives along the line."

Could Wordsworth have done better? It is true that he did not often expatiate upon the scenery; but, when he chose, he could call up a vision of nature which is unforgettable—

"Lo! where Maeotis sleeps, and hardly flows
The freezing Tanais thro' a waste of snows,"

We see, and we shiver. It cannot be denied that Pope wore a wig; it must even be confessed that there are traces, in his earlier work especially, of that inexpressive ornament in the rococo style, which was the bane of his age; but the true Pope was not there. The true Pope threw his wig into the corner of the room, and used all the plainest words in the dictionary He used them carefully, no doubt, very carefully, b. ae used them—one-syllabled, Saxon words, by no means pretty—they cover his pages; and some of his pages are among the coarsest in English literature. There are passages in the *Dunciad* which might agitate Mr. James Joyce. Far from being a scrupulous worshipper of the noble style, Pope was a realist—in thought and in expression. He could describe a sordid interior as well as any French novelist—

"In the worst inn's worst room, with mat half-hung,
The floors of plaster, and the walls of dung,
On once a flock-bed, but repair'd with straw,
With tape-tied curtains, never meant to draw,
The George and Garter dangling from that bed
Where tawdry yellow strove with dirty red,
Great Villiers lies. . . ."

But these are only the outworks of the citadel. The heart of the man was not put into descriptions of physical things; it was put into descriptions of people whom he disliked. It is in those elaborate Characters, in which, through a score of lines or so, the verse rises in wave upon wave of malice, to fall at last with a crash on the devoted head of the victim—

in the sombre magnificence of the denunciation of the great dead Duke, in the murderous insolence of the attack on the great living Duchess, in the hooting mockery of Bufo, in the devastating analysis of Addison—it is here that Pope's art comes to its climax. With what a relish, with what a thrill, we behold once more the impossible feat—the couplet, that bed of Procrustes, fitted exactly and eternally with the sinuous egoism of Addison's spirit, or the putrescent nothingness of Lord Hervey's. In the Character of Sporus, says the great critic and lexicographer, in memory of whom I have had the honour of addressing you today, Pope "seems to be actually screaming with malignant fury." It is true.

> "Let Sporus tremble!—What? that thing of silk,
> Sporus, that mere white curd of ass's milk?
> Satire or sense, alas! can Sporus feel?
> Who breaks a butterfly upon a wheel?
> —Yet let me flap this bug with gilded wings,
> This painted child of dirt, that stinks and stings;
> Whose buzz the witty and the fair annoys,
> Yet wit ne'er tastes, and beauty ne'er enjoys:
> So well-bred spaniels civilly delight
> In mumbling of the game they dare not bite.
> Eternal smiles his emptiness betray,
> As shallow streams run dimpling all the way.
> Whether in florid impotence he speaks,
> And, as the prompter breathes, the puppet squeaks,
> Or at the ear of Eve, familiar toad,
> Half froth, half venom, spits himself abroad
> In puns, or politics, or tales, or lies,
> Or spite, or smut, or rhymes, or blasphemies.
> His wit all see-saw, between that and this,
> Now high, now low, now master up, now miss,
> And he himself one vile antithesis.

276

Amphibious thing! that acting either part,
The trifling head, or the corrupted heart,
Fop at the toilet, flatterer at the board,
Now trips a lady, and now struts a lord.
Eve's tempter thus the Rabbins have expressed,
A cherub's face, a reptile all the rest;
Beauty that shocks you, parts that none can trust,
Wit that can creep, and pride that licks the dust."

It is true: Pope *seems* to be actually screaming; but let us not mistake. It is only an appearance; actually, Pope is not screaming at all; for these are strange impossible screams, unknown to the world of fact—screams endowed with immortality. What has happened then? Pope has waved his wand. He has turned his screams into poetry, with the enchantment of the heroic couplet.

1925.

7. The Eighteenth Century

DR. PAGET TOYNBEE[1] is to be congratulated on bringing to a close the monumental edition of Horace Walpole's Letters, the first volume of which appeared, under the editorship of Mrs. Toynbee, in 1903. The enormous and exquisite structure stands before us in all its Palladian beauty, and we can wander through it at our ease, conducted, as we go, by the most patient and accurate of scholars. This final volume is the third of the supplement and the nineteenth of the whole collection. Its contents are miscellaneous—the gleanings of the great correspondence: more than a hundred new letters by Walpole, together with a most interesting selection of those addressed *to* him by every variety of person, from the elder Pitt, at the height of his glory, to James Maclean, the highwayman. Walpole's own letters come from every period of his life. A delightful series to Sir Charles Hanbury Williams shows us the first sprightly runnings of that inimitable manner: one dip, and we are in the very middle of the eighteenth century. "My Lady Townshend," we learn, "has taken a room at Brompton to sleep in the air. After having had it eight days without having been there within six hours of the evening, she set out t'other night with Dorcas, and moveables and household stuff, and unnecessaries enough to have staid there a fortnight. Nightshifts, and drops, and her supper in a silver saucepan, and

[1] *Supplement to the Letters of Horace Walpole.* Edited, with notes and indices, by Paget Toynbee, M.A., D.Litt. Vol. III: 1744-1797. Oxford: Clarendon Press.

a large piece of work to do, four books, paper, and two hundred crow quills. When she came there it was quite dark: she felt her way up to her bedchamber, felt she did not like it, and felt her way down again. All this before the woman of the house could get candles. When she came down her coach was gone. . . ."

Then there are some excellent examples of the brilliant middle period: "The spring desires I would tell your Ladyship that it is waiting for you on this side of Chantilly": no one could mistake the author of that phrase. Finally, the mature virtuosity of Walpole's long old age is admirably represented. His last letter turns out not to be the famous one addressed on January 9, 1797, to Lady Ossory. Three days later the old connoisseur was able to dictate some lines to the Rev. Mark Noble. "Mr. Roscoe," he characteristically declared, "is, I think, by far the best of our historians, both for beauty of style and for deep reflections." So much for Mr. Gibbon! "I was sorry, sir, I missed the pleasure of seeing you when you called. . . . I should have been glad to see that coin or medal you mention of Lord Arundel. . . ." And so, as is fitting, with no particular flourish—with the ordinary amenity of a gentleman, the fascinating creature passes from our sight.

Amid so much that is perfect it may seem a little ungracious to make, or rather to repeat, a complaint. But it is the very perfection that raises one's standard and sharpens one's disappointment, when expectations, satisfied so long and so continuously, are suddenly dashed. The editor is still unable to resist meddling with his text. The complete edition is incomplete, after all. Apparently, we should blush too much were we to read the whole of Walpole's letters; those privileges have been reserved to Dr. Toynbee alone. It was impossible not to hope that, after so prolonged a *tête-à-tête* with his author, he would relent at last; perhaps, in this latest volume at any rate—but no! the powers of editorship must· be asserted to the bitter end; and the fatal row of asterisks and the fatal note, "passage omitted" occur, more than once, to exacerbate the reader. Surely it would have been kinder not to reveal the fact that any deletion had been made. Then one could have read on, innocent and undisturbed. As it is, when one's irritation has subsided, one's imagination, one's shocking imagination, begins to work. The question must be asked: do these explicit suppressions really serve the interests of the highest morality? Dr. Toynbee reminds one of the man who . . .[1] But enough; for, after all, it is not the fly but the ointment that claims our attention.

And, indeed, the ointment is rare and rich, of a subtle and delicious perfume. The aroma of a wonderful age comes wafting out from these few hundred pages, and enchants our senses. Why is it that the eighteenth century so particularly delights us? Are we perhaps simply reacting against a reaction? Is the twentieth century so fond of the eighteenth because the nineteenth disliked it so intensely? No doubt that is partly the reason; but the whole truth lies deeper. Every age has a grudge against its predecessor, and generally the grudge is well founded. The Romantics and the Victorians were probably right: they had good reason to dislike the eighteenth century, which they found to be intolerably rigid, formal, and self-satisfied, devoid, to an extraordinary degree, of sympathy, adventure, and imagination. All this was perfectly true. A world, for instance, in which Voltaire's criticism of Hamlet, or Walpole's of Dante—"a methodist parson in Bedlam"—could be meant seriously and taken seriously would certainly have been a most depressing world to live in. The nineteenth century, very properly, revolted, broke those chains, and then—proceeded to forge others of

[1] Passage omitted.

its own invention. It is these later chains that *we* find distressing. Those of the eighteenth century we cannot consider realistically at all; we were born—owing to the efforts of our grandfathers—free of them; we can afford to look at them romantically; we can even imagine ourselves dancing in them —stately minuets. And for the purposes of a historical vision, the eighteenth century is exactly what is wanted. What would have been, in fact, its most infuriating quality—its amazing self-sufficiency—is precisely what makes it, in retrospect, so satisfying; there hangs the picture before us, framed and glazed, distinct, simple, complete. We are bewitched by it, just as, about the year 2000, our descendants, no doubt, will cast longing eyes towards the baroque enchantments of the age of Victoria.

But, just now, to consider thus is to consider too curiously. With this book in one's hand, it is impossible to be anything but romantic: facts vanish; the hardest heart collapses before this triumph of superficial charm. There is a divine elegance everywhere, giving a grace to pomposity, a significance to frivolity, and a shape to emptiness. The English language takes on new shifts and guises. One discovers a subtle employment of *shall* and *should* as the future indicative in the formal third person singular—a truly beautiful usage, which must send a delicious shiver down the backbone of every grammarian. Nor is it only in the letters of the grand master, of Walpole himself, that these graces are evident; they are scattered everywhere over the pages of his correspondents. This is how, in those days of leisure and urbanity, a Prime Minister said, "Thank you for your kind letter":—

"The impressions I am under from the honour of your letter are too sensible not to call for expression. As often as I have read it, for ('tis best to confess) I do indulge myself in the frequent repetition, I am at some loss to decide which sort of pleasure such a letter is made to excite most; that delight which springs from wit, agrément and beauty of style, or the serious and deep-felt satisfaction which the possession of so kind and honourable a Testimony must convey."

It was annoying, doubtless, to be held up by highwaymen in the Park; but there were compensating advantages; one might receive, a few days later, a letter beginning as follows:—

"Sir, seeing an advertisement in the papers of to Day giving an account of your being Rob'd by two Highway men on wednesday night last in Hyde Parke and during the time a Pistol being fired whether Intended or Accidentally was Doubtfull Oblidges us to take this Method of assureing you that it was the latter and by no means Design'd Either to hurt or frighten you."

These are unusual occasions; it is in the everyday word, the casual gesture, that one perceives, still more plainly, the form and pressure of the time. The Duchess of Bedford asks Mr. Walpole to buy a bust of Faustina for her at a sale. "If it is tolerable," she adds; and nobly makes no mention of a price. And then—"Lord Huntingdon with his Compliments sends Mr. Walpole, according to promise, a little Spanish snuff. Having left off taking any, from finding that it disagreed with him, he hopes Mr. Walpole will be so much his friend as to keep possession of his box." Could delicate suavity go further? Sometimes the ladies' pens frisk and pirouette in irresponsible fantasy. Lady Lyttelton, in a mad letter, all dashes and exclamations, seems to forestall the style of Tristram Shandy; and Miss Mary Carter—unknown to fame—winds up an epistle full of vague and farcical melancholy, with—"I will not take up more of that precious stuff of which Life is composed but to assure You that I am with great Esteem and Respect yr most Obedt Moll Volatile Evaporated."

The precious stuff of which Life is composed flowed away gaily, softly, without any fuss whatever. The old letter writer and letter receiver, in his fortunate island, with his pens and paper, his Berrys, his gout and his memories, continued, as the century drew to its end, to survey the world with a dispassionate civility. There were changes, certainly; the French had become "a worse race than Chictaws and Cherokees"; but it hardly mattered. The young men stopped powdering their hair; even that could be met with a lifted eyebrow. Were there other, even more terrible revolutions brewing? Perhaps; but the Earl of Orford would not heed them. Machinery? Yes, he had indeed noticed it, and observed one day to Hannah More, in his clever fashion, that it might be used for making sugar, so that by its intervention "the poor negroes" could be saved from working. He passed on to more interesting subjects, his tranquillity unshaken; it remained unshaken to the end. He departed, happily unconscious that the whole system of his existence was doomed to annihilation—elegantly unaware of the implications of the spinning jenny.

1926.

8. Words and Poetry[1]

A STORY is told of Degas, who, in the intervals of painting, amused himself by writing sonnets, and on one occasion found that his inspiration had run dry. In his distress, he went to his friend Mallarmé. "I cannot understand it," he said; "my poem won't come out, and yet I am full of excellent ideas." "My dear Degas," was Mallarmé's reply, "poetry is not written with ideas; it is written with words."

Mr. George Rylands' book is a commentary on Mallarmé's dictum. Was it a platitude? Was it a paradox? Both and neither, perhaps, like most profound observations; and Mr. Rylands explains to us how this may be—explains with the delicate amplitude of sensitive enthusiasm and the fresh learning of youth.

It is pleasant to follow him, as he explains and explores. The wide rich fields of English literature lie open before us— the paths are flowery—the nosegays many and sweet. We are lured down fascinating avenues of surmises; we ask questions, and all is made clear by some cunningly chosen bunch that is put into our hands, full of unexpected fragrances, or, perhaps, by the moon. We begin to understand why it is that the glory of an April day cannot be fickle and must be uncertain; we realise the difference between hills and mountains; to our surprise we detect a connection between Dr.

[1] Originally published as an introduction to *Words and Poetry*. By George H. W. Rylands, M.A. The Hogarth Press. 1928.

284

Johnson and the Shropshire Lad. With such a clever guide,
we may well at last grow presumptuous and long to do a
little exploring on our own account.

But it is not an easy business. Perhaps of all the creations
of man language is the most astonishing. Those small articu-
lated sounds, that seem so simple and so definite, turn out,
the more one examines them, to be the receptacles of subtle
mystery and the dispensers of unanticipated power. Each one
of them, as we look, shoots up into

"A palm with winged imagination in it
And roots that stretch even beneath the grave."

It is really a case of Frankenstein and his monster. These
things that we have made are as alive as we are, and we
have become their slaves. Words are like coins (a dozen
metaphors show it), and in nothing more so than in this—
that the verbal currency we have so ingeniously contrived
has outrun our calculations, and become an enigma and a
matter for endless controversy. We say something; but we
can never be quite certain what it is that we have said. In a
single written sentence a hundred elusive meanings ob-
scurely palpitate. With Mr. Rylands' help we analyse the
rainbow; we dissect and compare and define; but the ultimate solution escapes us; we are entranced by an inexplicable beauty—an intangible loveliness more enduring than
ourselves.

The value of a word depends in part upon the obscure
influences of popular expression and in part upon the fiat
of poets and masters of prose. A great artist can invest a
common word with a miraculous significance—can suddenly
turn a halfpenny into a five-pound note. He can do more;
he can bring back a word that has been dead for centuries
into the life and usage of every day. What now passes as a
Bradbury was once—before the poet touched it with his mut-

tered abracadabra—a rusty bit of metal in a collector's cabinet. The romantic writers of the early nineteenth century
were the great masters of this particular enchantment; and
it is owing to them that today a multitude of words and
phrases go familiarly among us, which, no less familiar to the
Elizabethans, were unknown and unintelligible even to the
learned men of the age of Pope and Gray.

But neither can the poets themselves escape the thraldom
of their own strange handiwork. They, too, are the slaves
as well as the masters of words. Even the greatest of them
all, perhaps! There is one name that no English writer on
English literature can hope, or wish, to avoid for more than
a very few moments together. Before we are aware of it, we
all of us find that we are talking about Shakespeare. And
Mr. Rylands is no exception. Naturally, inevitably, he devotes the latter half of his book to a consideration of Shakespeare as a user of words, and to the history—the romance,
one might almost say—of his adventures among them.

It is curious that Shakespeare—by far the greatest word-
master who ever lived—should have been so rarely treated
of from this point of view. We know almost nothing of the
facts of his life; we can only conjecture, most hazardously,
about his opinions and his emotions; but there, fixed and
palpable before us, lie the vast accumulations of his words,
like geological strata, with all their wealth of information
laid bare to the eye of the patient and curious observer. How
very remarkable, for instance, is the development, which
Mr. Rylands points out to us—a late and unexpected development—in Shakespeare's use of prose! How extremely interesting is the story of his dealings with words of classical
derivation! The early youthful *engouement* for a romance
vocabulary, the more mature severity, and the recoil towards
Saxon influences, and then the sudden return to a premeditated and violent classicism—the splendid latinistic passion,

which, though it grew fainter with time, left such ineffaceable traces on all his later life!

A drama might almost be made of it—and a drama that could hardly have passed unconsciously in Shakespeare's mind. The supreme artist must have known well enough what was happening among those innumerable little creatures who did his bidding with so rare a felicity—his words. Did he, perhaps, for his own amusement, write an account of the whole affair? A series of sonnets . . . ? If an allegory must be found in those baffling documents, why should not this be the solution of it? One can fancy that the beautiful youth was merely a literary expression for the classical vocabulary, while the dark lady personified the Saxon one. Their relations, naturally enough, were strained, yet intimate. . . . The theory is offered gratis to the next commentator on the Sonnets. There have been many more far-fetched.

Shakespeare, certainly, knew what he was doing; and yet, in the end, he found that those little creatures were too much for him. So it appears; the geological strata put it almost beyond a doubt. The supreme word-master lorded it no less over character and drama; for many years he carried those three capacities together in an incredible combination, pushing them on from glory to glory; until something most unexpected happened: the words asserted themselves, and triumphed, with extraordinary results. In Shakespeare's later works character has grown unindividual and unreal; drama has become conventional or operatic; the words remain more tremendously, more exquisitely, more thrillingly alive than ever—the excuse and the explanation of the rest. The little creatures had absolutely fascinated their master; he had become their slave. At their bidding he turned Coriolanus from a human being into a glorious gramophone; they spoke, and a fantastic confusion, a beautiful impossibility, involved

287

the constructions of *The Winter's Tale* and *Cymbeline*. To please them, he called up out of nothingness, in *The Tempest*, an Island, not of Romance, but of Pure Style. At last, it was simply for style that Shakespeare lived; everything else had vanished. He began as a poet, and as a poet he ended. Human beings, life, fate, reality—he cared for such things no longer. They were figments—mere ideas; and poetry is not written with ideas; it is written with words.

1928.

9. Othello

WITH *Hamlet*, Shakespeare had reached one of the turning-points of his career; he had constructed a tragedy of character—an aesthetic form which had been unknown in Europe since the Greeks. But he had certainly not gone to the Greeks for a model. Romantic, metaphysical, complicated, *Hamlet* seems at times to be almost a psychological treatise, and at other times to be almost a novel. The achievement was vast—perhaps too vast—so Ben Jonson may have remarked, between a growl and a laugh at the Mermaid; and Shakespeare may well have felt that such a criticism was not unfounded. At any rate, he would not repeat himself; he would not write another *Hamlet*; on the contrary, his next work, while preserving the essential quality of the former—the interplay of character and tragic circumstance—should differ from it in almost every other respect; it should be simple, both in treatment and scope; it should avoid philosophical implications and spiritual mysteries; it should depend for its effect upon force, intensity, and concentration.

That·Shakespeare, this time, intentionally submitted himself to Greek influence may be a fanciful suggestion; but it is not an impossibility. Even if he could not read Greek, his "small Latin" was probably enough to enable him to go through one of the Latin translations of Sophocles, and to gather from it a perception, if not of the poetical sublimity, at least of the constructive principles, of the original. Be that as it may, there is undoubtedly a curious analogy between the basic scheme of *Othello* and that of the *Oedipus Tyrannus*. It might almost be said that the first is, in essence, the converse of the second. The dramatic idea of the *Oedipus* is that of a man who deliberately discovers a horror—a horror which is a fact and which, when he knows it, is his undoing. The play consists of this crescendo of discovery, leading to the foreseen and inevitable catastrophe. In *Othello,* on the other hand, the hero is gradually deluded into believing a horror—a horror which is a figment; and the culmination of the tragedy comes, not with the knowledge of a fact, but with the realisation of a delusion. The crescendo, this time, is one of *false* discovery; but in both cases the essence of the drama lies in a mental progression on the part of the hero— a progression whose actual nature and necessary conclusion is not understood by him, but is realised and foreseen at every point by the audience.

The comparison may be carried a step further: whether or no Shakespeare was aware of it, for us it is illuminating to observe the likeness and the contrast between, not only the situations, but the characters of the two heroes. Given the scheme of Sophocles's play, it is clear that it becomes a dramatic necessity for Oedipus to possess certain qualities. It is clear that he must be a very intelligent and an extremely self-willed man. It must be his nature to put two and two together, to refuse to be taken in, to insist with all the force of obstinacy and passion upon unravelling the mystery with which he is faced. A detective-autocrat, his ironic tragedy comes when, utterly unaware of what he is doing, he turns his power and his intellect against himself. One other quality he must have, to complete the effect of the story: he must be royal, not only in position but in nature; the soul that is overwhelmed by this strange nemesis must be a great one, if pity and terror are to reach their full height.

But what are the dramatic requirements for Othello's

situation? A great soul certainly; a passionate nature; but
his intellectual equipment must be exactly the reverse of
that of Oedipus—he must be simple-minded, unsuspicious,
easily thrown off his mental balance, a creature eminently
susceptible to deceit. The tragedy here is not ironical but
pathetic; and the pathos will be deepest if the victim whom
one watches led step by step to his ruin, is both magnificent
and blind.

Such, stated in the most general terms possible, is the
nucleus of the tragedy of *Othello*—the axiomatic starting-
point from which—given the genius of Shakespeare—the
whole of the rest of the play might be deduced. Actually, of
course, Shakespeare did not proceed in any such abstract
manner. According to his almost invariable habit, he found
the suggestion for his play in another work, which he used
as the rough material for his own construction. From this
point of view, the case of *Othello* is particularly informing,
since it is drawn from a single source, and we are thus able
to observe, without doubt or difficulty, the process of manip-
ulation which Shakespeare applied to his original. Cinthio's
story—the seventh in the third decade of his *Hecatommithi*
—is a "novella" written in the manner of Boccaccio, a perfectly straightforward narrative, which, brief, matter-of-fact,
with hardly a touch of colour or comment, might almost
be the report of an actual occurrence, based upon the pro-
ceedings of a police-court. In its main lines, the story, up
to the death of Desdemona, is nearly identical with Shakespeare's: the marriage of the Venetian lady and the Moorish
general; the plot of the Ancient to make the Moor believe
that his wife was guilty of adultery with the Captain; the
Captain's disgrace, and Desdemona's attempt to obtain his
forgiveness from the Moor; the incident of the stolen handkerchief; the Moor's determination to avenge himself by the
deaths of his wife and the Captain; and the wounding of

the Captain in the leg by the Ancient—all this is common
to the story and the play. But in Cinthio, Desdemona is
murdered by the Ancient at the instigation and in the presence of the Moor; after which they make her death appear a
natural one, so that the murder is undetected; then the
Moor and the Ancient quarrel; the Ancient persuades the
Captain that it was the Moor who wounded him in the
leg (which by this time had been amputated), with the result
that the Moor is arrested by the Signoria of Venice, is put
to the torture, and, on refusing to confess, is banished—to be
eventually slain by the kinsfolk of his wife. As for the
Ancient, in consequence of the failure of another of his plots,
his end comes in death following upon torture.

Certainly, to anyone who bears in mind what Shakespeare
made out of Cinthio's story, its most striking feature is its
lack of characterisation. The persons who, with the exception of the Venetian lady, Desdemona, are not even named,
are furnished with a few crude and obvious qualities, and
then set off into action. The Moor, we are told, was "molto
valoroso," he was "prò della persona," had given proof "nelle
cose della guerra, di gran prudenza e di vivace ingegno," and
had an "amore singolare" for his wife. She on her side was
"una virtuosa donna di maravigliosa bellezza," who "altro
bene non haveva al mondo che il Moro." Of the Captain we
simply learn that he was "carissimo al Moro," and of the
Ancient's wife that she was a "bella e honesta giovane."
The Ancient alone receives a slightly more elaborate label.
He was "di bellissima presenza, ma della più scelerata natura
che mai fosse huomo del mondo," and "quantunque egli
fosse di vilissimo animo, copriva nondimeno, coll'alte e
superbe parole e colla sua presenza, di modo la viltà ch'egli
chiudea nel cuore, che si scopriva nella sembianza un'Ettore
od un'Achille." Yet, with all this black and white, it is difficult to make sure where our sympathies are expected to

lie, or even if we are intended to have any. For when at last
Othello is killed, the author's casual comment is "com'egli
meritava"—a curious piece of moral bleakness, which reminds us once again of the magistrate's court.

Shakespeare's way was different: his persons are elaborate
human beings, towards whom our feelings are directed with
an extraordinary certainty and intensity. The Moor becomes
Othello; and, whether Shakespeare met with the name in
some obscure book of stories or whether he invented it, it
was certainly a marvellous *trouvaille*. The essential elements
of the character—grandeur and simplicity—are immediately
evoked: the bearer of such a name, one feels instinctively,
could never have been a clever, puny man. At the same
time, the suggestions aroused by the idea of a Moor—which
Cinthio had made no use of whatever—were seized upon by
Shakespeare with the greatest skill to reinforce his dominating intention. An Italian meant primarily to an Englishman
of those days a creature of unscrupulous cunning—a Macch-
iavel—and Othello was *not* an Italian; he was *not* a "super-
subtle Venetian"; he was—the point is constantly insisted
upon—utterly foreign to all that. Actually, of course, a Moor
might have been as unscrupulously cunning as any Italian;
but the antithesis, once established, is effective, and the imagination is set going on the required lines. Among a multitude of minor details, all introduced for the same purpose,
one in particular deserves remark. Othello—so Shakespeare
more than once gives us to understand—was not merely a
fighter and an explorer, he was a sailor; and a certain grand
simplicity is a sailor's obvious attribute. There is some reason to believe that, after the first production of the play,
Shakespeare decided to accentuate this note still further. At
one of the supreme moments of Othello's tragedy—when he
finally abandons himself to the delusion that destroys him—
Shakespeare put into his mouth the astonishing lines about

the Propontic and the Euxine. What manner of man is this? We need no telling: it is the mariner, whose mind, in the stress of an emotional crisis, goes naturally to the sea.

The delusion, yes; but it is time to consider the deluder. It is at this point that we find Shakespeare making, not merely expansions, but definite alterations in the material provided by Cinthio. The Ancient, in Cinthio's story, concealed his wickedness under a heroic guise; he wore the semblance of a Hector or an Achilles. Now it is obvious that, in Shakespeare's scheme, this would not do. To have had two heroic figures, a real one and a false one—as protagonists, would have turned the tragedy into something very like a comedy; and, though we can imagine Shakespeare treating such a theme in another mood—the mood of *Troilus and Cressida*, for instance—any such confusion of *genres* was now quite alien to his purpose. No; the cloak of Iago's villainy must be of an altogether different stuff; clearly it must be the very contrary of the heroic—the downrightness, the outspokenness of bluff integrity. This conception needed no great genius to come by—it might have occurred to half a dozen of the Elizabethan dramatists, even without Iago as a model—but Shakespeare's next readjustment is of quite another class. In Cinthio's story, the Ancient's motive for his villainy is—just what one would expect it to be: he was in love with the lady; she paid no heed to him; his love turned to hatred; he imagined, in his fury, that she loved the Captain; and he determined to be revenged upon them both. Now this is the obvious, the regulation plot, which would have been followed by any ordinarily competent writer. And Shakespeare rejected it. Why? In the first place, let us recall once more the nature of the theme, and let us put it this time less schematically: Othello is to be deluded into believing that Desdemona is faithless; he is to kill her; and then he is to discover that his belief was false. This is the situation, the horror of which is to be intensified in every possible way: the tragedy must be enormous, and unrelieved. But there is one eventuality that might, in some degree at any rate, mitigate the atrocity of the story. If Iago had been led to cause this disaster by his love for Desdemona, in that very fact would lie some sort of comfort; the tragedy would have been brought about by a motive not only comprehensible but in a sense sympathetic; the hero's passion and the villain's would be the same. Let it be granted, then, that the completeness of the tragedy would suffer if its origin lay in Iago's love for Desdemona; therefore let that motive be excluded from Iago's mind. The question immediately presents itself—in that case, for what reason are we to suppose that Iago acted as he did? The whole story depends upon his plot, which forms the machinery of the action; yet, if the Desdemona impulsion is eliminated, what motive for his plot can there be? Shakespeare supplied the answer to this question with one of the very greatest strokes of his genius. By an overwhelming effort of creation he summoned up out of the darkness a psychological portent that was exactly fitted to the requirements of the tragic situation with which he was dealing, and endowed it with reality. He determined that Iago should have no motive at all. He conceived of a monster, whose wickedness should lie far deeper than anything that could be explained by a motive—the very essence of whose being should express itself in the machinations of malignity. This creature might well suppose himself to have a motive; he might well explain his purposes both to himself and his confederate; but his explanations should contradict each, other; he should put forward first one motive, and then another, and then another still; so that, while he himself would be only half-aware of the falsity of his self-analysis, to the audience it would be clear; the underlying demonic impulsion would be manifest as the play developed, it would be seen to be no common affair of love and jealousy, but a tragedy conditioned by something purposeless, profound, and terrible; and, when the moment of revelation came, the horror that burst upon the hero would be as inexplicably awful as evil itself. This triumphant invention of the motive-lessness of Iago has been dwelt upon by innumerable commentators; but none, so far as I know, has pointed out the purpose of it, and the dramatic necessity which gave it birth. . . .

*   *   *   *   *   *   *

1931.

Index

297

INDEX

301